Frommer's®

PORTABLE

St. Maarten/ St. Martin, Anguilla & St. Barts

2nd Edition

by Alexis Lipsitz Flippin

Here's what critics say about Frommer's:

"Amazingly easy to use. Very portable, very complete."

—*Booklist*

"Detailed, accurate, and easy-to-read information for all price ranges."

—*Glamour Magazine*

WILEY

Wiley Publishing, Inc.

Published by:

WILEY PUBLISHING, INC.
111 River St.
Hoboken, NJ 07030-5774

ISBN: 978-0-470-33146-0

Editor: Jennifer Polland
Production Editor: Lindsay Conner
Cartographer: Andy Dolan
Photo Editor: Richard Fox
Production by Wiley Indianapolis Composition Services

For information on our other products and services or to obtain technical
support, please contact our Customer Care Department within the U.S. at
800/762-2974, outside the U.S. at 317/572-3993 or fax 317/572-4002.

Wiley also publishes its books in a variety of electronic formats. Some con-
tent that appears in print may not be available in electronic formats.

Manufactured in the United States of America

5   4   3   2   1

Contents

List of Maps

ACKNOWLEDGMENTS

I'd like to thank the following individuals for their enormous help and support: the Anguilla Tourism Board; Accelyn Connor; Sherry Marker; Marilyn Marx, Hans Maissen & Iain McCormack, Cap Juluca; Stephane Zaharia and David Lyon, CuisinArt; Caitlin Hickey and Marc Thézé, Guanahani, Camilla Stahl and Julia Barnes, La Samanna; Kristin Petrelluzzi, L'Esplanade; Brad Belding, Skipjack's; and finally, my husband, Royce Flippin, for his love and support.

—Alexis Lipsitz Flippin

ABOUT THE AUTHOR

Alexis Lipsitz Flippin is a freelance writer and former Frommer's Senior Editor. She has written and edited for consumer magazines and websites such as *Self, American Health,* CNN.com, Weather.com, and *Rolling Stone.*

AN INVITATION TO THE READER

In researching this book, we discovered many wonderful places—hotels, restaurants, shops, and more. We're sure you'll find others. Please tell us about them, so we can share the information with your fellow travelers in upcoming editions. If you were disappointed with a recommendation, we'd love to know that, too. Please write to:

Frommer's Portable St. Maarten/St. Martin, Anguilla & St. Barts, 2nd Edition
    Wiley Publishing, Inc. • 111 River St. • Hoboken, NJ 07030-5774

AN ADDITIONAL NOTE

Please be advised that travel information is subject to change at any time—and this is especially true of prices. We therefore suggest that you write or call ahead for confirmation when making your travel plans. The authors, editors, and publisher cannot be held responsible for the experiences of readers while traveling. Your safety is important to us, however, so we encourage you to stay alert and be aware of your surroundings. Keep a close eye on cameras, purses, and wallets, all favorite targets of thieves and pickpockets.

FROMMER'S STAR RATINGS, ICONS & ABBREVIATIONS

Every hotel, restaurant, and attraction listing in this guide has been ranked for quality, value, service, amenities, and special features using a **star-rating system.** In country, state, and regional guides, we also rate towns and regions to help you narrow down your choices and budget your time accordingly. Hotels and restaurants are rated on a scale of zero (recommended) to three stars (exceptional). Attractions, shopping, nightlife, towns, and regions are rated according to the following scale: zero stars (recommended), one star (highly recommended), two stars (very highly recommended), and three stars (must-see).

In addition to the star-rating system, we also use **seven feature icons** that point you to the great deals, in-the-know advice, and unique experiences that separate travelers from tourists. Throughout the book, look for:

Finds	Special finds—those places only insiders know about
Fun Fact	Fun facts—details that make travelers more informed and their trips more fun
Kids	Best bets for kids and advice for the whole family
Moments	Special moments—those experiences that memories are made of
Overrated	Places or experiences not worth your time or money
Tips	Insider tips—great ways to save time and money
Value	Great values—where to get the best deals

The following **abbreviations** are used for credit cards:

AE	American Express	DISC	Discover	V	Visa
DC	Diners Club	MC	MasterCard		

FROMMERS.COM

Now that you have this guidebook to help you plan a great trip, visit our website at **www.frommers.com** for additional travel information on more than 4,000 destinations. We update features regularly to give you instant access to the most current trip-planning information available. At Frommers.com, you'll find scoops on the best airfares, lodging rates, and car rental bargains. You can even book your travel online through our reliable travel booking partners. Other popular features include:

- Online updates of our most popular guidebooks
- Vacation sweepstakes and contest giveaways
- Newsletters highlighting the hottest travel trends
- Podcasts, interactive maps, and up-to-the-minute events listings
- Opinionated blog entries by Arthur Frommer himself
- Online travel message boards with featured travel discussions

The Best of St. Maarten/ St. Martin with Anguilla & St. Barts

St. Maarten/St. Martin and its neighbors Anguilla and St. Barts offer something for everyone: from pristine beaches and duty-free jewelry to amazing outdoors adventures and nocturnal life on the wild side. You can stay in charming Creole cottages or world-class resorts. And you can dine very well indeed at casual beach barbecues or grand temples of gastronomy. Whatever your tastes and budget, in this chapter I'll guide you to the best these beautiful islands have to offer.

1 Frommer's Favorite Experiences

- **Day-Tripping to Offshore Islands:** Take a trip to a real-life desert-island paradise when you visit one of the tiny offshore gems on St. Martin and Anguilla. Here you can snorkel in gin-clear waters, sip rum punches, and eat lobster and barbecue fresh off the grill. There are few more relaxing diversions than wading in the gentle lagoon at idyllic Îlet Pinel (Pinel Island) near St. Martin's Orient Beach, or taking similar day trips off-island to Anguilla's Scilly Cay, Sandy Island, and Prickly Pear. See p. 94 and 155.
- **Watching children dip their toes in the calm, clear waters at Le Galion Beach, St. Martin:** It's not called the "children's beach" for nothing. Gentle waves lap a white-sand beach, where the shallow waters seem to go on forever. It's the perfect place for kids to learn the delights of swimming in the sea. See p. 96.
- **Becoming a High-Flying Yachtsman, St. Maarten:** If you've ever dreamed of racing in an America's Cup yachting competition, here's your chance. St. Maarten's 12-Metre Challenge lets you race real America's Cup boats in one of four regattas a day.

St. Maarten/St. Martin, Anguilla & St. Barts

Dog I.

Prickley Pear Keys

ANGUILLA
(U.K.)

The Valley ✈

SAINT-MARTIN
(FRANCE)

✈

Marigot   Orleans

SINT MAARTEN
(NETHERLANDS)

Phillipsburg

C A R I B B E A N

S E A

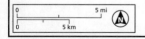

| 0 | | 5 mi |
| 0 | | 5 km |

DOMINICAN
REPUBLIC
San-Juan
VIRGIN ISLANDS
(U.S. & UK.)
see main
map
PUERTO
RICO
ST. KITTS
AND NEVIS
ANTIGUA AND
BARBUDA
MONTSERRAT
GUADELOUPE
DOMINICA
Caribbean Sea
MARTINIQUE
ST. LUCIA
L E S S E R
A N T I L L E S
ST. VINCENT
AND THE
GRENADINES
BARBADOS
NETHERLANDS
ANTILLES
GRENADA
Curaçao
Bonaire
*Isla la
Tortuga*
*Isla de
Margarita*
Tobago
Caracas
Port-of-Spain
TRINIDAD
AND TOBAGO
Trinidad
VENEZUELA

Scrub I.

I. Tintamarre

A T L A N T I C

O C E A N

I. Fourchue

I. Frégate
I. Toc Vers
I. Chevreau
La Tortue

SAINT BARTHÉLEMY
(FRANCE)
Gustavia

- **People-Watching at a Sidewalk Cafe:** Find yourself a prime seat on the Marigot waterfront, along the Front Street/Great Bay Boardwalk in Philipsburg (where leviathan cruise ships make the fishing dinghies look like toy boats), or in St. Barts' fairy-tale harbor town, Gustavia.

- **Dining in Grand Case, St. Martin:** This tiny fishing village has an appealing ramshackle style. But don't let its languourous style fool you: The "Gourmet Capital of the Caribbean" has an amazing concentration of top-notch eateries on one beachfront strip. See p. 76.

- **Visiting Loterie Farm, St. Martin:** Head over to this nature reserve to handle the zip lines or hike through virgin rainforest, followed by a meal at the lovely Hidden Forest Cafe. See p. 87.

- **Breakfast at La Samanna, St. Martin:** The view is extraordinary: You're high above Baie Longue, its white sands caressing the curve of the bay. The food isn't bad either; a grand buffet of breakfast favorites plus fresh island fruits and juices. See p. 64.

- **Horseback Riding, St. Maarten/St. Martin:** You actually dip into the water astride your horse during rides with **Bayside Riding Club** on the French side and **Lucky Stables** on the Dutch side (the latter also offers rugged 2-hr. jaunts down to Cay Bay). See p. 100.

- **Chilling in an Anguilla Beach Shack:** No place gets the beach-bar culture as right as Anguilla, where the vibe is laid-back, the food tasty, the music toe-tapping, and the setting sublime. It'll cure whatever ails you. See p. 152.

- **Dining Out in Anguilla:** You will not have a bad meal here, I guarantee it, whether you dine in one of the island's highly touted restaurants or at a barbecue buffet under the stars. See p. 147.

- **Kitesurfing in the Grand Cul-de-Sac on St. Barts:** This stretch of water is perfect for kitesurfing. It's a thrill to do, and a thrill to watch, as the billowing kites skim the clouds and the boards skate the glassy sea. See p. 190.

- **Beach-hopping in St. Barts:** Everyone does it, and they know *how* to do it. Grab a beach umbrella (your hotel can provide one for you)—shade is hard to find on St. Bart's beaches—towels, beach book, and delicious-smelling Ligne St. Barth coconut oil, and prepare for a day of luxuriating on some of the world's finest beaches. See p. 188.

- **Shopping in St. Barts:** When it comes to shopping, St. Barts wins the prize hands-down for the best in the Caribbean—it's Paris by the sea. And even better: It's duty- and tax-free. You can find stylish, high-quality clothing in even the most basic-looking shops. The pharmacies are shopping havens, where the famously exquisite French skincare lines and toiletries are a pleasure to browse. Even the grocery stores are a marvel, with imported French cheeses, pates, wine, and—ooh-la-la!—the French version of canned ravioli. See p. 191.

2 The Best Beaches

- **Orient Bay, St. Martin:** This happening strand may be clothing-optional, but it also happens to be a beautiful beach. If you're looking for water-sports action and a lively beach-bar scene, this is the place to find it. See p. 84.
- **Baie Longue, St. Martin:** The longest and perhaps most private stretch of sand on St. Martin, and a fine place to spot celebrities staying at La Samanna. See p. 92.
- **Baie de l'Embouchure/Galion Beach, St. Martin:** This crescent is encircled (and protected) by a reef, making it a prime family beach. But the steady breezes lure windsurfers too. It's a great place to glide, and learn. See p. 96.
- **Happy Bay, St. Martin:** It's a short hike to this remarkably pretty, remarkably deserted scimitar of blinding sand where you can act out Robinson Crusoe fantasies. See p. 95.
- **Pinel Island, St. Martin:** This tiny offshore cay makes for a wonderful day trip with a perfect lagoon to paddle around in. See p. 94.
- **Cupecoy Beach, St. Maarten:** This Dutch-side beach boasts gorgeous multihued cliffs pocked with caves, and the occasional green flash sighting at sunset. See p. 90.
- **Dawn Beach, St. Maarten:** The views of St. Barts, great beach bars, excellent windsurfing, and superb snorkeling enchant at any time of day. See p. 92.
- **Shoal Bay East, Anguilla:** Not to be confused with Shoal Bay West, this beach offers both rollicking activity and seclusion, with beach bars lining one section and great snorkeling on its less-trafficked eastern flank. See p. 156.
- **Rendezvous Bay, Anguilla:** This picture-perfect beach curls and stretches its sands for nearly 3 miles—it's a great swimming beach. See p. 156.

- **Maundays Bay, Anguilla:** The prime beach for the Cap Juluca resort, Maundys Bay has calm, sparkling waters that are perfect for swimming and snorkeling. See p. 156.
- **St-Jean Beach, St. Barts:** This beach is split into two beaches by the Eden Rock hotel, but it's lovely nonetheless. It's just steps away from great shopping and dining. See p. 188.
- **Flamands Beach, St. Barts:** This is a long, wide beach with little commercial activity and that rarity on St. Barts: a shady grove of lantana palms. See p. 188.

3 The Best Places to Get Away from It All

- **Hôtel L'Esplanade,** Grand Case, St. Martin (© **590/87-06-55**), is up on a bluff overlooking Grand Case and Grand Case beach, which you can see from your private terrace. This handsome hotel is pillowed in colorful flowers, and the rooms are utterly private and beautifully outfitted. You're just 5 minutes away from bustling Grand Case below, but this tranquil spot feels like a world apart. See p. 57.
- **Le Petit Hotel,** Grand Case, St. Martin (© **590/29-09-65**), is small and intimate indeed, yet its chic suites are fully equipped. Even though it sits right in the middle of the Grand Case gourmet strip, serenity prevails once you're inside—and the beachfront setting is glorious. See p. 59.
- **Hostellerie des Trois Forces,** Vitet, St. Barts (© **590/27-61-25**), isn't about cash and cachet: It's a genuinely serene spiritual retreat that lures seers and CEOs, thanks to owner/astrologer Hubert Delamotte (a Gemini). The mountaintop setting, seemingly miles from civilization, makes life's frenzied, frantic, frenetic pace melt away. Rooms are decorated according to each astrological sign's characteristics, and where else could you book past life regression therapy with a gourmet dinner? See p. 179.
- **Salines Garden Cottages,** Grande Saline, St. Barts (© **590/51-04-44**), is a cozy, comfortable, and arty retreat for romantics and self-sufficient types, just steps from a gorgeous, relatively tranquil beach. See p. 181.

4 The Best Luxury Hotels

- **La Samanna,** Baie Longue, St. Martin (© **800/237-1236**), is rare among resorts in its class (in both senses of the word), offering posh pampering with nary a hint of pretension. The main restaurant is set high up over Baie Longue—an unbelievably beautiful setting. See p. 58.

- **Cap Juluca,** Maundays Bay, Anguilla (© **888/858-5822**), is always at or near the top of everyone's "Best Of" lists. The Moroccan-themed digs, the beautiful landscaping, the wonderful rooms, and professional yet discreet service explain why it's a favorite of celebrities and captains of industry. But regular folks get the royal treatment, too. See p. 138.

- **Malliouhana,** Mead's Bay, Anguilla (© **800/835-0796**), has a cooler look and ambience than Cap Juluca, but it's just as luxe. It has twin beaches, gorgeous landscaping, sublime food, a lovely spa, stylish rooms, caring service, and owner Leon Roydon's collecting passions on display: Haitian art and arguably the Caribbean's finest wine cellar. See p. 140.

- **CuisinArt,** Anguilla (© **264/498-2000**), has a world-class beach, a lovely pool, a fabulous spa, and an amazing hydroponic farm, which supplies its on-site restaurants with fresh produce. It's a sunny, comfortable, well-managed resort, with service and amenities that just get better and better. See p. 139.

- **Eden Rock,** Baie de St-Jean, St. Barts (© **877/563-7105**), defines the old hotel mantra "location, location, location," its exquisite lodgings staggered on either side of the titular bluff that cleaves the bay, forming two perfect beaches. But delightful owners David and Jane Matthews never rest on their laurels, constantly improving one of the Caribbean's most elegant enclaves. See p. 173.

- **Hotel Guanahani & Spa,** Grand Cul-de-Sac, St. Barts (© **590/ 27-66-60**), is the ultimate spot to relax and unwind and let the pros pamper you. The vibrantly colored rooms are stuffed with state-of-the-art amenities, the beach looks out on beauteous Grand Cul-de-Sac bay, and the food is terrific. The capper? All this luxury is yours without pomp or attitude. See p. 174.

- **Hôtel St. Barth Isle de France,** Baie des Flamands, St. Barts (© **590/27-61-81**), is an award-winning boutique hotel (35 rooms) that is both luxurious and supremely comfortable. It opens right onto glorious Flamands beach. See p. 176.

5 The Best Restaurants

- **Temptation,** Cupecoy, St. Maarten (© **599/545-2254**), lives up to its admittedly silly if appropriate name with the island's most creative fare, not to mention an incredibly hip space. I have yet to experience a bad dish, let alone a mediocre meal. See p. 68.

- **Rare,** Cupecoy, St. Maarten (© **599/545-5714**), is the other brainchild of Temptation's wunderkind chef/owner, Dino Jagtiani. Aside from the witty decor and winning beef selection, his delightful side dishes are fun and inventive. See p. 68.

- **L'Hibiscus,** Grand Case, St. Martin (© **590/29-17-91**), is tiny and on the "wrong side" of Grand Case Boulevard, so it gets overlooked. But not by savvy locals, including rival restaurateurs, who appreciate the flavorful blend of classic French and Creole fare. See p. 78.

- **Spiga,** Grand Case, St. Martin (© **590/52-47-83**), proves that Grand Case (and St. Martin) can cook Italian with equal panache. From tuna carpaccio to tiramisu, everything is perfection. See p. 79.

- **Lolos,** St. Martin/St. Maarten, is a term for the basic outdoor shacks dishing out heaping helpings of heavenly Creole fare at unbelievably fair prices. The biggest concentration lies along the beach in Grand Case. See p. 77.

- **Malliouhana,** Anguilla (© **264/497-6111**), exemplifies why this tiny, scrubby British island rivals the best of the French West Indies in the dining department. The stellar French menu is personally supervised by two-star Michelin toque, Michel Rostang. The beachfront setting is simple yet stylish and the wine selection unparalleled. See p. 140.

- **Blanchards,** Anguilla (© **264/497-6100**), ranks high on everyone's list of top beachfront eateries. Owners Bob and Melinda Blanchard have become celebrities themselves, thanks to their witty books about the joys and perils of running a Caribbean restaurant. See p. 148.

- **Hibernia,** Anguilla (© **264/497-4290**), is an out-of-the-way gem whose owners brilliantly incorporate ingredients and techniques from their Asian travels into their exquisitely prepared and presented French fare. Their wanderings also inform the soothing, smart decor and adjacent gallery. See p. 149.

- **CuisinArt Barbecue Buffets,** Anguilla (© **264/498-2000**), will please both gourmands and the ultra-ravenous. It's an all-you-can-eat outdoor extravaganza, with grilled lobster, ribs, and chicken; fantastic sides (with produce from CuisinArt's own hydroponic farm); and scores of rich desserts—all of it unbelievably tasty. A string band will have your toes tapping. See p. 140.

- **Le Gaïac,** Anse de Toiny, St. Barts (© **590/27-88-88**), in the ultra-plush Le Toiny hotel, may be the last bastion of formal French dining on St. Barts. The ambience is swooningly romantic at dinner and the food sublime any time, but it's really a must for its extravagant Sunday brunches. See p. 188.
- **Le Sapotillier,** Gustavia, St. Barts (© **590/27-60-28**), now has Stéphane Guidal as its hot chef, and his credentials are impeccable—among other apprenticeships, Guidal worked with Alain Ducasse in Paris. Le Sapotillier remains a memorable fine-dining experience, where you spend the evening on the candlelit patio under a magnificent sapodilla tree or inside the clapboard-covered Creole cottage. See p. 184.

6 The Best Shopping

- **Front Street** in Philipsburg is a mind-boggling display of rampant consumerism. And it's all duty-free, from luxury watches to diamonds to Delft china. See p. 105.
- **Le West Indies Mall** and **Plaza Caraïbes** in Marigot feature the hautest of couture, well, at any rate prettily priced *prêt-à-porter* and accessories from such design legends as Cartier and Hermès. See p. 106.
- **Artists' ateliers** on the French side are particularly notable, showcasing Gallic expats working in a variety of media and traditions. Many open their studios to visitors, offering a wonderful insight into the creative process. See chapter 6.
- **Ma Doudou,** Cul de Sac, St. Martin (© **590/87-30-43**), offers a series of delectably infused, charmingly bottled rums, which for my money (or yours) beats the more famous Guavaberry liqueurs for flavor. See p. 115.
- **La Ligne St. Barth,** Lorient, St. Barts (© **590/27-82-63**), produces skin care, scents, and cosmetic products creatively crafted from Caribbean ingredients. The appetizing aroma in the traditional Creole cottage/factory surpasses that at many a restaurant. See p. 192.
- **Made in St-Barth,** St-Jean, St. Barts (© **590/27-56-57**), is a fine source for local artworks and crafts, including superb intricate straw-work, as well as locally made essential oils and infused rums. See p. 192.

7 The Best Nightlife

- **Bamboo Bernie's,** St. Maarten (© **599/545-3622**), is a sushi bar. No, it's a tiki bar. No, it's a grade-A meat market. Well, it's a pleasure palace, with fishbowl drinks, swimsuit competitions, even a climbing wall and movie screenings in its Kuta Beach "nightclub" section: something for almost everyone. See p. 120.
- **Bliss,** St. Maarten (© **599/545-3936**), sounds like a spa, but it's actually Bernie's equally sizzling neighbor, another multi-purpose beachfront nightclub-cum-restaurant-cum-live-music-venue. See p. 117.
- **Casino Royale,** St. Maarten (© **599/545-2590**), is the island's largest and glitziest casino, but really gets the nod over its competitors for its Vegas-style showroom and upstairs high-tech disco throwback, **Q-Club.** See p. 126.
- **Celine,** St. Maarten (© **599/545-3961**), and her skipper/builder, Neil Roebert, offer a unique experience. During Celine's Lagoon Pub Crawl, you sail to three Simpson Bay hot spots for drinks and appetizers. See p. 98.
- **Sunset Beach Bar,** St. Maarten (© **599/545-3998**), on the same beach as Bernie's and Bliss, is one of those places you either love or hate, but it's a "must" experience. A dive in the best or worst sense of the word, Sunset is famous for watching the planes take off and land right above your head. See p. 121.
- **Cheri's Café,** St. Maarten (© **599/545-3361**), is one of those institutions that manages to avoid becoming a cliché or a tourist trap: good relatively inexpensive food, congenial crowd, and fun entertainment. See p. 122.
- **Johnno's Beach Stop,** Sandy Ground, Anguilla (© **264/497-2728**), is another enduringly popular haunt that draws everyone from locals to Hollywood elite for great barbecue and live music on the beach. See p. 152.
- **Dune Preserve,** Rendezvous Bay, Anguilla (© **264/497-2660**), is a multi-tiered beachfront bar that was crafted out of old boats and beach salvage. It's got lots of interesting nooks and crannies and now serves food from one of the island's best cooks, Dale Carty. It's owned by Anguilla's best-known singer, "Bankie" Banx, and jammed when he performs. See p. 153.
- **Nikki Beach,** Baie de St-Jean, St. Barts (© **590/27-64-64**), may be that chain's most absurdly decadent, debauched exclusive outpost. The A-list makes a beeline here to spray each other

with champagne and canoodle in canopied four-poster beds on the sand, the paparazzi's popping bulbs (and everyone else's popping eyes) be damned. See p. 194.

- **Le Ti St. Barth,** Pointe Milou, St. Barts (© **590/27-97-71**), serves up uneven but often scrumptious food in a sensuous torchlit setting that lures the merely wealthy and beautiful for sizzling theme nights. See p. 194.

2

Planning Your Trip to St. Maarten/St. Martin with Anguilla & St. Barts

Dickens may have had his *A Tale of Two Cities,* but St. Maarten/St. Martin spins a tale of two nations, indeed two lifestyles, in just 96 sq. km (37 sq. miles)—the world's smallest land mass shared by two sovereign states, France and the Netherlands. So friendly are their relations that you don't even clear Customs when passing between them; only flags and welcome signs (BIENVENUE À PARTIE FRANÇAISE) stand guard over the obelisk marking the border at Mount Concordia. Everything about the island is similarly user-friendly. Though the euro and Netherlands Antilles florin are the official currencies, the dollar is accepted everywhere and English spoken throughout.

Returning visitors who haven't been to the island for a while are often shocked by today's St. Maarten. No longer a sleepy Caribbean backwater, it's now a boomtown (administered as part of the semi-autonomous Dutch Caribbean territory of the Netherlands Antilles). Much has been lost to the bulldozer, and it isn't for those who hate crowds, especially when cruise-ship hordes retake **Philipsburg,** the Dutch capital. Indeed, a fellow travel writer once described St. Maarten as Cleveland with palm trees; his wife quickly retorted that Cleveland had cleaned up its act.

In some respects, that uncharitable comment is true. Although Dutch St. Maarten has its share of pastoral pockets, alluring beaches, and historic ruins, per square foot the Dutch side is one of the Caribbean's most developed islands: Strip malls have stripped the landscape of character, and even residents joke that the local flower is the satellite dish. Indeed, the island is more notable for what it lacks: It has no major art museums, the native folk and craft traditions are disintegrating, and everything has become increasingly homogenized. Ironically, that makes St. Maarten ideal entry-level Caribbean, cannily blending familiarity and exoticism. Despite

A Little History

Excavations suggest St. Maarten was settled around 2,500 years ago by American Indian Arawaks. Christopher Columbus sighted the island during his second voyage in November 1493, naming it without setting foot on land. The Spaniards couldn't spare the expense of military maintenance after several devastating European wars, so they literally abandoned it in 1648, enabling opportunistic French and Dutch settlers from, respectively, St. Kitts and St. Eustatius, to claim the island. After initial skirmishes, mostly political, the two nations officially settled their differences later that year. Even so, St. Maarten changed hands 16 times before it became permanently Dutch, while the French side endured the usual colonial tugs-of-war through the Napoleonic era. Alas, there appears to be no truth to the colorful legend of a wine-drinking Frenchman and gin-guzzling Dutchman walking the island to determine the border.

problems like crime, occasional storms, traffic congestion, and corruption, St. Maarten continues to attract massive numbers of visitors who want a Caribbean island vacation with a splash of Las Vegas. And Philipsburg is in the throes of a serious beautification initiative, and its waterfront boardwalk is a pleasure to stroll.

The French side (currently governed from Guadeloupe though it has petitioned for its separate status) remains quieter, more subtly European: a tropic St. Tropez. White stucco houses adorned with flowerpots and red-tile roofs cling to sapphire coves, the inimitable scent of galettes and Gauloises hanging in the air. Police officers wear *kepis,* towns have names like Colombier and Orléans, and the French flag flies over the *gendarmerie* in **Marigot,** the capital. Advocates cite French St. Martin as more sophisticated, prosperous, stylish, and cosmopolitan than its fellow *départements d'outre-mer,* Guadeloupe and Martinique.

The pace on Dutch St. Maarten resembles a frat party by comparison, with neon-accented action at its casinos and clubs. Both sides offer watersports aplenty, superb dining (you'll find not just some of the finest French fare outside La Belle France, but everything from rigatoni to *rijstaffel*), and duty-free shopping.

And underneath that splashy shell beats the heart of the islands' African roots. They emerge in the snatch of a racy reggae ditty along

St. Maarten: A Bigger, Better Cruise-Ship Port

St. Maarten's booming cruise-ship business has gotten even bigger, with a late-2007 deal between Carnival Cruise Lines and the St. Maarten government to build a new two-berth cruise-ship pier at the Port of St. Maarten, in Point Blanche, just outside Philipsburg. This will give St. Maarten a total of six dedicated cruise berths—making it one of the Caribbean's largest cruise-ship ports. For more about the port, go to **www.portofstmaarten.com**.

a street; in the brightly colored shirts and shifts that replace the crisp starched school uniforms at a weekend picnic; in the spices that enliven the local cuisine; in Carnival's colorful jambalaya of sights, sounds, and smells.

It all adds up to a tale of two nations that offers the best of both worlds: activity and leisure. If you're seeking fun in the sun, even R&R *à deux,* they fit the bill.

1 The Islands in Brief

ST. MAARTEN/ST. MARTIN   In the early 1990s, this little island exploded in popularity as a tourist destination thanks to easy air access from the eastern U.S. and a boom in timeshare development. It's also one of the Caribbean's duty-free (and tax-free) shopping meccas. Its unique political situation and remarkably varied populace (census figures allegedly list around 130 nationalities) lend it a cosmopolitan air even when it's overrun by cruise ship passengers, who tend to cluster on the more developed Dutch side. In high season, the large number of tourists and constant building (and the six-times-daily opening of the Simpson Bay bridge to let boat traffic through) combine to create traffic snarls around the airport. **Philipsburg,** the capital of Dutch St. Maarten, is lined with duty-free shops selling luxury watches, cameras, and other high-end goods—catnip to the cruise-ship passengers who descend on the port city with increasing frequency. On French St. Martin, **Marigot** is not quite the same size as its Dutch counterpart and has little of its sometimes frenzied pace—but it does have a rich cache of duty-free shops and tony international brands (Chanel, Cartier, Hermes). In fact, Marigot looks like a French village transplanted to the Caribbean. If you climb the hill over this little port, you'll be rewarded with a view from the old fort. About 15 minutes by car beyond Marigot is

Grand Case, a small, charming Creole fishing village that's an outpost of French civilization, with a number of excellent restaurants and a handful of recommended hotels.

ANGUILLA Just 20 minutes by ferry from Marigot, flat, arid, scrubby Anguilla has become one of the Caribbean's choicest destinations, despite its unprepossessing landscape and comparative lack of colonial grandeur. The reasons are obvious: The island resembles one big sugary-sand beach surrounded by luminous turquoise seas. The locals are friendly and laid-back, all beneficiaries of the excellent British education system. You'll find almost no hawking, pushiness, or overt poverty—and correspondingly low crime rates. The leading resorts and villa complexes define luxury, and the food is some of the finest in the Caribbean. And yet the vibe is pleasingly laid-back in even the toniest resorts; it's barefoot luxury at its least pretentious.

ST. BARTS A quick flight or ferry ride 24km (15 miles) east of St. Maarten/St. Martin, this rugged, hilly, 21-sq.-km (8-sq.-mile) island ("St. Barths," to the locals) is practically synonymous with international glamour and glorious beaches. The cost for effortless chic is astronomical (especially for Americans, whose dollar has plummeted against the euro), but the jet set (once nicknamed the Concorde Horde) has never minded. Despite its forbidding prices and luxury reputation—and its sometimes ostentatious display of wealth—St. Barts has retained its xxx French soul and sunny, easy-going West Indian heart. The 8,000 locals—many descended from the original hardy Norman and Breton settlers—remain matter-of-fact and supremely unimpressed by the jet-setting crowd. And why not? Their cultural traditions are firmly entrenched in a fairy-tale capital, **Gustavia;** the Caribbean equivalent of the Riviera, **St-Jean;** exceptionally pretty fishing villages as **Colombier** and **Corossol;** and along a gnarled coastline that harbors some of the world's most beautiful **beaches.**

2 Visitor Information

For the latest information on **Dutch St. Maarten** and **French St. Martin,** go to **www.st-maarten.com** or **www.st-martin.org,** respectively. You can also contact the St. Maarten/St. Martin Tourist Office, 675 Third Ave., Suite 1807, New York, NY 10017 (© **800/ 786-2278** or 212/953-2084 for the department servicing the Dutch side, and © **877/956-1234** or 212/475-8970 for the department servicing the French side). In Canada, the office for information about the Dutch side of the island is located at 703 Evans Ave., Suite

106, Toronto, ON M9C 5E9 (℡ **416/622-4300**). For information about the French side of the island, contact 1981 Ave. McGill College, Suite 490, in Montréal (℡ **514/288-4264**).

Once on St. Maarten, go to the **Tourist Information Bureau,** Vineyard Office Park, 33 W. G. Buncamper Rd., Philipsburg, St. Maarten, N.A. (℡ **599/542-2337**), open Monday to Friday from 9am to 5pm.

The tourist board on French St. Martin, called the **Office du Tourisme,** is at Route de Sandy Ground, Marigot, 97150 St. Martin (℡ **590/87-57-21**), open Monday to Friday from 8am to 1pm and 2:30 to 5:30pm.

For details on Anguilla and St. Barts, see chapters 8 and 9, respectively.

3 Entry Requirements & Customs

ENTRY REQUIREMENTS
PASSPORTS

U.S. and Canadian citizens must have a passport or a combination of a birth certificate and photo ID, plus a return or ongoing ticket, to enter the country. Citizens of the United Kingdom, Commonwealth countries of the Caribbean, the Republic of Ireland, and E.U. countries must also have a current passport.

All travelers coming from the Caribbean, including Americans, are now required to have a passport to enter or re-enter the United States. Those returning to Canada are also required to show passports. Cruise ship passengers have until June 1, 2009, to meet the requirement. You'll certainly need identification at some point, and a passport is the best form of ID for speeding through Customs and Immigration. Driver's licenses are not acceptable as a sole form of ID.

CUSTOMS

Generally, you're permitted to bring in items intended for your personal use, including tobacco, cameras, film, and a limited supply of liquor—usually 40 ounces.

Just before you leave home, check with the St. Maarten/St. Martin Customs or Foreign Affairs department for the latest guidelines—including information on items that are not allowed to be brought into your home country—since the rules are subject to change and often contain some surprising oddities.

Visitors to St. Maarten/St. Martin (as well as St. Barts and Anguilla) may not carry any form of firearm, spear guns, pole spears, illegal drugs, live plants or cuttings, and raw fruits and vegetables.

Visitors over 18 may bring in—duty-free—items intended for personal use (generally up to 4 liters of alcohol, a carton of cigarettes or 25 cigars), as well as laptops, cell phones, and cameras.

You should collect receipts for all purchases made abroad. You must also declare on your Customs form the nature and value of all gifts received during your stay abroad.

If you use any medication that contains controlled substances or requires injection, carry an original prescription or note from your doctor.

For specifics on what you can bring back, download the invaluable free pamphlet *Know Before You Go* online at **www.customs. ustreas.gov**. (Click on "Travel," then go to "Travel Smart" and click on "Know Before You Go.") Or contact the **U.S. Customs and Border Protection (CBP),** 1300 Pennsylvania Ave. NW, Washington, DC 20229 (✆ **877/287-8667**), and request the pamphlet.

For a clear summary of **Canadian** rules, write for the booklet *I Declare,* issued by the **Canada Border Services Agency** (✆ **800/ 461-9999** in Canada, or 204/983-3500; www.cbsa-asfc.gc.ca).

U.K. citizens should contact **HM Customs & Excise** at ✆ **0845/ 010-9000** (✆ 020/8929-0152 from outside the U.K.), or consult its website at www.hmce.gov.uk.

Citizens of **Australia** should request a helpful brochure available from Australian consulates or Customs offices called *Know Before You Go.* For more information, call the **Australian Customs Service** at ✆ **1300/363-263,** or log on to www.customs.gov.au.

For **New Zealand** Customs information, contact **New Zealand Customs** at ✆ **04/473-6099** or 0800/428-786, or log on to www. customs.govt.nz.

4 Money
CURRENCY
Despite the dominance of the euro since January 2002 within the mother country, Holland, the legal tender on the Dutch side is still the **Netherlands Antilles florin (NAf);** the official exchange rate is NAf 1.79 for each $1. U.S. dollars are widely accepted, and prices in hotels and most restaurants and shops are often designated in dollars as well. On the French side (as well as on St. Barts), the official monetary unit is the **euro,** with most establishments widely quoting and accepting either dollars or NAf guilders as well. At press time, the U.S. dollar was trading at $1.50 to the euro. **Anguilla**'s official currency is the **Eastern Caribbean Dollar,** though U.S. dollars are

accepted everywhere; the exchange rate is set permanently at roughly 2.70EC to $1. (Just before you leave home, you can check the current exchange rates at **www.xe.com/ucc**.) Prices throughout this book are given in U.S. dollars for establishments on the Dutch side and Anguilla, and in either euros or U.S. dollars for establishments on the French side and St. Barts according to whether establishments quoted their prices in euros or dollars at the time of publication.

As the dollar is much weaker than the euro, some establishments on St. Barts and French St. Martin advertise a 1-to-1 exchange rate if you use cash. Always confirm before you get the bill.

ATMs

The easiest and best way to get cash away from home is from an ATM. Banks affiliated with the **Cirrus** (© **800/424-7787;** www. mastercard.com) and **PLUS** (© **800/843-7587;** www.visa.com) ATM networks are located on St. Maarten/St. Martin. Check the following banks' websites for locations of ATMs (also called ABMs for "automated banking machines"): **Windward Island Bank** (http://wib-bank.net); **Scotiabank** (www.scotiabank.com); **First-Caribbean** bank (www.firstcaribbeanbank.com); and **RBTT N.V.** (www.rbtt.com). The international airport in St. Maarten has two ATMs (WIB and RBTT) on the Arrivals floor. A Scotiabank branch is located at the cruise terminal building at Pointe Blanche, St. Maarten.

Note: Keep in mind that ATMs in St. Maarten give you a choice of dollars or euros, while ATMs on St. Martin only dispense euros.

For bank and ATM information on St. Barts and Anguilla, see chapters 8 and 9.

Be sure you know your personal identification number (PIN) and your daily withdrawal limit before you leave home. Also keep in mind that many banks impose a fee every time a card is used at a different bank's ATM, and that fee can be higher for international transactions than for domestic ones. And if you use a debit card, the fees may be higher still—again, check with your bank before you leave home. On top of this, the bank from which you withdraw cash may charge its own fee. For international withdrawal fees, ask your bank before you leave home.

TRAVELER'S CHECKS

You can get traveler's checks at almost any bank. They are offered in denominations of $20, $50, $100, $500, and sometimes $1,000. Generally, you'll pay a service charge ranging from 1% to 4%.

The most popular traveler's checks are offered by American Express (© **800/807-6233** or 800/221-7282 for cardholders—this number accepts collect calls, offers service in several foreign languages, and exempts Amex gold and platinum cardholders from the 1% fee); **Visa** (© **800/732-1322**)—AAA members can obtain Visa checks for a $9.95 fee (for checks up to $1,500) at most AAA offices or by calling © **866/339-3378;** and **MasterCard** (© **800/223-9920**).

If you carry traveler's checks, be sure to keep a record of their serial numbers separate from your checks in the event that they are stolen or lost. You'll get a refund faster if you know the numbers.

CREDIT CARDS

Credit cards are widely accepted at businesses in St. Maarten/St. Martin. Credit cards are a safe way to carry money, they provide a convenient record of all your expenses, and they generally offer relatively good exchange rates. You can also withdraw cash advances from your credit cards at banks or ATMs, provided you know your PIN. Keep in mind that you'll pay interest from the moment of your withdrawal, even if you pay your monthly bills on time. Also note that many banks now assess a 1% to 3% "transaction fee" on all charges you incur abroad (whether you're using the local currency or your native currency).

Almost every credit card company has an emergency toll-free number that you can call if your wallet or purse is stolen. Credit card companies may be able to wire cash advances immediately, and in many places they can deliver an emergency credit card in a day or two. **Citicorp Visa**'s U.S. emergency number is © **800/336-8472.** **American Express** cardholders and traveler's check holders should call © **800/221-7282** for all money emergencies. **MasterCard** holders should call © **800/307-7309.**

5 When to Go

THE HIGH & LOW SEASONS

Hotels on all three islands charge their highest rates during the peak winter season, from mid-December to mid-April. Christmas week rates may double those tariffs. You should make reservations months in advance for Christmas and February, especially over Presidents' Day weekend.

The off-season on all three islands runs roughly mid-April to mid-December (though exact dates vary according to hotel). It's one big summer sale: Most hotels, inns, condos, and villas slash their prices 20% to 50%. The beaches are less crowded and many top lodgings and restaurants shutter for one, even two months as the owners take their own vacation or perform necessary renovations. Be sure to request a room away from noise if the hotel remains open during construction. We provide closing dates wherever possible, but visitors should double-check before booking.

WEATHER

High season on all three islands features a temperate climate, rarely exceeding 90°F (32°C), with lower humidity and the famed cooling trade winds blowing in from the northeast. It's ideal beach weather, with the occasional cloudy day. Usually rain showers are brief: Islanders call them "liquid sunshine."

Rainy season runs from late May to mid-November. This doesn't mean it rains for days at a time or even every day. But this also roughly corresponds to the official Atlantic hurricane season, June 1 to November 30. Fortunately, satellite surveillance provides enough advance warning to take precautions and, rarely, evacuate.

St. Maarten/St. Martin Average Daily Temperature & Rainfall

	Jan	Feb	Mar	Apr	May	June	July	Aug	Sept	Oct	Nov	Dec
Temp. (°F)	77	77	77	79	81	81	83	83	83	81	80	79
Temp. (°C)	25	25	25	26	27	27	28	28	28	28	27	26
Rainfall (in.)	2.5	1.3	1.6	2.3	2.3	3.8	3.8	3.5	3.7	4.4	3.8	3.7

ST. MAARTEN/ST. MARTIN CALENDAR OF EVENTS

For Anguilla and St. Barts, see chapters 8 and 9.

January & February

Carnival. Festivities on St. Martin last for nearly 2 months starting the second Sunday in January with parade rehearsals and band tryouts.

Carnival reaches its frenzied peak on the French side in February, with jump-ups, barbecues, and pageants. It all leads to J'ouvert, the weekend before Mardi Gras and lasts until Ash Wednesday. The wild dancing-in-the-streets parades represent the culmination of an entire year's preparation from creating the feathered, sequined costumes to writing the unique musical themes. The streets are crowded with young and old following trucks with enormous sound systems in Marigot until everyone congregates at "Carnival Village" come nightfall for concerts and events, including the crowning of the Carnival King and Queen.

March

Heineken Regatta. This annual series of major boat races debuted in 1980. More than 200 vessels, from converted family fishing dinghies to race prototypes, compete in several categories. It's a prime excuse for partying, particularly on the Dutch side. For details, go to www.heinekenregatta.com. First weekend of March.

Anglers Big Fishing Tournament. This is the first of several year-round fishing competitions that lures an international roster. Last weekend of March.

April

Carnival. The Dutch side chimes in with its own, even more extravagant version, beginning the Wednesday after Easter Sunday and continuing for 15 riotous days of beauty pageants, costume and calypso competitions, Mas bands, parades, shows, and assorted revels.

The Carnival Village features stands dishing out spicy local fare and an enormous stage where local and international musicians perform nightly. J'ouvert, the opening jump-up, showcases local and international bands and thousands of revelers line the streets and follow the bands until they arrive at Carnival Village.

More parades are held the next morning, and the grandest of all takes place on the Queen's Birthday. Crowds pack the streets of Philipsburg vying for a spot to see the musicians, the outrageous costumes, and the colorful floats. The Last Lap, the grand finale of the Carnival, includes a symbolic burning of King Momo, a straw figure who embodies the spirit of Carnival. Island legend claims that burning the King in effigy will purge the sins and consequent bad luck of the village. Check www.stmaartencarnival. com for more information.

St. Maarten Open Golf Tournament. Residents and visitors alike are invited to participate in this 3-day 54-hole event at Mullet Bay Golf Resort. For details, go to www.stmaartengolf.com. First weekend in April.

May

Ecotourism Day. Nature discovery organizations, activity operators, artisans, and local entertainers take over the Bellevue Estate on the French side for this event. You can indulge in free sea kayaking, scuba diving, horseback tours, mountain bike riding, hiking, and treasure hunts. Cultural and culinary traditions are displayed: spice-growing, pottery-making, coffee-roasting. Typical island dishes and local bands are also on the menu. Go to www.st-martin.org for updates. Usually second or third weekend of May.

Fête du Nautisme. This watersports festival organized by METIMER, the St. Martin Sea Trades Association, focuses on (re)discovering the rich marine environment. Free activities include yacht and motorboat excursions and regattas, jet-skiing, kayaking, and windsurfing, with lessons available. Usually second or third weekend of May.

June
Billfish Tournament. One of the Caribbean's most prestigious fishing competitions lasts nearly the entire week, attracting anglers from Europe and the Caribbean. About 30 fishing boats battle at the Marlin Boulevard area, rich fishing grounds about 48km (30 miles) east of St. Maarten. Go to www.billfish-tournament.com for details. Usually second week of June.

July
Bastille Day. The French holiday is celebrated island-wide with fanfare and fireworks, races and revelry. July 14.

Schoelcher Day. Boat and bike races are held in honor of Victor Schoelcher, a Frenchman, who fought against slavery. July 21.

November
St. Maarten's Day. Christopher Columbus named the island St. Maarten/St. Martin because he discovered it in 1493 on November 11, the feast day of St. Martin of Tours. Island residents on both sides still celebrate it as an official holiday, organizing various sporting events, parades, and jump-ups over 2 to 3 days. November 11.

December
MYBA St. Maarten Charter Show. One of the Caribbean's premier boat shows, now run by worldwide yachting association MYBA, is a chance for brokers to display their leviathan ships to potential bookers. It's also an excuse for lots of partying on and off the water. For details, go to www.mybacaribbeanshow.com. First week of December.

6 Travel Insurance

Check your existing insurance policies and credit card coverage before you buy travel insurance. You may already be covered for lost luggage, canceled tickets, and/or medical expenses.

The cost of travel insurance varies widely, depending on the cost and length of your trip, your age and health, and the type of trip you're taking, but expect to pay between 5% and 8% of the vacation itself. You can get estimates from various providers through **Insure MyTrip.com.** Enter your trip cost and dates, your age, and other information for prices from more than a dozen companies.

TRIP-CANCELLATION INSURANCE   Trip-cancellation insurance helps you get your money back if you have to back out of a trip, if you have to go home early, or if your travel supplier goes bankrupt. Permissible reasons for cancellation can range from sickness to natural disasters to the State Department declaring your destination unsafe for travel.

For information, contact one of the following recommended insurers: **Access America** (© 866/807-3982; www.accessamerica. com), **Travel Guard International** (© 800/826-4919; www.travel guard.com), **Travel Insured International** (© 800/243-3174; www.travelinsured.com), or **Travelex Insurance Services** (© 888/ 457-4602; www.travelex-insurance.com).

MEDICAL INSURANCE   For travel overseas, most health plans (including Medicare and Medicaid) do not provide coverage, and the ones that do often require you to pay for services upfront and reimburse you only after you return home. As a safety net, you may want to buy travel medical insurance, particularly if you're traveling to a remote or high-risk area where emergency evacuation is a possible scenario. If you require additional medical insurance, try **MEDEX Assistance** (© 410/453-6300; www.medexassist.com) or **Travel Assistance International** (© 800/821-2828; www.travelassistance. com; for general information on services, call the company's Worldwide Assistance Services, Inc., at © 800/777-8710).

LOST-LUGGAGE INSURANCE   On flights within the U.S., checked baggage is covered up to $2,500 per ticketed passenger. On international flights (including U.S. portions of international trips), baggage coverage is limited to approximately $9.07 per pound, up to approximately $635 per checked bag. If you plan to check items more valuable than the standard liability, see if your homeowner's policy covers your valuables, get baggage insurance as part of your comprehensive travel-insurance package, or buy Travel Guard's "BagTrak" product.

If your luggage is lost, immediately file a lost-luggage claim at the airport, detailing the luggage contents. Most airlines require that you report delayed, damaged, or lost baggage within 4 hours of arrival. The airlines are required to deliver luggage, once found, directly to your house or destination free of charge.

7 Health & Safety

STAYING HEALTHY
GENERAL AVAILABILITY OF HEALTHCARE
There are no particular health concerns on St. Maarten/St. Martin, Anguilla, or St. Barts. The best medical facilities are on St. Maarten/St. Martin, with good clinics on Anguilla and St. Barts. Emergency airlift to Puerto Rico is available from all three destinations.

It's fairly easy to obtain major over-the-counter medication, though the brands might be manufactured in Europe under unfamiliar names. Some leading prescription drugs for such common ailments as allergies, asthma, and acid reflux are also available over the counter, albeit by European pharmaceutical companies.

Contact the **International Association for Medical Assistance to Travelers (IAMAT; ℂ 716/754-4883,** or in Canada 416/652-0137; www.iamat.org) for tips on travel and health concerns on the islands you're visiting and lists of local English-speaking doctors. The **United States' Centers for Disease Control and Prevention** (℃ **800/311-3435;** www.cdc.gov) provides up-to-date information on health hazards by region or country and offers tips on food safety. The website **www.tripprep.com**, sponsored by a consortium of travel-medicine practitioners, may also offer helpful advice.

COMMON AILMENTS
BUGS, BITES & OTHER WILDLIFE CONCERNS The biggest menaces on all three islands are mosquitoes (none are disease vectors) and no-see-ums, which appear mainly in the early evening. Window screens aren't always sufficient, so carry insect repellent.

SUN EXPOSURE The tropical sun can be brutal. Wear sunglasses and a hat, and apply sunscreen liberally. Increase your time on the beach gradually. If you do overexpose yourself, stay out of the sun until you recover. Sun and heatstroke are possibilities, especially if you engage in strenuous physical activity. See a doctor immediately if fever, chills, dizziness, nausea, or headaches follow overexposure.

WHAT TO DO IF YOU GET SICK AWAY FROM HOME
It's easy to find good English-speaking doctors on all three islands. You can find **hospitals** and **emergency numbers** under "Fast Facts"

SPECIALIZED TRAVEL RESOURCES

on p. 38. For Anguilla and St. Barts, refer to p. 135 and p. 170, respectively.

If you suffer from a chronic illness, consult your doctor before your departure. If you worry about getting sick away from home, you might want to consider medical travel insurance (see the section on travel insurance, above)

You may have to pay all medical costs upfront and be reimbursed later. See "Medical Insurance," under "Travel Insurance," above.

STAYING SAFE
Violent crime is rare on Anguilla and St. Barts, though isolated incidents are reported on St. Maarten/St. Martin. Petty crime has become an issue of concern on St. Maarten, however, with thefts and break-ins an increasing problem. Travelers are urged to lock their cars and lodging doors and windows at all times. Visitors should exercise common sense and take basic precautions, including being aware of one's surroundings, avoiding walking alone after dark or in remote areas, and locking all valuables in a rental or hotel safe.

8 Specialized Travel Resources
TRAVELERS WITH DISABILITIES
Most disabilities shouldn't stop anyone from traveling. There are more options and resources out there than ever before. Unfortunately, the islands aren't on the vanguard, though larger hotels usually offer handicap-accessible rooms. It's always advisable to call the hotel of your choice and personally discuss your needs before booking a vacation.

Many travel agencies offer customized tours and itineraries for travelers with disabilities. **Access-Able Travel Source** (② 303/232-2979; www.access-able.com) offers access information and advice for traveling around the world with disabilities.

Organizations that offer assistance to disabled travelers include **MossRehab** (www.mossresourcenet.org); the **American Foundation for the Blind** (AFB; ② 800/232-5463; www.afb.org); and **SATH** (**Society for Accessible Travel & Hospitality**; ② 212/447-7284; www.sath.org).

GAY & LESBIAN TRAVELERS
The Caribbean in general isn't the LGBT-friendliest destination perhaps because of regrettably rampant "on the DL" hypocrisy in local communities. Anguilla, like many a British colony, is quite conservative in attitude, but individual deluxe resorts welcome gay and lesbian

Frommers.com: The Complete Travel Resource

Planning a trip or just returned? Head to **Frommers.com,** voted Best Travel Site by *PC Magazine*. We think you'll find our site indispensable before, during, and after your travels—with expert advice and tips; independent reviews of hotels, restaurants, attractions, and preferred shopping and nightlife venues; vacation giveaways; and an online booking tool. We publish the complete contents of over 135 travel guides in our **Destinations** section, covering over 4,000 places worldwide. Each weekday, we publish original articles that report on **Deals and News** via our free **Frommers.com Newsletters.** What's more, **Arthur Frommer** himself blogs 5 days a week, with cutting opinions about the state of travel in the modern world. We're betting you'll find our **Events** listings an invaluable resource; it's an up-to-the-minute roster of what's happening in cities everywhere—including concerts, festivals, lectures, and more. We've also added weekly **podcasts, interactive maps,** and hundreds of new images across the site. Finally, don't forget to visit our **Message Boards,** where you can join in conversations with thousands of fellow Frommer's travelers and post your trip report once you return.

travelers. St. Barts is by far the most open of the islands covered in this book.

The French and Dutch are generally tolerant, but St. Maarten/St. Martin is a mixed bag. Its self-proclaimed reputation as the Friendly Island took a beating after a horrific gay-bashing on April 6, 2006. Two men were attacked with tire irons, allegedly by four thugs shouting anti-gay epithets. Authorities on both sides, mindful of negative publicity and its impact on tourism, took action and apprehended the suspects within a month.

The International Gay and Lesbian Travel Association (IGLTA; © **800/448-8550** or 954/776-2626; www.iglta.org) is the trade association for the gay and lesbian travel industry, and offers an online directory of gay- and lesbian-friendly travel businesses; go to their website and click on "Consumer Site."

SENIOR TRAVEL

Though the major U.S. airlines flying to St. Maarten no longer offer senior discounts or coupon books, some hotels extend deals, especially during slower periods. Members of **AARP** (formerly known as the American Association of Retired Persons), 601 E St. NW, Washington, DC 20049 (© **888/687-2277;** www.aarp.org), get discounts on hotels, airfares, and car rentals. AARP offers members a wide range of benefits, including *AARP The Magazine* and a monthly newsletter. Anyone over 50 can join.

FAMILY TRAVEL

St. Maarten/St. Martin has several kid-friendly activities, and many restaurants feature kids' menus. The absence of American-style kid-centric attractions like theme parks doesn't keep families away from Anguilla and St. Barts, popular (if pricey) family destinations where kids are heartily welcomed in even the toniest resorts.

To locate accommodations, restaurants, and attractions that are particularly kid-friendly, refer to the "Kids" icon throughout this guide.

9 Getting There

BY PLANE

There are two airports on the island. St. Maarten's **Princess Juliana International Airport (PJIA)** (© **599/54-67542;** www.pjiae.com) is the second-busiest airport in the eastern Caribbean, topped only by San Juan, Puerto Rico, and your likely arrival point. Princess Juliana is a thoroughly modern facility, with restaurants, snack bars, ATMs, and car-rental kiosks. The smaller **L'Espérance Airport,** in Grand Case on French St. Martin (© **590/87-10-36**), caters largely to smaller commuter airlines.

American Airlines (© **800/433-7300** in the U.S. and Canada; www.aa.com) offers more options and more frequent service into St. Maarten than any other airline—two daily nonstop flights from New York's JFK and one from Miami. Additional nonstop daily flights into St. Maarten are offered by American and its local affiliate, **American Eagle** (same number), from San Juan. Ask about American's package tours, which can save you a bundle.

Continental Airlines (© **800/231-0856** in the U.S. and Canada; www.continental.com) has daily nonstop flights out of its hub in Newark, New Jersey, during the winter months (flight times vary in low season). **Delta Airlines** (© **800/241-4141** in the U.S.

and Canada; www.delta.com) flies in from New York City, and **United** (𝄪 **800/538-2929**; www.united.com) also offers flights from New York. Both leave from JFK airport.

US Airways (𝄪 **800/428-4322** in the U.S. and Canada; www. usairways.com) offers nonstop daily service from Philadelphia and Charlotte to St. Maarten.

JetBlue Airways (𝄪 **800-JETBLUE/538-2583** in the US; www. jetblue.com) has introduced one daily nonstop flight from New York's JFK into St. Maarten.

Spirit Airlines (𝄪 **800/772-7117** in the U.S. and Canada; www.spiritair.com) has begun nonstop service from Fort Lauderdale to St. Maarten.

Caribbean Airlines (𝄪 **800/920-4225** in the U.S. and Canada, or 599/54-67660 on St. Maarten; www.caribbean-airlines.com), the new national airline of Trinidad and Tobago (replacing the now-defunct BWIA) has flights from New York, Miami, Toronto, and London with connections to St. Maarten.

The regional airline **LIAT** (𝄪 **888/844-5428** in the U.S. and Canada; www.liatairline.com), now partnered with Caribbean Star, has direct daily 40-minute flights and connecting flights into St. Maarten from its hub in Antigua. From St. Martin, LIAT offers ongoing service to a number of other islands, including Antigua, St. Croix, Puerto Rico, St. Kitts, and Dominica.

One airline specializes in flying the short routes of the northeastern Caribbean islands, from Tortola to Montserrat. **Winair** (𝄪 **888/ 255-6889** in the U.S. and Canada, or 599/54-54237; www.fly-winair. com) offers 10 to 20 flights daily (depending on the season) on the short 10-minute hop between St. Maarten and St. Barts, as well as other island trips from its main gateway at the Princess Juliana International Airport.

For more information on getting to Anguilla and St. Barts, see "Getting There" in chapters 8 and 9.

GETTING INTO TOWN FROM THE AIRPORT

BY TAXI   Most visitors use taxis at some point to get around the island. Since they are unmetered on both sides of the island, always agree on the rate before getting into a cab.

Rates are slightly different depending on which side of the island the taxi is based, though both Dutch and French cabs service the entire island. **St. Maarten taxis** have minimum fares for two passengers, and each additional passenger pays $4 extra. One piece of luggage per person is allowed free; each additional piece is $1 extra.

> ### *Tips* Getting Through the Airport
>
> - Arrive at the airport 1 hour before a domestic flight and 2 hours before an international flight; if you show up late, tell an airline employee and he or she will probably whisk you to the front of the line.
> - Beat the ticket-counter lines by using airport electronic kiosks or even online check-in from your home computers, from where you can print out boarding passes in advance. Curbside check-in is also a good way to avoid lines.
> - Bring a passport. Children under 18 are also now required to have passports to enter or re-enter the U.S.
> - Speed up security by removing your jacket and shoes before you're screened. In addition, remove metal objects such as big belt buckles. If you've got metallic body parts, a note from your doctor can prevent a long chat with the security screeners.
> - Use a TSA-approved lock for your checked luggage. Look for Travel Sentry certified locks at luggage or travel shops and Brookstone stores (or online at www.brookstone.com).
> - Follow Transportation Security Administration (TSA) regulations when packing your carry-on luggage. Follow the agency's "3-1-1" policy, which limits the volume of liquids, gels, and aerosols to bottles 3 ounces or smaller (or 100 ml), in 1 quart-sized zip-top bag, and 1 bag per traveler. Log on to **www.tsa.gov/travelers/ index.shtm** for details.

Typical fares around the island are as follows: Queen Juliana Airport to Grand Case: $25 for up to two passengers and all their luggage; Marigot to Grand Case, $15; Queen Juliana airport to anywhere in Marigot, $15 to $20; Queen Juliana Airport to the Maho Beach Hotel, $6; and from Queen Juliana Airport to Philipsburg, about $15. *Note:* Fares are 25% higher between 10pm and midnight, and 50% higher between midnight and 6am.

St. Martin taxi fares are also for two passengers, but you should plan to add about $1 for each suitcase or valise and $2 for each additional person. These fares are in effect from 6am to 10pm; after that, they go up by 25% until midnight, rising by 50% after midnight. On the French side, the fare from Marigot to Grand Case is $15, from Queen Juliana Airport to Marigot and from Queen Juliana Airport to La Samanna, $15.

For late-night cab service on St. Maarten, call ℂ **147. Taxi Service & Information Center** operates at the port of Marigot (ℂ **590/87-56-54**) on the French side of the island.

BY RENTAL CAR   I highly recommend renting a car to get around St. Maarten/St. Martin, and it's not a bad idea to go ahead and pick up a car when you fly into Princess Juliana International Airport in St. Maarten. A number of car-rental agencies offering competitive rates are located at the airport. For specifics on renting a car and driving in general on St. Maarten/St. Martin, go to "Getting Around St. Maarten/St. Martin," below.

FLYING FOR LESS: TIPS FOR GETTING THE BEST AIRFARE

You can often save money by buying your airfare as part of a vacation package. In most cases, a package to St. Maarten/St. Martin will include airfare, hotel, and transportation to and from the airport— (read the section "Packages for the Independent Traveler," below). But if a package isn't for you and you need to book your airfare on your own, keep in mind these money-saving tips:

- *When* **you fly makes all the difference.** If you fly in late spring, summer, and early fall, you're guaranteed substantial reductions on airfares. Passengers who can book their tickets long in advance, who can stay over Saturday night, or who fly midweek or at less-trafficked hours may pay a fraction of the full fare. If your schedule is flexible, say so, and ask if you can secure a cheaper fare by changing your flight plans.
- **Buy early, not late.** The cheapest seats are snagged by the early birds, so book as far in advance as possible.
- **Search the Internet for cheap fares.** The most popular online travel agencies are **Travelocity** (**www.travelocity.com** or www.travelocity.co.uk); **Expedia** (**www.expedia.com**, www. expedia.co.uk, or www.expedia.ca); and **Orbitz** (**www.orbitz. com**). In addition, most airlines offer online-only fares that even their phone agents know nothing about.
- **Keep an eye out for sales.** Check newspapers for advertised discounts or call the airlines directly and ask if any promotional rates or special fares are available. You'll almost never see a sale during the peak winter vacation months of February and

March, or during the Thanksgiving or Christmas seasons; but in periods of low-volume travel, you should find a discounted fare. If you already hold a ticket when a sale breaks, it may even pay to exchange your ticket, which usually incurs a $50 to $75 charge. *Note:* The lowest-priced fares are often nonrefundable, require advance purchase of 1 to 3 weeks and a certain length of stay, and carry penalties for changing dates of travel.

- **Consolidators,** also known as bucket shops, are great sources for international tickets. Start by looking in Sunday newspaper travel sections; U.S. travelers should focus on the *New York Times, Los Angeles Times,* and *Miami Herald.* U.K. travelers should search in the *Independent,* the *Guardian,* or the *Observer. Beware:* Bucket-shop tickets are usually nonrefundable or rigged with stiff cancellation penalties, often as high as 50% to 75% of the ticket price, and some put you on charter airlines, which may leave at inconvenient times and experience delays. Several reliable consolidators are worldwide and available online. **Lowestfare.com** (© **800/FLY-CHEAP;** www.1800flycheap.com), owned by package-holiday megalith MyTravel, has especially good fares to sunny destinations. **AirTicketsDirect** (© **800/858-8884;** www.airticketsdirect.com) is based in Montreal.

- **Join frequent-flier clubs.** Frequent-flier membership doesn't cost a cent, but it does entitle you to better seats, faster response to phone inquiries, and prompter service if your luggage is stolen or your flight is canceled or delayed, or if you want to change your seat. And you don't have to fly to earn points; **frequent-flier credit cards** can earn you thousands of miles for doing your everyday shopping. With more than 70 mileage awards programs on the market, consumers have never had more options. Consider which airlines have hubs in the airport nearest you, and, of those carriers, which have the most advantageous alliances, given your most common routes. To play the frequent-flier game to your best advantage, consult Randy Petersen's **Inside Flyer** (www.insideflyer.com). Petersen and friends review the programs in detail and post updates on policies and trends.

GETTING TO ANGUILLA & ST. BARTS BY FERRY
ANGUILLA — Ferries run between the ports of Marigot Bay, French St. Martin, and Blowing Point, Anguilla, every 30 to 45 minutes. The trip takes 20 to 25 minutes. The first ferry leaves St. Martin at 8am

and the last at 7pm; from Blowing Point, the first ferry leaves at 7:30am and the last at 6:15pm. The one-way fare is 15€ or $15 ($10 children 2 and over) plus a $3 departure tax. No reservations are necessary; schedules and fares, of course, are always subject to change.

A number of **private charter boats or shuttle ferries** also take passengers between St. Maarten/St. Martin and Anguilla and can even pick up and drop off passengers at the Princess Juliana airport in St. Maarten. For details, go to chapter 8.

ST. BARTS   The **Voyager** vessels (*©* **590/87-10-68;** www.voyager-st-barths.com) make frequent (usually daily, sometimes twice a day) runs between St. Barts and either side of St. Maarten/St. Martin. The schedule varies according to the season (and the seas), but the *MV Voyager II* usually departs Marigot Harbor for St. Barts every morning and evening. *MV Voyager I* travels from Oyster Pond to Gustavia. Advance reservations are a good idea; fares run around 50€ to 58€ ($75–$87) adults, 30€ ($45) children 2–12 one way (plus taxes). The trip can take around 45 minutes and can be rough; it's recommended that those with queasy tummies take Dramamine for the trip.

The technologically advanced, speedier, more luxurious, and stable 68-foot hydrofoil *Rapid Explorer* (*©* **590/27-60-33;** www.st-barths.com/rapid-explorer) offers three daily 45-minute crossings between St. Maarten's Bobby's Marina in Philipsburg and Gustavia. Reservations are essential; the fare is 59€ ($88) adults, 47€ ($70) child one way (plus taxes).

For additional details on Anguilla and St. Barts, see "Getting There" in chapters 8 and 9.

10 Packages for the Independent Traveler

For value-conscious travelers, packages are often the smart way to go because they can save you a ton of money. Especially in the Caribbean, package tours are *not* the same thing as escorted tours. You'll be on your own, but in most cases, a package will include airfare, hotel, and transportation to and from the airport—and it'll cost you less than just the hotel alone if you booked it yourself.

You'll find an amazing array of packages to the islands. Check out some of the big **online travel agencies**—Expedia, Travelocity, Orbitz, and Lastminute.com—which do a brisk business in packages. Remember to comparison shop among at least three different operators, and always compare apples to apples.

One good source of package deals is the airlines themselves. Most major airlines offer air/land packages, including **American Airlines Vacations** (© 800/321-2121; www.aavacations.com), **Delta Vacations** (© 800/221-6666; www.deltavacations.com), **Continental Airlines Vacations** (© 800/301-3800; www.covacations.com), and **United Vacations** (© 888/854-3899; www.unitedvacations.com).

Of course, don't forget to check the **hotel or resort websites** for very desirable package deals, especially in the off season. No, these packages rarely include airfares, but they're packed with extra amenities (or a night free) if you book a block of vacation time, say, 5 or 7 days. These packages often include meals, spa treatments, or water sports excursions along with lodging.

11 Getting Around St. Maarten/St. Martin

BY RENTAL CAR

A car is the best way to experience and explore St. Maarten/St. Martin. And renting a car here couldn't be easier; car-rental agencies are a dime a dozen, with locations at the airports and throughout the island. It's also a cost-efficient way to see the island, with rates starting around $30 a day, with unlimited mileage, and short distances between towns.

Many visitors rent cars when they arrive at Princess Juliana International Airport. A good number of car-rental agency kiosks are located on the Arrivals floor of the airport and along Airport Road. To get around the law (strictly enforced by St. Maarten taxi drivers' union) that forbids anyone from picking up a car at the airport, every rental agency parks its cars at a location nearby. When you rent a car at one of the agency kiosks on the Arrivals floor of the Princess Juliana airport, you will be taken by company shuttle 5 to 10 minutes away to pick up your car. *Note:* Always ask how far away from the airport the rental cars are located; some of the smaller agencies are a couple of miles away—which can turn into a long trip when traffic is heavy around the airport.

Car rental agencies at the airport include **Budget** (© **800/472-3325** in the U.S. and Canada; or 599/545-4030 on the Dutch side; www.budget.com); **Avis** (© **800/331-1212** in the U.S. and Canada, 599/545-2847 on the Dutch side, or 590/87-50-60 on the French side; www.avis.com), **Hertz** (© **800/654-3001** in the U.S. and Canada; www.hertz.com), **Thrifty** (© **800/367-2277** in the U.S. and Canada; www.thrifty.com), **National** (© **800/328-4567** in the

U.S. and Canada, or 599/545-5552 on the Dutch side; www.national car.com); **Best Deal Car Rental** (© **599/545-3061**); **Safari Car Rental** (© **599/554-2102**); or **Empress Rent-a-Car** (© **599/551-1708**).

All these companies charge roughly equivalent rates. The major car-rental agencies require that renters be at least 25 years old.

Many rental agencies will also deliver cars directly to your hotel, where an employee will complete the paperwork. Some hotels, like La Samanna, actually have a fleet of cars to rent on the premises—but try to reserve well in advance because supply is limited.

Budget (© **599/543-0431**) also has an office at the cruise-ship terminal.

Driving is on the right side of the road on St. Maarten/St. Martin and on St. Barts; it's on the left side of the road on Anguilla. Seat belts and child car seats are mandatory. International road signs are observed, and there are no Customs formalities at the border between the French and Dutch sides—in fact, you might not even realize you crossed the border.

Expect traffic jams near the major towns and tourist areas on St. Maarten/St. Martin—particularly in the Simpson Bay area when the Simpson Bay bridge is raised to let bridge traffic through (six times daily in high season; three times daily in low season). Tune your car radio to **Island 92** (91.9FM) for traffic updates.

For information on renting cars on Anguilla and St. Barts, see "Getting Around" in chapters 8 and 9.

BY TAXI

Most visitors use taxis at some point to get around. Since they are unmetered on both sides of the island, always agree on the rate before getting into a cab. For information on taxi rates, go to "Getting into Town from the Airport," earlier in this chapter.

If you find a driver you like, ask for his card and call on him during your trip—especially if you need a nighttime drop-off and pickup from a restaurant or casino. Taxi drivers are happy to provide sightseeing tours of the island or take you to grocery stores to let you stock up on basics. One driver we recommend is **Jules Gumb** (© **0670-27-38-88**).

BY BUS

Traveling by minibus or minivan is a reasonable means of transport on St. Maarten/St. Martin if you don't mind some inconvenience and overcrowding. Buses run daily from 6am to midnight and serve most of the major locations on both sides of the island. The most popular run is from Philipsburg on the Dutch side to Marigot on the French side. Privately owned and operated, minibuses tend to follow specific routes; the fare is $1.50 (buses accept both dollars and euros).

12 Tips on Accommodations

SAVING ON YOUR HOTEL ROOM

The **rack rate** is the maximum rate that a hotel charges for a room. I list these simply as a guideline. Hardly anybody pays this price, however, except in high season or on holidays. To lower the cost of your room:

- **Dial direct.** When booking a room in a chain hotel, you'll often get a better deal by calling the individual hotel's reservation desk rather than the chain's main number.
- **Book online.** Many hotels offer Internet-only discounts, or supply rooms to Travelocity, Hotels.com, Priceline, Hotwire, Orbitz, or Expedia at rates much lower than the ones you can get through the hotel itself.
- **Remember the law of supply and demand.** Island hotels have high- and low-season prices, and booking even 1 day after high season ends can mean big, big discounts. Resort hotels are most crowded and often most expensive on weekends, so discounts may be available for midweek stays.
- **Avoid excess charges and hidden costs.** Use your own cellphone, pay phones, or prepaid phone cards instead of dialing direct from hotel phones, which usually have exorbitant rates. The room's minibar offerings can also add up. Finally, ask about local taxes and service charges, which can increase the cost of a room by 15% or more.
- **Consider a meal plan.** Many resorts with full restaurant service offer meal plans. If you enjoy eating out and sampling the local cuisine, it makes sense to choose a **Continental Plan (CP),** which includes breakfast only, or a **European Plan (EP),** which doesn't include any meals and allows maximum flexibility. If you're more interested in saving money, opt for a **Modified American Plan (MAP),** which includes breakfast and one meal, or the **American Plan (AP),** which includes three meals. If you must choose a MAP, see if you can get a free lunch at your hotel if you decide to do dinner out.

Villas & Timeshare Rentals

Villas are particularly popular on St. Barts and, to a lesser degree, Anguilla and St. Maarten/St. Martin. **Wimco** (© 800/932-3222; www.wimco.com) is a reputable company handling properties on all three islands. For villas in St. Barts, St. Barth Properties (© 800-421-3396; www.stbarth.com) is affiliated with Sotheby's. (For other suggestions for Anguilla and St. Barts, see chapters 8 and 9.) St. Maarten is (in)famous for its timeshare/condo complexes; see chapter 3. Members of **RCI** (© 317/805-9000; www.rci.com) or **Interval International** (© 888/784-3447; www.intervalworld.com) can look into the feasibility of exchanges.

- **Book an efficiency.** Most hotel and resort rooms have full or partial kitchens. A room with a kitchenette allows you to shop for groceries and cook your own meals, as well as store cold drinks and perishables. This is a big money saver, especially for families on long stays.

Refer to chapter 3 for information on St. Maarten/St. Martin lodging options and taxes/surcharges. For Anguilla and St. Barts, refer to chapters 8 and 9, respectively.

LANDING THE BEST ROOM

Somebody has to get the best room in the house—it might as well be you. When you make your reservation, ask if the hotel is renovating; if it is, request a room away from the construction. Ask about nonsmoking rooms, rooms with views, and rooms with twin or queen- or king-size beds. If you're a light sleeper, request a quiet room away from restaurants, bars, and discos. Ask for one of the rooms that have been most recently renovated or redecorated.

If you aren't happy with your room when you arrive, say so. If another room is available, most places will be willing to accommodate you. Ask these questions before you book a room:

- What's the view like? Cost-conscious travelers may be willing to pay less for a room without an ocean view, especially if they don't plan to spend much time in their room.
- Does the room have air-conditioning or ceiling fans? Do the windows open? If they do, and the nighttime entertainment takes place alfresco, you may want to find out when show time is over.

- What's included in the price? Your room may be moderately priced, but if you're charged for the use of water-sports equipment, fitness centers, and other amenities that you get gratis at pricier resorts, you could end up spending more than you bargained for.
- How far is the room from the beach and other amenities? If it's far, is there transportation to and from the beach?

13 Tips on Dining

All three islands in this book are renowned for their fine dining. For St. Maarten/St. Martin specifics, see chapter 4. Consult chapters 8 and 9 for details on Anguilla and St. Barts.

To save money on St. Maarten/St. Martin, get take-out food for picnics and buy basics (snacks, soft drinks, milk, beer) at local grocery stores. See "Resources for Self-Catering," in chapter 4. Several restaurants take the sting from the euro's strength by offering 1€=$1 exchange rates for customers paying cash (this rarely applies to credit card users). Several restaurants, especially on the Dutch side, provide Internet coupons for free drinks or a second main course at half price. Lunch is generally less expensive, and the menu selection often simpler. Look for multicourse prix-fixe menus; these can represent bargains, often including a beverage. Tipping is usually hassle-free (the menu will state whether service is included), but always confirm whether gratuities are added (and what the percentage is) and give a little extra when you feel the staff warrants it. If there's no service charge, add 15% to 20% to your bill.

Note: Entrée is actually the French term for appetizer; *plat* means main course.

14 Recommended Books, Films & Music

The Caribbean has produced numerous fine authors, including Nobel Prize laureate Derek Walcott (St. Lucia), V. S. Naipaul (Trinidad), Anthony Winkler (Jamaica), Jean Rhys (Dominica), and Jamaica Kincaid (Antigua). Alas, none of the three islands in this book boast noted native writers. But there are a few literal "beach" reads worth mentioning. *The Captain's Fund* (Resource Power Publishing) by Raina Wissing Harris, a very purple "romance suspense" novel of murder, heiresses-in-distress, and black market diamonds is notable for its St. Maarten/St. Martin setting with such familiar landmarks as Friar's Beach Café, the Horny Toad Guesthouse, and

Joe's Jewelry International. St. Martin inspired celebrity chef/author Anthony Bourdain's *Gone Bamboo* (Villard/Bloomsbury USA).

Melinda and Bob Blanchard's *A Trip to the Beach: Living on Island Time in the Caribbean* (Clarkson Potter/Three Rivers Press) is the true-life restaurateurs' hilarious yet sympathetic, ungarnished version of Herman Wouk's riotous fictional account of an American hotelier in the Antilles, *Don't Stop the Carnival.* The Blanchards' most recent guide is *Changing Your Course: The 5-Step Guide to Getting the Life You Want* (Sterling). *Murder in St. Barts* (Beachfront Publishing) is a passable Gendarme Trenet novel by J. R. Ripley (note that teasing last name, mystery aficionados), better known for the Tony Kozol whodunits. Jimmy Buffet's *Tales from Margaritaville* (Fawcett Books) offers fictional short stories of West Indian life, many based on his years of St. Barts residency.

FAST FACTS: St. Maarten/St. Martin

American Express None of the three islands has an official AmEx representative.

Area Codes The country and area code for French St. Martin and St. Barts is 590/590, for Dutch St. Maarten 599, and for Anguilla 264.

ATM Networks See "Money" on p. 17.

Business Hours On the Dutch side, most banks are open Monday to Friday from 8:30am to 3:30pm, Saturday from 9am to noon. On the French side, they are usually open Monday to Friday 8:30am to 1:30pm. It's easy to find ATMs. On the Dutch side, several banks are clustered along Front Street in Philipsburg. On the French side, most banks are along rue de la République in Marigot. Store hours vary, but the French side shops generally are open 10am to 5pm (closing for lunch), while Dutch side shops often stay open continuously and as late as 11pm.

Car Rentals See "Getting Around St. Maarten/St. Martin" on p. 33.

Currency See "Money" on p. 17.

Driving Rules See "Getting Around St. Maarten/St. Martin" on p. 33.

Drugstores Both sides have several pharmacies, though none are open 24 hours. On the **French** side, try **Pharmacie du Port**

(rue de la Liberté, Marigot; ℂ 590/87-50-79; Mon–Sat 8am–
7:30pm, Sun hours vary). On the **Dutch** side, try **Philipsburg
Pharmacy** (4 E. Voges St., Philipsburg; ℂ 599/542-3001; Mon–
Fri 7:30am–7pm, Sat 9am–1pm, Sun 10am–noon), **Simpson Bay
Pharmacy** (Simpson Bay Yacht Club, 163 Welfare Rd.; ℂ 599/
544-3653; Mon–Fri 8:15am–7pm, Sat 9am–1pm, Sun 5–7pm),
and **the Druggist** (Airport Rd., Simpson Bay; ℂ 599/545-2777;
Mon–Fri 8:30am–7:30pm, Sat noon–7pm, Sun 1–3pm). For
pharmacies on Anguilla and St. Barts, see p. 136 and p. 170.

Electricity Dutch St. Maarten and Anguilla use the same volt-
age (110-volt AC, 60 cycles) with the same electrical configurations as the United States, so adapters and transformers are
not necessary. However, on French St. Martin and St. Barts,
220-volt AC prevails, so you'll usually need transformers and
adapters. To simplify things, many hotels on both sides of the
island have installed sockets suitable for both European and
North American appliances.

Embassies & Consulates There is no U.S. diplomatic represen-
tation on Anguilla. **U.S. citizens** are advised to register with
the consulates at Bluff House, English Harbour on Antigua
(ℂ 268/463-6531; ryderj@candw.ag), or Georgetown, Barbados (visit http://bridgetown.usembassy.gov or https://travel
registration.state.gov/ibrs/home.asp). Likewise **Canadian
citizens** should register with the Canadian High Commission
on Barbados. **Australian citizens** can register with the Australian High Commission in Port-of-Spain, Trinidad and
Tobago (ℂ 868/628-4732). On St. Maarten/St. Martin, **citizens
of the U.S.** are represented by its consulate at St. Anna Boulevard, Willemstad, Curaçao (ℂ 599/961-3066). There is a Canadian conuslate at 16A Topaz Dr., St. Maarten (ℂ 599/544-
5023). **Citizens of the U.K.** can register with the consulate at
38 Jan Sofat in Willemstad, Curaçao (ℂ 599/747-3322).

Emergencies On the **Dutch** side, call the **police** at ℂ 542-2222
or an **ambulance** at ℂ 542-2111; to report a **fire,** call ℂ 911 or
120. On the **French** side, you can reach the **police** by dialing
ℂ 17 or 87-50-10. In case of **fire,** dial ℂ 18. For an **ambulance**
dial ℂ 15 or 29-04-04. For Anguilla and St. Barts, see "Fast
Facts" on p. 135 and p. 170, respectively.

Etiquette & Customs Despite the clothing-optional beaches
on St. Martin, St. Maarten, and St. Barts, flaunting (or any fla-
grant display) is frowned upon, especially on proper British

Anguilla. Except at casual beach bars, men should wear some kind of shirt, women a wrap. Smart resort wear is recommended for most restaurants, especially at dinner. "Sunday dress" is appropriate when visiting churches, though ties aren't mandatory for men. In general, profanity is frowned upon.

Holidays National holidays are New Year's Day, January 1; Epiphany, January 6 (French side); Carnival, early February; Good Friday and Easter Monday, usually April; Labor Day, May 1; Ascension Day, early May; Bastille Day, July 14 (French side); Schoelcher Day, July 21 (French side); Assumption Day, August 15; All Saints' Day, November 1; Concordia Day and St. Martin Day, November 11; Christmas Day, December 25; and Boxing Day, December 26. For more information, see "St. Maarten/St. Martin Calendar of Events," earlier in this chapter.

Hospitals On the Dutch side, go to the **St. Maarten Medical Center,** Welegen Road, Cay Hill (© 599/543-1111; www.sint maartenmedicalcenter.com). On the French side, the local hospital is **Hospital Louis-Constant Fleming,** near Marigot in Concordia (© **590/52-25-25**). For Anguilla and St. Barts, refer to "Fast Facts" on p. 135 and p. 170, respectively.

Internet Access Cybercafes can be found in both Marigot and Philipsburg, and most hotels have a computer center and/or high-speed Internet access.

Newspapers & Magazines In addition to several local newspapers (*The Daily Herald* is the leading English-language publication), visitors can pick up one of several useful tourist magazines including *St. Maarten Nature, St. Maarten Events, Discover St. Martin/St. Maarten, St. Maarten Nights, Ti Gourmet,* and *Vacation St. Maarten.* For Anguilla and St. Barts, see "Fast Facts" in chapters 8 and 9.

Passports Allow plenty of time before your trip to apply for a passport; processing normally takes 3 weeks but can take longer during busy periods (especially spring). And keep in mind that if you need a passport in a hurry, you'll pay a higher processing fee.

For Residents of Australia: You can pick up an application from your local post office or any branch of Passports Australia, but you must schedule an interview at the passport office to present your application materials. Call the **Australian Passport Information Service** at © **131-232,** or visit the government website at www.passports.gov.au.

For Residents of Canada: Passport applications are available at travel agencies throughout Canada or from the central **Passport Office,** Department of Foreign Affairs and International Trade, Ottawa, ON K1A 0G3 (© **800/567-6868;** www. ppt.gc.ca).

For Residents of Ireland: You can apply for a 10-year passport at the **Passport Office,** Setanta Centre, Molesworth Street, Dublin 2 (© **01/671-1633;** www.irlgov.ie/iveagh). Those under 18 and over 65 must apply for a 12€ 3-year passport. You can also apply at 1A South Mall, Cork (© **021/272-525**), or at most main post offices.

For Residents of New Zealand: You can pick up a passport application at any New Zealand Passports Office or download it from their website. Contact the **Passports Office** at © **0800/ 225-050** in New Zealand or 04/474-8100, or log on to www. passports.govt.nz.

For Residents of the United Kingdom: To pick up an application for a standard 10-year passport (5-year passport for children under 16), visit your nearest passport office, major post office, or travel agency, or contact the **United Kingdom Passport Service** at © **0870/521-0410** or search its website at www.ukpa.gov.uk.

For Residents of the United States: Whether you're applying in person or by mail, you can download passport applications from the U.S. State Department website at **http:// travel.state.gov**. To find your regional passport office, either check the U.S. State Department website or call the **National Passport Information Center** toll-free number (© **877/487- 2778**) for automated information.

Police See "Emergencies," above.

Restrooms Public facilities are few and far between other than a couple of options in Marigot, Philipsburg, and Orient Beach. Hotel lobbies and restaurants are the best options, though technically you should be a guest or customer.

Safety See "Health & Safety," earlier in this chapter.

Smoking While many larger properties offer nonsmoking rooms, there are no regulations against smoking—for now. Legislation has recently been proposed to ban smoking in all St. Maarten restaurants, bars, and casinos—check to see if the law has been passed.

Taxes For departures to international destinations from Princess Juliana Airport on the Dutch side, there's a departure tax of $30 ($10 if you're leaving the island for St. Eustatius or Saba; if you're leaving by ferry from Marigot Pier to Anguilla, the departure tax is $4). There is a 3€ ($4.50) departure tax for departures from L'Espérance Airport on the French side. *Note:* The departure tax is often included in the airfare. On the Dutch side, a government tax of between 5% and 8%, depending on the category of hotel you stay in, is added to hotel bills. On the French side, hotels must levy a *taxe de séjour* (hotel tax); this differs from hotel to hotel, depending on its classification, but is often 5% a day. In addition to these taxes, most hotels add a (mandatory) service charge of around 10% to 15% to your hotel bill. For Anguilla and St. Barts, refer to "Fast Facts" (chapters 8 and 9).

Telephones To call St. Maarten/St. Martin, Anguilla, and St. Barts:

1. Dial the international access code: 011 from the U.S.; 00 from the U.K., Ireland, or New Zealand; or 0011 from Australia.
2. Dial the country code 599 for St. Maarten and 590 for St. Barts and St. Martin.
3. Dial the city code 590 (a second time) and then the six-digit number on St. Barts and St. Martin. The St. Maarten city code is 54, then dial the five-digit number. Dialing Anguilla from the U.S. doesn't require 011, just 1, then the 264 area code, followed by the seven-digit number.
4. To call the French side from the Dutch side and vice versa is an expensive international "long distance" call, going through Byzantine routing to Europe and back. From the French to Dutch side, dial 00, then 599, 54 and the five-digit number. From the Dutch to the French side (and St. Barts), dial 00, then 590590 (590690 for cell phones) and the six-digit number.

To make international calls: From St. Maarten/St. Martin and St. Barts, first dial 00 and then the country code (U.S. or Canada 1, U.K. 44, Ireland 353, Australia 61, New Zealand 64). Next dial the area code and number. For example, if you wanted to call the British Embassy in Washington, D.C., you would dial 00-1-202-588-7800. From Anguilla to the U.S., dial 1, then the number.

On the Dutch side there are facilities for overseas calls, but from the French side you cannot make collect calls to the States and there are no coin-operated phones. At the Marigot post office you can purchase a *Telecarte,* giving you 40 units. A typical 5-minute call to the States takes up to 120 units. There are two public phones at the Marigot tourist office from which it's possible to make credit card calls. There are six public phones at the post office.

For directory assistance: Dial 150 if you're looking for a number inside St. Maarten/St. Martin, and dial 0 for numbers to all other countries.

For operator assistance: If you need operator assistance in making a call, dial 0 if you're trying to make an international call and a number within St. Maarten/St. Martin.

Toll-free numbers: There are no toll-free numbers on St. Maarten/St. Martin, Anguilla, or St. Barts, and calling a 1-800 number in the States from them is not toll-free. In fact, it costs the same as an overseas call.

Time Zone St. Maarten/St. Martin, Anguilla, and St. Barts operate on Atlantic Standard Time year-round. Thus in winter, if it's 6pm in Philipsburg, it's 5pm in New York. During daylight saving time in the United States, the islands and the U.S. East Coast are on the same time.

Tipping See "Tips on Dining," earlier in this chapter, for restaurant guidelines. Otherwise, porters and bellmen expect $1 per bag. Taxi drivers should receive 10% of the fare, more if they offer touring or other suggestions.

Useful Phone Numbers **U.S. Dept. of State Travel Advisory:** ⓒ 202/647-5225 (manned 24 hr.); **U.S. Passport Agency:** ⓒ 202/647-0518; **U.S. Centers for Disease Control International Traveler's Hot Line:** ⓒ 404/332-4559.

Water The water on St. Maarten/St. Martin, Anguilla, and St. Barts is safe to drink. In fact, most hotels serve desalinated water.

3

Where to Stay on St. Maarten/St. Martin

Despite its small size, St. Maarten/St. Martin offers a surprising range of accommodations: large high-rise all-inclusive resorts, medium-size chain hotels catering to tour groups, small "bourgeois" hotels, locally owned guesthouses ranging from boutique-y to budget, not to mention villas, apartments, and, of course, timeshare complexes. As you leave the airport, it seems you can't go more than a few feet without someone hawking a new or expanded development. Remember, a government tax of between 5% and 8%, plus a service charge of 10% to 15% will be added to your hotel bill. Ask whether it's included in the original rates you're quoted.

Renting a Villa

An increasingly popular lodging option on St. Maarten/St. Martin is villa rentals. Expect to pay anywhere from $1,000 to $68,000 per week in high season—but you can save big if you're flexible enough to travel in the low or even shoulder season. Villas can be a great money-saver for large groups or families and are a smart option for travelers looking for a more private vacation experience. **Wimco** (© **800/932-3222** or 800/449-1553; www.wimco.com) is the acknowledged king of Caribbean villa living and represents dozens of properties from one- to nine-bedrooms. For high-end properties, look no further than **Pierres Caraïbes,** affiliated with Christie's Great Estates (on the French side: rue Kennedy, Marigot, © **590/29-21-46;** on the Dutch side: Plaza del Lago, Simpson Bay Yacht Club, © **599/544-2622;** www.pierres-caraibes.com). **Jennifer's Vacation Villas** (Plaza del Lago, Simpson Bay Yacht Club; © **599/544-3107;** www.jennifersvacationvillas.com) arguably boasts the largest selection, with both villas and condos for rent, and caters to all budgets. All three companies will source drivers, chefs, even personal trainers.

1 Dutch St. Maarten

Remember, a government tax of between 5% and 8%, plus a service charge of 10% to 15% will be added to your hotel bill. Ask whether it's included in the original rates you're quoted to save yourself a shock when you check out.

VERY EXPENSIVE

Divi Little Bay Beach Resort ✦   Built on a peninsula about a 10-minute drive east of the airport, this hotel is consistently ranked as one of the best family-vacation resorts in the Caribbean. It originated as a simple guesthouse in 1955 and soon became famous as the vacation home of the Netherlands' Queen Juliana, Prince Bernhard, and Queen Beatrix. It was severely damaged during the hurricanes of the early 1990s, and was rebuilt in 1997 as the flagship of the Divi chain. The rooms and public spaces have been nicely renovated and freshened up. The architecture evokes a European seaside village, with stucco walls and terra-cotta roofs, with some Dutch colonial touches. In the upper reaches of the property are the ruins of Fort Amsterdam, once Dutch St. Maarten's most prized military stronghold and today a decorative historical site. Gardens are carefully landscaped, and Divi improved the nearby beach after it suffered massive erosion.

Accommodations are airy, accented with ceramic tiles and pastel colors, and each has its own private balcony or patio; suites (and studios) have fully equipped kitchens—the only units that don't have kitchens are the beachfront doubles. The newly upgraded luxury Casita one-bedroom suites even have iPod docking stations. The resort offers a variety of meal plans, including an all-inclusive option.

Little Bay (P.O. Box 961), Philipsburg, St. Maarten, N.A. ② **800/367-3484** in the U.S., or 599/54-22333. Fax 599/54-24336. www.divilittlebay.com. 225 units. Winter $277–$288 double, $286–$328 1-bedroom suite, $475 2-bedroom suite; off season $206–$218 double, $296–$308 1-bedroom suite, $355 2-bedroom suite. Children under 15 stay free in parent's room. AE, DC, MC, V. **Amenities:** 3 restaurants; bar; 3 outdoor pools; 2 lit tennis courts; gym; spa; watersports center; dive shop; jet skis; kayaks; sailing; snorkeling; water-skiing; windsurfing; activities coordinator; car rental (Thrifty); salon; laundry service; coin-operated laundry; nonsmoking rooms. In room: A/C, flatscreen TV (DVD in some), kitchens (in suites), beverage maker, hair dryer, iron, safe, Jacuzzi (in suites).

Princess Heights ✦ *Finds*   In the hills above Dawn Beach, which is just across the road, this boutique all-suites condo hotel is an intimate hideaway with great panoramic views. It's reached after a 10-minute drive from Philipsburg. Opening onto St. Barts in the distance, the

St. Maarten/St. Martin

Pointe
Arago

Pointe
du Bluff

See Marigot
map, p 57

Baie de
Marigot

Marigot

Baie Nettlé

Nettlé Beach

Marigot
Fort

Pointe
du Plum
Baie aux
Prunes **2**

Baie Rouge

3 4 **5** **6**

7

Baie Longue **1**

Simpson Bay Lagoon

Cupecoy Bay
Beach

57

Mullet Bay Beach

55
56

Princess Juliana
International
Airport

Border
Monument

54
53

52

49

43

47

46

45

Maho Bay Beach

50
48

Simpson
Bay Beach

42 **41** **44**

Koolbaai

51

Kimsha Beach

39 **40**

Caribbean
Sea

38

Cole
Bay

Airport ✈
Beach
Mountain ▲

| 0 | | 1 Mile |
| 0 | | 1 Kilometer |

N

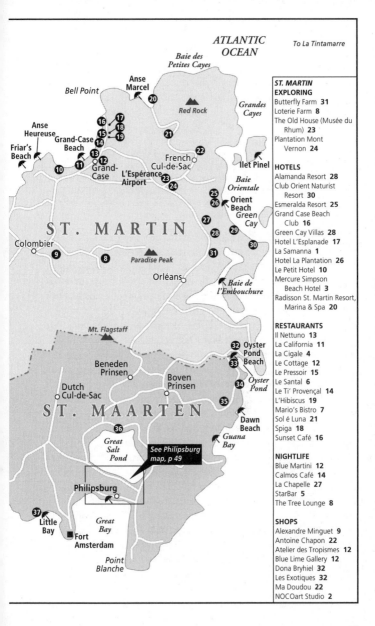

ATLANTIC OCEAN

To La Tintamarre

Baie des Petites Cayes

Anse Marcel

Bell Point

Grandes Cayes

Red Rock

Anse Heureuse

Grand-Case Beach

Friar's Beach

French Cul-de-Sac

Grand-Case

L'Espérance Airport

Ilet Pinel

Baie Orientale

Orient Beach Green Cay

ST. MARTIN

Colombier

Paradise Peak

Orléans

Baie de l'Embouchure

Mt. Flagstaff

Oyster Pond Beach

Beneden Prinsen

Boven Prinsen

Oyster Pond

Dutch Cul-de-Sac

ST. MAARTEN

Dawn Beach

Great Salt Pond

See Philipsburg map, p 49

Guana Bay

Philipsburg

Little Bay

Fort Amsterdam

Great Bay

Point Blanche

large suites are tastefully furnished, each containing one or two bedrooms, with separate living rooms opening onto balconies. Granite-topped counters, clay-tiled terraces, lots of marble, and well-crafted, fully equipped kitchens make for fine living, and the hillside location spells privacy. At press time 18 new ocean-view deluxe suites had opened for business, the rooms more spacious and luxurious than the originals and located on the hillside slightly above the original building.

156 Oyster Pond Rd., Oyster Pond, St. Maarten, N.A. ℂ **599/54-36906.** Fax 599/54-36007. www.princessheights.com. 33 units. Winter $285–$335 studio, $350–$500 suite; off season $160–$210 studio, $225–$375 suite. Children (two maximum) under 12 stay free in parent's room. Extra person $35–$45. AE, DISC, MC, V. **Amenities:** Outdoor pool; fitness center; car rental; limited room service; massage; babysitting; laundry service; dry cleaning; high-speed Internet access. *In room:* A/C, flatscreen TV, kitchen, minibar, safe, washer/dryer (in some).

Sonesta Maho Beach Hotel & Casino 𝓰   Separated into three distinct sections, this megaresort, practically a self-contained village with its sprawling convention facilities, is the island's largest hotel. It's the closest thing on either the Dutch or French side to a Las Vegas–style blockbuster resort. It has a rather anonymous feeling (it's always full of conventioneers and giant tour groups), but it's modern and up-to-date, thanks to continual upgrades and renovations. Set on a 4-hectare (10-acre) tract that straddles the busy, and often congested, coastal road adjacent to the crescent-shaped Maho Beach, the hotel's scattered structures are painted a trademark cream and white. The large rooms are conservatively but comfortably furnished. Each has wicker and rattan furniture, Italian tiles, plush upholstered pieces, a walk-in closet, pillow-top mattresses, and good soundproofing (important, since planes taking off at the nearby Princess Juliana airport thunder overhead several times a day).

The hotel contains three separate, directly managed restaurants (the **Point** is excellent but avoid the **Palms,** where karaoke blasts louder than the jets), with another half-dozen on-site that are independently operated but accept all-inclusive guests. The glitzy Casino Royale, across the street from the accommodations, includes a cabaret theater for glittery shows and **Q Club,** the island's splashiest late-night dance spot. On the resort's street front, the Maho Promenade is filled with several dozen shops open late, restaurants (including Cheri's Café), an Internet center, a scuba-diving center, dance club, piano bar, even a classy gentleman's club. Ask about the all-inclusive option, which includes breakfast, lunch, and dinner, all drinks, and other amenities, with the room rates.

Philipsburg

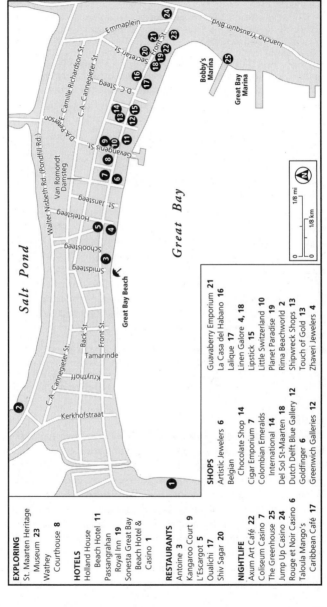

EXPLORING
St. Maarten Heritage
  Museum **23**
Wathey
  Courthouse **8**

HOTELS
Holland House
  Beach Hotel **11**
Passangrahan
  Royal Inn **19**
Sonesta Great Bay
  Beach Hotel &
  Casino **1**

RESTAURANTS
Antoine **3**
Kangaroo Court **9**
L'Escargot **5**
Oualichi **17**
Shiv Sagar **20**

NIGHTLIFE
Axum Art Café **22**
Coliseum Casino **7**
The Greenhouse **25**
Jump Up Casino **24**
Rouge et Noir Casino **6**
Taloula Mango's
  Caribbean Café **17**

SHOPS
Artistic Jewelers **6**
Belgian
  Chocolate Shop **14**
Cigar Emporium **7**
Colombian Emeralds
  International **14**
Del Sol St-Maarten **18**
Dutch Delft Blue Gallery **12**
Goldfinger **6**
Greenwich Galleries **12**
Guavaberry Emporium **21**
La Casa del Habano **16**
Lalique **17**
Linen Galore **4, 18**
Lipstick **15**
Little Switzerland **10**
Planet Paradise **19**
Rima Beachworld **2**
Shipwreck Shops **13**
Touch of Gold **13**
Zhaveri Jewelers **4**

49

Maho Beach, 1 Rhine Rd., St. Maarten, N.A. ℂ **800/223-0757** in the U.S., or 599/ 54-52115. Fax 599/54-53180. www.sonesta.com/mahobeach. 527 units. Winter $290–$390 double, $425–$590 suite, from $780 2-bedroom unit; off season $225–$295 double, $330–$400 suite, from $660 2-bedroom unit. AE, DC, DISC, MC, V. **Amenities:** 3 restaurants; 2 outdoor pools; casino; nightclub; golf (nearby); 4 tennis courts; fitness center; spa; business services; shopping promenade; babysitting; laundry service; rooms for those w/limited mobility. *In room:* A/C, TV, high-speed Internet access, fridge (in some), beverage maker (in some), hair dryer, safe.

Westin St. Maarten, Dawn Beach Resort & Spa ✺   This sprawling resort opened in early 2007. One local said it looked like a prison had been plopped down on Dawn Beach, but to be fair, its colonnaded beachfront facade is much more elegant than its character-free backside. And the freshwater infinity pool is lovely. The lobby has a spiffy Frank Lloyd Wright feel, and is adjoined by a clanging casino. The 310 mostly oceanview guest rooms (and 15 suites) have all the state-of-the-art trappings you'd expect from a high-end chain like Westin, including its trademark Heavenly Bed mattresses—and the rates cover a range of budgets. Facilities include a full-service, European-style **Hibiscus Spa,** fitness center, retail shops with duty-free shopping, two oceanfront restaurants, watersports, and meeting facilities. Kids get the royal treatment at Westin Kid's Club—Camp Scallywag. All the rooms are nonsmoking.

144 Oyster Pond Rd., St. Maarten, N.A. ℂ **800/WESTIN-1 [937-8461]** or 599/54-36700. Fax 599/54-36004. www.starwoodhotels.com. 325 units. Winter $380–$749 double, $1,050–$3,150 suite; off season $149–$549 double, $735–$1,200 suite. AE, MC, V. **Amenities:** 4 restaurants/lounges; pool snack bar; outdoor pool; casino; tennis courts; fitness center; spa; dive shop; concierge desk; business services; shops; 24-hr. room service; babysitting; laundry; valet service; rooms for those w/limited mobility. *In room:* A/C, TV, high-speed Internet access, minibar, fridge, coffee- and tea-making facilities, hair dryer, safe.

EXPENSIVE

Holland House Beach Hotel ✺   The lobby of this well-run "city" hotel runs uninterrupted from bustling Front Street to Great Bay Beach. The public areas are quite stylish, with rotating local and Dutch artworks for sale on the walls. The lively global clientele enjoys the little touches (free international newspapers, beach chairs, and freshwater beach shower). Most rooms have gorgeous polished hardwood floors and large, arched balconies. The muted color scheme favors cream and canary yellow. The one-bedroom penthouse includes kitchenette, large-screen TV, DVD, and fax machine. The $36 surcharge is well worth it for the popular oceanview rooms; but weekly stays in any unit lasso huge savings.

The newly renovated beachfront restaurant and bar (crowned by a billowing tent) rock weekends with live jazz; the regular menu is surprisingly good, but opt for the chef's creative, affordable tapas (including Dutch finger food, Vietnamese spring rolls, and Spanish meatballs).

43 Front St. (P.O. Box 393), Philipsburg, St. Maarten, N.A. © 800/223-9815 in the U.S., or 599/542-2572. Fax 599/542-4673. www.hhbh.com. 54 units. Winter $155–$280 double, $315–$350 1-bedroom suite, $365–$450 penthouse; off season $170–$225 double, $325 1-bedroom suite, $390 penthouse. Weekly rates available. AE, MC, V. **Amenities:** Restaurant; bar; snorkeling; salon; massage; Wi-Fi throughout; computer with Internet access; conference room. *In room:* A/C, ceiling fan, TV, Wi-Fi, kitchenette, hair dryer, iron, safe, Jacuzzi (in some).

The Horny Toad Guesthouse 🌟 (Value) This homey, welcoming place is run by an expatriate from Maine, Betty Vaughan. Unfortunately, the hotel is near the airport, but the roar of jumbo jets is heard only a few times a day. Children 7 and under are not allowed, but families with older children often come here to avoid the megaresorts, and second-timers quickly become "part of the family."

Seven well-maintained units are in an amply proportioned beachside house originally built in the 1950s as a private home by the island's former governor. The eighth room is in half of an octagonal "round house," with large windows and views of the sea. Guest rooms range from medium-size to spacious, and each has a fully equipped kitchen, and a king-size bed. The guesthouse has no pool, no restaurant, and no organized activities of any kind. However, the beach is a few steps away, and there are often impromptu get-togethers around the pair of gas-fired barbecues.

2 Vlaun Dr., Simpson Bay, St. Maarten, N.A. © 800/417-9361 in the U.S., or 599/54-54323. Fax 599/54-53316. www.thehornytoadguesthouse.com. 8 units. Winter $198 double; off season $107 double. Extra person $40 in winter, $25 off season. MC, V. No children under 7 allowed. **Amenities:** Laundry service; nonsmoking rooms. *In room:* A/C (in some), ceiling fan, kitchen, fridge, safe, no phone.

Mary's Boon Beach Plantation 🌟 (Finds) Mary's Boon is one of those endearing places that draws loyal guests year after year. It's the kind of intimate, relaxed spot where you actually *talk* to people, whether in the small, convivial bar or on your porch as you gaze out at the beach. But even though it enjoys direct access to one of the best beaches on St. Maarten, with powdery white sand, this oldtimer is showing its age. Luckily, a new owner, Raul Max Brown, is on the scene and busy doing all the right things—refreshing and upgrading the rooms and public spaces, adding beach cabanas and spa services, and going as green as possible on an island that doesn't yet recycle. Not to worry: The cat still lazes on the easy chair, people walk barefoot through the lobby, and local business folk drop in for happy hour. The aim is not to undermine the charming, laidback ambience but to keep Mary's Boon from becoming a rusted relic.

One thing Max Brown *can't* do is curb the daily jet noise. Mary's Boon is right near the airport, so you do get the sounds of jets taking off a few times a day. But it's also only minutes from casinos, shops, and restaurants. Each room varies architecturally, but all have verandas or terraces; a number have big cherrywood beds and Balinese woodcarvings. Those facing the sea directly are breezy, high-ceilinged, and comfortably unpretentious. A couple of oceanfront rooms upstairs have already been renovated; they are now big, airy rooms that are equipped with full fridges, granite countertops, stainless steel appliances, and flatscreen TVs. Ask for room 105, 106, 107, or 108, which are nice and spacious and open up to the garden on the one side and the sea on the other. **Tides,** the simple but tasty beach restaurant and bar, offers good-value food that reveals a sure hand in the kitchen—it should; the head chef, Leona, has been cooking here for 36 years!—and its perch over the beach with the sea breeze wafting in is as good as it gets.

117 Simpson Bay Rd., St. Maarten, N.A. (or P.O. Box 523882, Miami, FL 33152). ⓒ **599/54-57000.** Fax 599/54-53403. www.marysboon.com. 36 units. Winter $125–$300 double (studios and one-bedroom suites; $250–$525 two-bedroom suites; off season $75–$275 double, $135–$415 two-bedroom suites. Extra person $30. AE, MC, V. Take the first right-hand turn as you head from the airport toward Philipsburg, then follow the signs to Mary's Boon. **Amenities:** Restaurant; bar; outdoor pool; limited room service; babysitting; Wi-Fi. *In room:* A/C, ceiling fan, TV, kitchenette, fridge, beverage maker, hair dryer, iron, safe.

Oyster Bay Beach Resort ⟨ᴿ⟩   At the end of a twisting, scenic road, a 1-minute walk from Dawn Beach, this retreat was originally designed for vacationers who don't like overly commercialized megaresorts; now it's largely timeshare. Once an intimate inn, it's been growing by leaps and bounds, having witnessed a five-fold increase in size since it was established in the 1960s. It can't be considered intimate anymore, but it's still not overwhelming. On a circular harbor on the eastern shore, near the French border, the fortresslike structure stands guard over a 14-hectare (35-acre) protected marina. There's a central courtyard and an alfresco lobby. Two new additions should be completed by the time this book goes to press: an 18-unit condominium (with a rooftop infinity pool) and a 40-unit timeshare pavilion.

More than half the units have kitchens, and most have West Indian decor with lots of rattan and wicker. The bedrooms offer balconies overlooking the pond or sea; the deluxe and superior rooms are preferable to the tower suites. Rooms are airy and fairly spacious, and suites have a bathroom with a tub and a shower.

The resort restaurant, **Jade,** serves international and Asian (mostly Indonesian) food for breakfast, lunch, and dinner. **Beau Beau's,** on the beach, serves seafood and international fare at lunch and dinner.

10 Emerald Merit Rd., Oyster Pond (P.O. Box 239), St. Maarten, N.A. © 866/978-0212 in the U.S., or 599/54-36040. Fax 599/54-36695. www.oysterbaybeachresort.com. 178 units (of those, 153 are timeshares). Winter $225–$300 double, $325–$675 suite; off season $150–$250 double, $250–$520 suite. Extra person $50–$60. Children under 12 stay free in parent's room. AE, DISC, MC, V. **Amenities:** 2 restaurants; 2 bars; outdoor pool; 4 tennis courts; fitness center; car rental; activities desk; babysitting; coin-operated laundry; 1 room for those w/limited mobility. *In room:* A/C, TV, dataport, kitchen (in most), fridge, beverage maker, hair dryer, iron, safe.

Sonesta Great Bay Beach Hotel & Casino ⊛ This property, ideally located a few minutes' walk from downtown Philipsburg, reopened in 2005 after a $10-million renovation. Virtually every area was completely refurbished; several facilities, including the fine **La Cucina Eatery** and a splendid infinity pool with swim-up bar, were added or expanded. Handsome Art Deco touches enliven the public spaces and halls, though the sizable rooms (more than half with an ocean view) feature standard decorative tropical trappings. Studios and one- and two-bedroom suites include kitchens and Murphy or sofa beds. Friendly management, extensive facilities (including a full-service spa), and an enviable location make this a fine bet for honeymooners and families alike.

19 Little Bay Rd. (P.O. Box 910), Philipsburg, St. Maarten, N.A. © 800/223-0757 in the U.S., or 599/542-2446. Fax 599/544-3008. www.sonesta.com/greatbay. 257 units. Winter $240–$350 double ($410–$550 all-inclusive), $490–$625 suite ($720–$880 all-inclusive); off season $180–$290 double ($350–$470 all-inclusive), $390–$550 suite ($600–$790 all-inclusive). AE, DISC, MC, V. **Amenities:** 3 restaurants; 4 bars; 3 outdoor pools; casino; lighted tennis court; fitness center; spa; 2 outdoor whirlpool tubs; activity center; boating; jet-skiing; snorkeling; windsurfing; scuba clinic; car rental; business services; babysitting; wedding facilities; Internet cafe. *In room:* A/C, ceiling fan, satellite TV, Wi-Fi, kitchenette (in some), fridge (in some), coffeemaker, hair dryer, iron/ironing board safety deposit box, private balcony or terrace.

MODERATE/INEXPENSIVE

La Vista This small West Antillean–style timeshare complex lies at the foot of Pelican Cay. For a fee, guests can use the more elaborate facilities of the nearby Pelican Resort, with its casino, shops, and spa.

The resort consists of two parts—La Vista Resort, a 2-minute walk from a good sandy beach, and La Vista Beach Resort, whose units open directly on the beach with studios and 2-bedroom apartments. Rooms with a view come in seven different categories, including a junior suite, deluxe suite, penthouse, or cottage. Accommodations feature fully equipped kitchenettes. Our preference is the one-bedroom Antillean cottage with its front porch (suitable for occupancy by four).

The **Hideaway Restaurant** serves well-prepared French cuisine adjacent to the pool, with live entertainment several nights a week. Wednesday nights feature barbecue beach parties.

53 Billy Folly Rd., Pelican Cay (P.O. Box 2086), Simpson Bay, St. Maarten, NA ℂ **599/54-43005.** Fax 599/54-43010. www.lavistaresort.com. 50 suites. Winter $180 double, $210–$330 suites for 4; off season $140 double, $160–$225 suites for 4. Children under 12 stay free when sharing with 2 adults. AE, DISC, MC, V. **Amenities:** Restaurant; bar; large outdoor pool; sundries shop; coin-operated laundry. *In room:* A/C, TV, kitchenette, fridge, beverage maker, hair dryer, iron, safe.

Pasanggrahan Royal Guest House ✶ *Value*   This vintage West Indian–style guesthouse has a prime spot on the beach in Philipsburg, sandwiched between the busy, narrow main street of Philipsburg and the harbor. It's set back and shaded under tall trees, a charming relic from another time. In fact, this was once the summer home of the Dutch Queen Wilhelmina, and the interior has a gracious, late-19th-century feel, with peacock bamboo chairs, Indian spool tables, and a gilt-framed oil portrait of the Dutch queen. The small- to medium-size accommodations have queen-size, double, or king-size beds with four-poster designs; some are in the main building and others are in an adjoining annex. The finest have genuine colonial flair, with antique secretaries and four-posters swaddled in mosquito netting, madras valances, hand-stitched quilts, beamed ceilings, and still life paintings.

Set among lush palms is the harborfront **Pasanggrahan Restaurant,** which specializes in fresh fish caught by the hotel's own deep-sea charter fishing boat and family-style dinners. Even if you don't stay here, this is a lovely, peaceful oasis for lunch or a drink after a day wrestling the cruise-ship hordes in downtown Philipsburg. The food is good and fresh, and the view of the harbor from the old wooden veranda, with Fort Amsterdam in the distance, never quits.

19 Front St. (P.O. Box 151), Philipsburg, St. Maarten, N.A. ℂ **599/54-23588.** Fax 599/54-22885. www.pasanhotel.com. 30 units. Winter $158–$250 double; off season $98–$165 double. Extra person winter $75, offseason $55. DISC, MC, V. Closed Sept. **Amenities:** Restaurant; 2 bars; car/scooter rental; gift shop; laundry service. *In room:* A/C, ceiling fan, TV, dataport, kitchenette (in some), fridge, beverage maker (in some), iron/ironing board, safe (in some).

Turquoise Shell Inn *(Value)*   The surrounding area isn't as nice and clean (or safe) as this trim yellow-and-white apartment complex steps from Simpson Bay Beach, but the price and location are right. Each one-bedroom suite has a fully equipped kitchen, though the restaurants and bars along the Simpson Bay "strip" are easy walking distance (not recommended if you're alone after a night's carousing). The plumbing is noisy, the A/C patchy, the shower-only bathrooms cramped, and the decor unassuming, but the friendly, obliging management keeps everything tidy.

34 Simpson Bay Rd., Simpson Bay, St. Maarten, N.A. © 599/545-2875 or 545-5642. Fax 599/545-2846. www.tshellinn.com. 10 units. Winter $145 double; off season $95–$115 double. MC, V. **Amenities:** Pool. *In room:* A/C, ceiling fan, TV, Wi-Fi.

2 French St. Martin

Hotels on French St. Martin add a 10% service charge and a *taxe de séjour.* This visitors' tax on rooms differs from hotel to hotel, depending on its classification, but is often $4 a day. Expect higher rates during Christmas week. Rates are quoted in either euros or dollars depending upon how establishments quoted them at the time of publication.

VERY EXPENSIVE

Alamanda Resort *(★)*   Small and intimate, like a European beachfront inn, the Alamanda opens onto Orient Bay's beautiful beach. The resort is a cluster of Creole *cazes,* or little houses, surrounding a lushly landscaped outdoor pool quite near the beach. The Alamanda has few drawbacks, one being that not all rooms have ocean views. Bedrooms are spacious and done up in soothing earth tones, with decorative accents in bold colors from sunflower yellow to tomato red, or pineapple patterns. The king-size beds are elegantly carved, often a four-poster. The best accommodations are the 2-bedroom duplexes with a second bathroom. Our favorite place to dine here is at **Kakao Beach** restaurant, featuring both Creole and European specialties in a laid-back Caribbean atmosphere. A less expensive choice is the **Alamanda Café,** with an inventive tropical cuisine served at poolside.

Baie Orientale, St. Martin, F.W.I. © 800/622-7836 in the U.S., or 590/52-87-40. Fax 590/52-87-41. www.alamanda-resort.com. 42 units. Winter $330–$495 double, $530 2-bedroom duplex, $710–$790 suite. Off season $270–$340 double, $440 2-bedroom duplex, $450–$500 suite. Extra person $30. AE, MC, V. Closed Sept. **Amenities:** 2 restaurants; 2 bars; outdoor pool; 2 tennis courts; gym; car rental; limited room service; massage; babysitting; laundry service; dry cleaning; Wi-Fi. *In room:* A/C, ceiling fan, TV, dataport, kitchenettes, hair dryer, iron/ironing board, safe.

Esmeralda Resort ✦   Originally conceived as a site for a single private villa, and then for a semiprivate club, this hillside housing development gives the appearance of a well-maintained compound of Creole-inspired villas on sloping terrain that's interspersed with lush gardens. It lies within a 25-minute taxi ride northeast of Princess Juliana airport. Opening onto Orient Beach, the Esmeralda blossomed into a full-scale resort in the early 1990s, offering views over Orient Bay and a decidedly French focus. Each of the 18 Spanish mission–style, tile-roofed villas can be configured into four separate units by locking or unlocking the doors between rooms. Each individual unit contains a king-size or two double beds, a kitchenette, a terrace, and a private entrance. Each villa has a communal pool, which creates the feeling of a private club. The suites are luxuriously spacious.

Astrolabe, with its award-winning chef, Stephane Decluseau, serves fine French and Caribbean specialties at breakfast and dinner daily. At lunch, the hotel issues an ID card that can be used for discounts at any of a half-dozen restaurants along the nearby beach.

Parc de la Baie Orientale (B.P. 5141), 97071 St. Martin, F.W.I. ℂ **590/87-36-36.** Fax 590/87-35-18. www.esmeralda-resort.com. 65 units. Winter $330–$495 double, $605–$715 suite; off season $240–$320 double, $370–$440 suite. Children under 12 free in parent's suite. AE, MC, V. Closed Sept. **Amenities:** 2 restaurants; bar; 18 outdoor pools; 2 tennis courts; parasailing; scuba diving; snorkeling; water-skiing; horseback riding (nearby); car rental desk; boutique; limited room service; massage; babysitting; laundry service; library. *In room:* A/C, ceiling fan, TV, dataport, kitchenette, fridge, beverage maker, hair dryer, safe.

Green Cay Villas ✦   This gated hillside community overlooking the sweep of Orient Bay features 16 fully equipped, three-bedroom, 418-sq.-m (4,500-sq.-ft.) villas with private pools at—comparatively—bargain rates, especially off season. Each can be configured into individual units; even the one-bedroom contains a modern kitchen. The design emphasizes cool blue, pristine off-whites, and rich tropical accents mirroring sea, sand, and sunset. White and natural wicker and hardwood furnishings are juxtaposed with boldly hued art naïf, throw pillows, fabrics, ceramics, and whimsical touches like painted parrots dangling from the high coffered ceilings. Daily maid service and breakfast are included.

Parc de la Baie Orientale (B.P. 3006), St. Martin, F.W.I. ℂ **866/592-4213** in the U.S., or 590/87-38-63. Fax 590/87-39-27. www.greencayvillas.com. 16 units. Winter $605–$739 1-bedroom suite, $713–$871 2-bedroom suite, $810–$990 3-bedroom villa; off season $362–$442 1-bedroom, $427–$521 2-bedroom, $522–$574 3-bedroom. Rates include continental breakfast. Minimum stay 5 nights. MC, V. **Amenities:** 16 pools; gym; Jacuzzis; airport shuttle; Wi-Fi. *In room:* A/C, TV, VCR, Internet, Wi-Fi, kitchen, beverage maker, hair dryer, safe.

Marigot

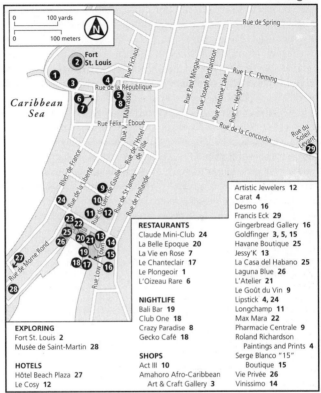

RESTAURANTS
Claude Mini-Club **24**
La Belle Epoque **20**
La Vie en Rose **7**
Le Chanteclair **17**
Le Plongeoir **1**
L'Oizeau Rare **6**

NIGHTLIFE
Bali Bar **19**
Club One **18**
Crazy Paradise **8**
Gecko Café **18**

SHOPS
Act III **10**
Amahoro Afro-Caribbean
    Art & Craft Gallery **3**

EXPLORING
Fort St. Louis **2**
Musée de Saint-Martin **28**

HOTELS
Hôtel Beach Plaza **27**
Le Cosy **12**

Artistic Jewelers **12**
Carat **4**
Desmo **16**
Francis Eck **29**
Gingerbread Gallery **16**
Goldfinger **3, 5, 15**
Havane Boutique **25**
Jessy'K **13**
La Casa del Habano **25**
Laguna Blue **26**
L'Atelier **21**
Le Goût du Vin **9**
Lipstick **4, 24**
Longchamp **11**
Max Mara **22**
Pharmacie Centrale **9**
Roland Richardson
    Paintings and Prints **4**
Serge Blanco "15"
    Boutique **15**
Vie Privée **26**
Vinissimo **14**

Hôtel L'Esplanade ✸✸ This lovely, beautifully managed small hotel just gets better and better. Along with its sister hotel, Le Petit—located directly on Grand Case Beach—it's easily one of the most pleasant places to stay on the entire island. Everything is wonderfully maintained; you won't see a tatter here, a loose thread there. With a collection of suites set on a steeply sloping hillside above the village of Grand Case, it almost has the feel of a boutique inn in the French Alps. Flowered vines frame terraces with gorgeous views of the village and sea below. The resort is connected by a network of steps and terraced gardens, and cascades of bougainvillea drape white walls accented with hand-painted tiles and blue slate roofs. The lovely pool is just steps down the hill, and access to a beach is via a 6-minute walk on a winding pathway. There's no restaurant, but you can order a delicious lunch prepared by a local cook at the pool bar; in any case, the village of Grand Case is famous for its fine restaurants.

All guest rooms have private terraces that angle out toward the sea and the sun setting behind Anguilla. Each individually decorated unit contains a kitchen with up-to-date cookware, Italian porcelain tile floors, beamed ceilings, plasma-screen TVs, DVDs, mahogany and wicker furniture, and very comfortable queen- or king-size beds (many four-poster). Slate and tumbled marble bathrooms are beautifully equipped. The loft suites on the upper floors are worth the extra charge—they include a sofa bed downstairs, an upstairs master bedroom with a king-size bed, and a partial bathroom downstairs. The cordial owners, Marc and Kristin Petrelluzzi have completely redone each suite; additional, even posher villas are in the works.

Grand-Case (B.P. 5007), 97150 St. Martin, F.W.I. ℂ 866/596-8365 in the U.S., or 590/87-06-55. Fax 590/87-29-15. www.lesplanade.com. 24 units. Winter $395 double studio, $445–$495 loft, $495 suite; off season $245 double studio, $295–$345 loft, $345 suite. Extra person winter $70, off season $50. AE, MC, V. **Amenities:** Bar (winter season); outdoor pool; car rental; boutique; babysitting; laundry service; rooms for those w/limited mobility. *In room:* A/C, ceiling fan, TV, dataport, kitchen, minibar, beverage maker, hair dryer, iron, safe.

La Samanna ⭐⭐⭐ With low-lying Mediterranean-style villas spread out over a long stretch of one of St. Martin's finest beaches, La Samanna has earned a reputation as a world-class complex where the cognoscenti come to relax and unwind. The resort is indeed lovely (the views from the hotel's signature restaurant are divine), and the colonial-style lobby and bar are handsomely atmospheric. An Orient-Express hotel, La Samanna is currently upgrading its rooms, and good thing: Despite the elegance of its artworks, the luxuriousness of the bathrooms, and the close proximity of all villas to the beach, the rooms decor is a tad uninspired, and some guests report that maintenance is not quite what it should be. The construction of extravagant new privately owned villas on its southeastern flank may cause some temporary noise.

That said, it's still pretty swell: Regardless of their size, most rooms feature private terraces. Suites and villas have spacious bedrooms with luxurious beds, fully equipped kitchens, living and dining rooms, and large patios. The bathrooms are spacious and well designed, with bidets and hand-painted Mexican tiles. Seven gorgeous specialty villas have rooftop terraces with magnificent views; four have private plunge pools.

Despite the price tag, La Samanna isn't stuffy; everyone is treated royally here. Guests enjoy superb cuisine alfresco on a candlelit terrace spectacularly perched above Baie Longue—the ambience is pure French Riviera. (Note that children under 7 are not permitted in the main restaurant for dinner). The amazing wine cellar, **Le Cave,** has expanded its inventory and now holds some 14,000 bottles. The poolside grill serves lunch daily and dinner 2 nights a week. If you can't make dinner in the main restaurant, you can enjoy the same great views at the buffet breakfasts, as delicious as the setting. With the curve of Baie Longue stretched out before you, there are few better ways to start the day.

Baie Longue (B.P. 4077), 97064 St. Martin CEDEX, F.W.I. ℂ **800/237-1236** in the U.S., or 590/87-64-00. Fax 590/87-87-86. www.lasamanna.com. 81 units. Winter $995 double, $1,825–$4,800 suite or villa; off season $450–$680 double, from $850 suite or villa. Extra person $75. Children and under stay free in parent's room. Rates include full buffet breakfast. AE, MC, V. Closed late Aug–late Oct. **Amenities:** 2 restaurants; 2 bars; outdoor pool; 3 tennis courts; fitness center; spa; sailing; snorkeling; water-skiing; windsurfing; 24-hr. room service; babysitting; laundry service; dry cleaning; nonsmoking rooms; library; wine cellar. *In room:* A/C, ceiling fan, TV, DVD, minibar, beverage maker, hair dryer, iron, safe, plunge pool (in some).

Le Petit Hotel 𝕽𝕽 *(finds)* This well-managed, thoughtfully designed hotel opens directly onto the sands of Grand Case Beach. It practically defines quiet chic, starting with the hand-painted tiles throughout the public spaces and hallways. It shares the same strong management, meticulous attention to detail, and sense of stylish comfort that distinguishes its splendid sister property, L'Esplanade (see above). Furnishings and accents are sourced from around the globe, including Balinese teak and Brazilian mahogany; natural wicker beds are topped with white down duvets and pillows. Luxurious touches include Frette linens and Damana toiletries. The smallish bathrooms are mostly shower-only, and the kitchenettes have a microwave, fridge, and a two-burner stovetop, but no oven. Each has a huge, beautifully appointed terrace or balcony overlooking the sand. The overall effect is of serene sanctuary. Though there's no restaurant, the warm, gracious staff offers advice on the town's many superb dining options.

248 bd. de Grand-Case, Grand-Case, 97150 St. Martin, F.W.I. ℂ **590/29-09-65.** Fax 590/87-09-19. www.lepetithotel.com. 10 units. Winter $415–$455 double, $525 suite; off season $265–$305 double, $375 suite. Extra person (including children) $50–$70. Rates include continental breakfast. AE, MC, V. **Amenities:** Activities desk; babysitting; laundry service; 1 room for those w/limited mobility. *In room:* A/C, ceiling fan, TV, Wi-Fi, kitchenette, fridge, beverage maker, hair dryer, iron, safe.

EXPENSIVE

Club Orient Naturist Resort ✿   Occupying an isolated spot, this is the only true nudist resort in the French West Indies, but it's definitely *not* a wild, swinging, party place. Celebrating 30 years of business in 2008, it's very clean, decent, middle-class, even family-friendly. Very few singles check in, so "Club O" won't stimulate those seeking titillation. Despite their lack of clothing, many of the guests are older and very conservative—just looking for a quiet, reclusive getaway with like-minded nudists. There's no pool on the premises, but the chalets are right on an excellent beach, with plentiful activities to facilitate hanging out (in every sense). Accommodations, set in red-pine chalets imported from Finland, sport a basic IKEA-meets-campground-cabin look, though the decor has been spruced up. All have outside showers and most have both front and back porches. At **Papagayo Restaurant** you can dine alfresco; the popular 5 to 7pm happy hour allows guests to compare . . . notes. However, each unit has a kitchenette and there's a general store, **La Boutique,** on-site if you want to cook your own meal.

1 Baie Orientale, 97150 St. Martin, F.W.I. © **800/690-0199** in the U.S., or 590/87-33-85. Fax 590/87-33-76. www.cluborient.com. 136 units. Winter 215€–270€ ($322–$405) studio and suite, 330€–395€ ($495–$593) chalet, 1,000€ ($1,500) villa; off season 125€–200€ ($188–$300) studio and suite, 185€–220€ ($275–$330) chalet, 600€ ($900) villa. Children under 12 stay for free. AE, DC, DISC, MC, V. **Amenities:** Restaurant; 2 bars; gym; spa; kayaks; sailboats; snorkeling; windsurfing; car rental; general store and boutique; babysitting; laundry service; coin-operated laundry; library; minimart; 1 room for those w/limited mobility. *In room:* A/C, ceiling fan, Ethernet access, kitchen, beverage maker, safe.

Grand Case Beach Club ✿   This bundling of bougainvillea-draped buildings sits between two beaches just a short stroll from the action in "downtown" Grand Case. There are several different room categories, including duplex units, but all have well-stocked kitchens with granite counters and private balconies or patios (the best offering smashing views of Anguilla). The property is immaculately maintained, and you can't beat the views. Families will particularly appreciate the gated entrance (making the lovely "Petite Plage" practically private) and 24-hour security guard and video surveillance. Little extras include a sampling of island CDs and a bottle of wine at check-in. The general manager is conscientious, cordial, and helpful, qualities he inculcates in the staff.

The **Sunset Cafe,** set spectacularly on the rocks overlooking the water, serves a delicious breakfast, lunch, and dinner.

Grand Case 97150, St. Martin, F.W.I. © **800/344-3016** in the U.S., or 590/87-51-87. Fax 590/87-59-93. www.grandcasebeachclub.com. 73 units. Winter $310–$385 studio double, $365–$425 1-bedroom suite, $520–$555 2-bedroom suite; off season $145–$175 studio double, $160–$190 1-bedroom suite, $270–$285 2-bedroom suite. Continental breakfast included. Children under 12 stay free in parent's room. Extra person $35. AE, MC, V. **Amenities:** Restaurant; bar; outdoor pool; tennis court; fitness room; dive shop; sailing; snorkeling; kayaking; water-skiing; car rental; laundry facilities; computer with Internet access. *In room:* A/C, ceiling fan, TV, CD player, dial-up Internet access, kitchen, hair dryer, iron/ironing board, safe.

Hotel Beach Plaza ⓡ   This is the best hotel within a reasonable distance of Marigot's commercial heart. A three-story building that centers on a soaring atrium festooned with live banana trees and climbing vines, it's within a cluster of buildings mostly composed of condominiums. Built in 1996, and painted in shades of blue and white, it's set midway between the open sea and the lagoon, giving all rooms water views. The white interiors are accented with varnished, dark-tinted woods and an inviting tropical motif. Each room contains a balcony, tile floors, native art, and simple hardwood furniture, including a writing desk and comfortable beds.

   The hotel's restaurant, **Le Corsaire,** serves French food except for the all-you-can-eat buffets on Tuesday and Friday nights, which feature Creole and seafood, respectively.

Baie de Marigot, 97150 St. Martin, F.W.I. © **590/87-87-00.** Fax 590/87-18-87. www.hotelbeachplazasxm.com. 144 units. Winter $221–$391 double, $508–$601 suite; off season $174–$250 double, $394–$406 suite. Rates higher between Christmas and New Year's. Rates include buffet breakfast. AE, MC, V. **Amenities:** Restaurant; 2 bars; outdoor pool; jet skis; kayaks; scuba diving; snorkeling; bike rental; car rental; limited room service; babysitting; laundry service; nonsmoking rooms; rooms for those w/limited mobility. *In room:* A/C, TV, minibar, fridge, hair dryer, safe.

Mercure Simson Beach Hotel ⓥ̶ᵃˡᵘᵉ   This is a good-value hotel on the French side of the island. The complex occupies a flat, sandy stretch of land between a saltwater lagoon and the beach, 8km (5 miles) west of Princess Juliana Airport. Decorated throughout in bold, Creole-inspired hues, its five three-story buildings are each evocative of a large, many-balconied Antillean house. In its center, a pool serves as the focal point for a bar built out over the lagoon, an indoor/outdoor restaurant, and a flagstone terrace that hosts steel bands and evening cocktail parties. Each unit offers, in addition to a kitchenette, a terrace with a view. The most desirable accommodations, on the third (top) floor, contain sloping ceilings sheltering sleeping lofts, and two bathrooms. Ask about the hotel's all-inclusive plan.

Baie Nettlé (B.P. 172), Marigot, 97052 St. Martin, F.W.I. ℂ **800/221-4542** in the U.S., or 590/87-54-54. Fax 590/87-92-11. www.mercuresimsonbeach.com. 178 units. Winter $294 studio for 2, from $323 duplex; off season $205 studio for 2, $244 duplex. Rates include buffet breakfast. AE, DC, MC, V. **Amenities:** Restaurant; bar; outdoor pool; tennis court; dive center; kayaking; snorkeling; water-skiing; wind-surfing; beach volleyball; billiards; car rental; boutique; babysitting; laundry service; dry cleaning; rooms for those w/limited mobility. *In room:* A/C, TV, dataport, minibar, beverage maker (in some), hair dryer (in some), safe.

Radisson St. Martin Resort, Marina & Spa ✿

Formerly Le Meridien/L'Habitation de Lonvilliers, this new property, which opened in August 2008, is the beneficiary of a $60-million invest-ment that reworked and updated the existing building and grounds—grounds that include a sweet stretch of beach along Anse Marcel, one of St. Martin's prettiest coves, surrounded on three sides by volcanic hills. The 252 units feature all the latest amenities, from flatscreen TVs to complimentary Wi-Fi. Facilities include two pools, one of which is a "lazy river" pool; a spa; a watersports center and dive shop; two restaurants; and a lounge. Oh, and did I mention a full-service 150-slip marina?

Anse Marcel (B.P. 581), 97056 St. Martin, F.W.I. ℂ **800/333-3333** in the U.S. or Canada, or 590/87-67-00. Fax 590/87-30-38. www.radisson.com/stmartin. 252 units. 189€–269€ ($283–$403) double, 349€–499€ ($523–$748) suite. AE, DC, MC, V. **Amenities:** 2 restaurants; 2 bars; 2 pools; fitness center; spa; watersports center; dive center; banana boats; kayaking; sailing; snorkeling; water-skiing; windsurfing; car rental; babysitting; laundry service; dry cleaning; water taxi service; rooms for those w/limited mobility. *In room:* A/C, flatscreen TV, DVD, Wi-Fi, minibar, coffeemakers, hair dryer, safe, robes.

MODERATE/INEXPENSIVE

Hotel La Plantation ✿

Although it requires a few minutes' walk to reach the gorgeous white-sand beach, this is one of the most attrac-tive and appealing hotels at Orient Bay. It's set on a steep, carefully landscaped slope. Seventeen colonial-style villas are scattered around the tropically landscaped grounds and pool; each villa contains a suite and two studios, which can be rented separately or combined. The spacious units are stylishly furnished in a colorful Creole theme, com-plete with hand-painted or hand-stenciled murals, and each sports its own ocean-view terrace. Studios have kitchenettes and queen-size or twin beds; the suites have separate bedrooms with king-size beds, spa-cious living rooms, full kitchens, and beautifully tiled full bathrooms.

Café Plantation serves French and Creole dinners. At lunch, clients use an in-house "privilege card" to buy French/Creole/inter-national meals at any of five beachfront restaurants loosely associated with the resort.

C 5 Parc de La Baie Orientale, Orient Bay, 97150 St. Martin, F.W.I. ℭ **590/29-58-00.** Fax 590/29-58-08. www.la-plantation.com. 52 units. Winter $245 studio for 2, from $360 suite; off season $160–$185 studio, from $245 suite. Children under 12 stay free in parent's room. Rates include breakfast. DISC, MC, V. Closed Sept 1 to mid-Oct. **Amenities:** Restaurant; beach bar and grill; outdoor pool; 2 tennis courts; health club; diving; jet ski; parasailing; windsurfing; bike rental; horseback riding; boutique; high-speed Internet access; massage. *In room:* A/C, ceiling fan, TV, kitchen, fridge, beverage maker, hair dryer, safe.

Le Cosy   In the commercial center of Marigot (and favored by business travelers), Le Cosy's concrete facade is enlivened with gingerbread fretwork and magenta awnings. A bar with a soaring tent serves drinks to guests relaxing on wicker and bentwood furniture. The small bedrooms are arranged around a landscaped central courtyard with a fish-shaped fountain and funky island murals. A lime or cherry throw pillow suffices for decor in the worn, minimalist rooms, most of them duplexes with mahogany-trimmed stairs climbing to a sleeping loft. Tiny bathrooms are shower-only.

The simple restaurant serves dinner only. The traditional French cuisine is served in a charming open-air rooftop location.

Rue du Général-de-Gaulle (B.P. 679), Marigot, 97150 St. Martin, F.W.I. ℭ **590/87-63-93.** Fax 590/87-43-95. www.lecosyhotel.com. 12 units. Year-round 78€–90€ ($117–$135) double. MC, V. **Amenities:** Restaurant. *In room:* A/C, TV, minibar.

4

Where to Dine on St. Maarten/St. Martin

Without a doubt, St. Maarten/St. Martin has some of the best food in the Caribbean. Although both the French and Dutch sides offer epicurean experiences galore, with nearly 500 restaurants, it's the French side that gets the nod for overall excellence. St. Martin has drawn a number of classically trained culinary wizards and become a competitive training ground for Michelin-bound chefs. The Dutch side is more uneven and much more Americanized (you'll spot KFC and Burger King, among others), but some of the island's most exciting restaurants are opening up here.

Truth be told, the standards are so high on both sides of this tiny island that few restaurateurs can get away with mediocrity for long; even the hotel restaurants are better than most. Speaking of which, I'd like to mention a couple of hotel restaurants that for space issues aren't reviewed below. La Samanna's **The Restaurant** ✸✸ (www. lasamanna.com) offers a sublime fine-dining experience in a setting that's truly hard to beat: high above curving Baie Longue. At the other end of the dining spectrum is the **Tides,** a modest, old-fashioned dining room with a spectacular beachside setting at Mary's Boon Plantation (www.marysboon.com/marysboon). The head chef, Leona, has been cooking here for 36 years, and the food is delicious and the experience surprisingly satisfying.

Yes, you can eat well pretty much wherever you go, but as you might suspect, many of the top restaurants are located in the most highly trafficked areas. You'll find great dining in **Marigot,** in atmospheric restaurants lining the waterfront and at Marina Port la Royale. **Philipsburg,** for all its slightly tawdry tendencies, has a number of truly fine eateries on and around Front Street. Numerous excellent options have sprouted in St. Maarten's **Maho district,** while its neighbor **Simpson Bay** has dozens of casual but topnotch watering holes overlooking the lagoon where fresh seafood reflects the community's longtime fishing heritage. But the island's true culinary mecca is the charming little fishing village of **Grand Case,** perched near the

La Belle Créole

Befitting its turbulent colonial history, St. Maarten/St. Martin is a rich culinary melting pot. The local cuisine, symbol of the island's voyage on many levels, is primarily a savory blend of Arawak (the indigenous people), French, African, even East Indian influences. The Arawaks contributed native tubers like yuca (aka cassava) and dasheen (whose leaves, similar to spinach, are also used), as well as cilantro, lemon grass, and achiote for flavoring. The slave ships introduced plantains, sweet potato, green pigeon peas, and assorted peppers. The various European influences bore fruit in fresh garden staples like onions (and breadfruit imported from Tahiti because it proved cheaper for feeding slaves). The East Indians brought curry with them, an essential ingredient of Colombo, a meat or chicken dish of Tamil origin, as well as exotic spices.

True Creole cuisine is fast vanishing: It requires patience and work, long hours marinating and pounding. But you can still find authentic dishes whose seasonings ignite the palate. Look for specialties such as *crabe farci* (stuffed crab), *féroce* (avocado with shredded, spicy codfish called *chiquetaille*), *accras* (cod fritters), *blaff* (seafood simmered in seasoned soup), *boudin* (spicy blood sausage), *bébélé* and *matéte* (tripe dishes stewed with anything from breadfruit to bananas). Conch *(lambi)* and whelks are found in fritters and stews with fiery *sauce chien.* Wash them down with local juices: mango, guava, papaya, and less familiar flavors like the tart tangy tamarind; milky mouth-puckering soursop; pulpy passion fruit; bitter yet refreshing mauby (made from tree bark); and the milkshakelike, reputedly aphrodisiacal sea moss. And try a *ti' punch* aperitif: deceptively sweet, fruit-infused 100-proof rum.

—Jordan Simon

northern tip of St. Martin: No other Caribbean town offers so many wonderful restaurants per capita, sitting cheek-by-jowl along the narrow mile-long main road fronting Grand Case Beach.

1 In Dutch St. Maarten

PHILIPSBURG

EXPENSIVE

Antoine ✪ FRENCH   In a lovely seaside setting, Antoine serves fine, comfortably retro-bistro food with sophistication and style. The

Tips **Mapping It**

For locations of dining establishments listed in this chapter, please refer to the St. Maarten/St. Martin, Marigot, or Philipsburg maps on p. 46, p. 57, and p. 49, respectively.

handsome room decked with jungle-themed Haitian masterworks, Delft tile, hurricane lanterns, old phonographs, and towering floral arrangements further sets the scene for romance. I always start with the chef's savory kettle of fish soup, escargots de Bourgogne, or the almost translucent sea scallops Nantaise. You can't go wrong with the baked red snapper filet delicately flavored with shallots and a white-wine butter sauce, shrimp scampi flambéed with Pastis, or grilled local lobster. And desserts are satisfyingly sinful. Antoine occasionally opens for basic lunches (though some dinner items are available).

119 Front St., Philipsburg. ✆ **599/542-2964.** www.antoinerestaurant.com. Reservations recommended. Main courses lunch $8–$20, dinner $20–$40; lobster thermidor $46. AE, DISC, MC, V. Daily 11am–10pm.

L'Escargot FRENCH   You can't miss the wildly painted shutters and tropical Toulouse-Lautrec murals of revelers (and snails in toques) on the otherwise yellow exterior of this 160-year-old Creole cottage. The high spirits continue within, thanks to the mellow staff, which does double duty performing the Friday-night cabaret drag show, "La Cage aux Folles." Owners channel Kenny Rogers and Dolly Parton on "Islands in the Stream," and divas—Cher, Christina Aguilera, Donna Summers, Tina Turner—sashay in gold lamé and wigs whose colors don't exist in nature. The chef smartly sticks to hearty bistro classics like Dover sole meunière, duck terrine, quiche Lorraine, herbed rack of lamb, veal chops, and roast duck with the restaurant's signature pineapple/banana sauce. And oh yes, snails, with at least six preparations on the menu (try the sampler plate): *millefeuille* (phyllo pastry) with saffron sauce to *profiteroles aux escargots forestière* (wild mushrooms, shallots, white wine).

96 Front St., Philipsburg. ✆ **599/542-2483.** www.lescargotrestaurant.com. Reservations recommended. Main courses $20–$35. AE, DISC, MC, V. Daily noon–2pm and 6–10:30pm.

MODERATE

Oualichi ✿ FRENCH/INTERNATIONAL   Ideally situated on the boardwalk (there's even beach service), this French-owned brasserie is a local favorite frequented by island dignitaries and a big yachter hangout during boat shows and regattas. ("Oualichi" was the island's original Arawak name, meaning "land of women" after its curvaceous hills.) The jungle interior (glass bar embedded with shells, sand, and driftwood) is fun, but I prefer sitting on the patio, listening to occasional live music wafting across the courtyard and counting berths on the cruise ships. The menu offers fabulous mahimahi tartare, tuna sashimi, chicken breast in coconut curry, or escargots in garlic butter, as well as perfectly fine burgers, pizzas, and the like. A bucket of beers is $10, and drinks include the eponymous house specialty (vodka, Myer's rum, passion fruit, strawberry).

St. Rose Arcade, Front St., Philipsburg. ✆ 599/542-4313. Main courses $13–$30. AE, MC, V. Daily 11:30am–11pm.

Shiv Sagar INDIAN   The island's first Indian eatery remains its best, emphasizing Kashmiri and Mughlai specialties. The best tables in the large second-floor split-level space overlook Front Street. Black lacquer chairs, hand-carved chess tables, and traditional Indian silkscreens depicting scenes from such great epics as the *Mahabharata* set the stage for tempting tandooris, Madras fish curry, and vegetarian dishes like *saag panir* (spinach in garlicky curried yogurt), hearty enough to convert even the most dedicated carnivore.

20 Front St., Philipsburg. ✆ 599/542-2299. www.shivsagarsxm.com. Main courses $12–$20. AE, DISC, MC, V. Mon–Sat noon–10pm; Sun noon–3pm.

INEXPENSIVE

Kangaroo Court SANDWICHES/SALADS   This down-to-earth coffeehouse is set on a side street between Front and Back streets, adjacent to the historic Wathey Courthouse (named for the owners' forebears). The thick red-brick and black-stone walls, crafted 200 years ago from the ballast bricks of ships that sailed to the island for salt, have withstood many an act of God and war. Within an interior that's splashed in vibrant Creole colors, you'll find display racks loaded with fresh-baked pastries and constantly chugging espresso machines. Sandwiches and salads (including sesame chicken, or shrimp, avocado, and papaya) are sold at a roaring pace, mostly to passengers from the nearby cruise-ship docks, throughout the day. Continue through the back to a more tranquil interior garden courtyard with blue canvas chairs and nets strategically slung to catch leaves falling from shady almond and banyan trees. The pizzas are yummy (try the roast chicken pizza with mangoes, red onions, and black olives), as are the sweet potato fries with garlic pepper.

10 Hendrickstraat, Philipsburg. ✆ 599/542-7557. Sandwiches and salads $8–$13. AE, DISC, MC, V. Mon–Fri 8am–5pm; Sat 8am–4pm.

MAHO & CUPECOY BEACH AREAS
VERY EXPENSIVE

Rare 🌂🌂 STEAKHOUSE   Dino Jagtiani, the whiz behind the adjacent Temptation (see below) opened this take on the classic chophouse in 2005. The futuristic-yet-retro space is wittily design-infected. The only steakhouse in St. Maarten to carry USDA Prime dry-aged CAB (certified Angus beef), Rare offers choices from a 12-ounce filet mignon to a 28-ounce porterhouse that can be deconstructed several ways. Those seeking lighter fare can savor sashimi-grade tuna with wasabi mash, or Parmigiano-crusted salmon. Anyone could make a meal of the home-baked bread and dips (hummus, pesto, tapenade). Dino's creativity truly shines in sauces (nine including chipotle-ketchup and spicy peanut). Desserts include an inspired s'mores cobbler, with chocolate, graham crackers, marshmallow crust, caramel, and vanilla ice cream.

Atlantis Casino, Cupecoy. © **599/545-5714**. www.dare-to-be-rare.com. Reservations required. Main courses $25–$45. AE, DISC, MC, V. Mon–Sat 6:30–10:30pm.

Temptation 🌂🌂🌂 CONTEMPORARY   The name may sound like a strip club, but this innovative gem is one of the finest restaurants on island. Owner/chef Dino Jagtiani, who hails from a multi-generational East Indian family, is the only native St. Maarten grad of the prestigious Culinary Institute of America (C.I.A.). His mother Asha graciously greets diners "as if it were our house, only for 100 guests." Dino's "nouvelle Caribbean" cuisine is exciting, even unusual, often utilizing unorthodox pairings. Witness such witty dishes as seared foie gras "PB&J" (roasted peanut sauce and Port-fig jelly), his take on surf and turf (sea scallops in vanilla sauce with Italian sausage and curried lentil), or the McDino (Granny Smith apple tempura with honey-thyme ice cream and caramel sauce). He brilliantly juxtaposes flavors and textures. If they're on the menu, try tempura mussel shooters with coconut curry and *wakame* (seaweed), duck with mashed sweet potatoes and red cabbage (sweet and sour), or arugula-mushroom ravioli in basil jelly. You'll find the perfect wine complement on one of the island's top wine lists, with extremely pricey if intriguing boutique selections from producers such as Didier Dagueneau and Napa's Philip Togni. (Alas, it regrettably apes *Wine Spectator* by listing its scores as if gospel.)

Atlantis Casino, Cupecoy. © **599/545-2254**. www.nouveaucaribbean.com. Main courses $28–$37. AE, MC, V. Tues–Sun 6:30–10:30pm.

EXPENSIVE

Le Montmartre ⭐ FRENCH   This very Parisian bistro has new management, but chef Thiery Delauny is still running the very capable kitchen. Art Nouveau–inspired lamps, pilasters, crown moldings, and Second Empire–style furnishings set the tone for equally classic fare. Start with sautéed duck foie gras "Normandie style"—with onion jam with apple juice and frozen Calvados liquor—tuna carpaccio, or lobster bisque. Main courses include superbly executed standards (tournedos Rossini, beef filet with a foie gras medallion and truffles in brioche; classic French sweetbreads in a creamy mushroom sauce; a seafood cassoulet; and roasted French seabass). Many items are filleted or carved tableside with a flourish by an enthusiastic waitstaff. Decadent desserts include some of the best crème brûlées and soufflés on island. The wine list is comprehensive and fairly priced.

Atlantis Casino, Cupecoy. ✆ **599/545-3939.** www.lemontmartre.com. Reservations recommended. Main courses $22–$42. AE, MC, V. Daily 6–10:30pm.

MODERATE

La Gondola ⭐ ITALIAN   This traditional trattoria offers Mamma Mia Italian, all garlic and attitude, unfortunately at non-*paisano* prices. But I can overlook the pretension, prices, and overdone decor (neoclassical Davids, cherubs, gilt frames) if the food is good. And it is, with excellent versions of standards such as lasagna, linguini in clam sauce, veal Milanese, and desserts from tiramisu to *tartufo*. They also do a very nice risotto here; try the seafood risotto or the version with homemade *salsiccia* (sausage) and pan-fried Portobello mushrooms. The warm, attentive service is another plus.

Atlantis Casino, Cupecoy. ✆ **599/545-3938.** www.lagondola-sxm.com. Reservations recommended. Pastas and main courses $18–$34. AE, MC, V. Daily 6–10:30pm.

Peg Leg Pub & Steakhouse ⭐ AMERICAN/STEAKHOUSE In its new location just inside the casino entrance at Princess Port de Plaisance, this tavern hopes to continue to do a brisk business in beer (more than 35 available at one of the Caribbean's longest bars). It's assumed that the décor—a marriage of clubby steakhouse with Jolly Roger kitsch (model boats, peg legs dangling from rafters)—will be transplanted to its new location. Kitsch or no, the food is delicious, offering a wide range of entrees from filet mignon to fettucine Alfredo and a garlic shrimp platter. Even pub grub (coconut shrimp, beer-battered onion rings, fried calamari) is elevated to an art form. Lunch features salads, hearty deli sandwiches, and burgers.

Princess Port de Plaisance, Union Rd., Cupecoy. ⓒ **599/544-5859.** www.peglegpub.
com. Main courses $18–$39. AE, DISC, MC, V. Daily noon–11pm. Closed Sun lunch.

SIMPSON BAY AREA
EXPENSIVE
Saratoga ⓕ INTERNATIONAL/SEAFOOD   This cutting-edge
restaurant run by C.I.A. (Culinary Institute of America) grad John
Jackson occupies a beautiful setting, resembling a Spanish colonial
structure from the outside, and lined with rich mahogany inside.
Seating is either indoors or on a marina-side veranda. The food is
beautifully presented. Although the menu changes frequently, it
leans toward light and healthy: Witness the roasted eggplant, leek,
and tomato soup or the grilled red snapper filet served with tropical
fruit salsa. Not that fat is banned: If you're looking for good and rich,
opt for the linguine primavera, here prepared with both smoked ham
and bacon. Yum. It dips into Thai and classic Chinese preparations,
including the salt and pepper fried whole black seabass.

Simpson Bay Yacht Club, Airport Rd. ⓒ **599/544-2421.** Reservations recommended.
Main courses $24–$37. AE, MC, V. Mon–Sat 6:30–10pm. Closed Aug to mid-Oct.

MODERATE
Halsey's ⓕ INTERNATIONAL   Just south of the drawbridge on
Simpson Bay, this waterfront restaurant takes an unfussy approach to
fine dining (its motto is "fine food unrefined") and is adept at subtly updating classic dishes. Start with the prosciutto-wrapped sea
scallops served with black truffle cream sauce, the maguro sashimi,
or the smoked-salmon-wrapped asparagus. Fresh fish features largely
in the main course, with your choice of blackened mahimahi, pan-
seared grouper, or Asian tuna. You can also get good steaks, grilled
veal chops, or rack of Colorado lamb. The flavors change nightly, but
homemade ice cream is the smart finish. A Saturday 3–5pm happy
hour features a special sushi menu and $5 martinis.

86 Welfare Rd., Simpson Bay. ⓒ **599/544-2882.** www.halseysrestaurant.com.
Main courses $19–$32. AE, MC, V. Daily 6–10pm; lounge opens earlier.

Jimbo's Rock & Blues Café (Kids TEX-MEX   "Party and eat
hearty" could be the motto of this rollicking family-friendly frat-
house masquerading as a restaurant. The huge neon guitar at the
entrance hints at the ambience, reinforced by the amazing sound system, cocktails with *cojones* (try the 32-ounce "megarita"), and fun
watery decor: split-level platforms surrounding fountains and a pool
with swim-up bar (if you forgot your bathing suit, try the boutique).
Yes, you'll find lots of kids splashing about here—during the day.

Come happy hour (with numerous specials), anything goes, as the place devolves into a meat market. Food is surprisingly good, emphasizing mesquite-grilled items like fajitas and babyback ribs, and more creative fare such as grouper stuffed with chipotle crab cake or goat cheese–roasted pepper enchiladas. The menu also has lots of salads for the calorie- and cholesterol-conscious. You earn one Jimbo Dollar per drink (five gets a freebie, and some folks stockpile them for a last-night bender).

Plaza del Lago, Airport Rd., Simpson Bay. ℂ 599/544-3600. www.jimboscafe.com. Main courses $9–$27. AE, MC, V. Mon–Sat 11am–midnight; Sun 5pm–midnight.

SkipJack's Seafood Grill, Bar & Fish Market ✪ SEAFOOD
Of the many shipshape seafood spots on Simpson Bay, this pleasant, breezy spot is one of the best. You can pick your fish on ice and both Maine and Caribbean lobster from a tank and pool, then enjoy the breezes (and live music Wed and Fri) on the handsome and expansive wooden deck, where you can watch the big yachts muscle their way in and out of Simpson Bay. The entrees taste like they jumped from the sea to your plate, from blackened grouper to shrimp pot pie. The steamed shrimp, hot and piled on the plate, was some of the best I've ever had. Other excellent starters include tuna carpaccio, a hearty New England clam chowder, a lobster and crab salad, and crab cakes with caper mayo. SkipJack's does justice to its namesake, the old-time single-mast fishing boats that plied the Chesapeake.

Airport Rd., Simpson Bay. ℂ 599/544-2313. www.skipjacks-sxm.com. Main courses $18–$25. MC, V. Daily noon–10:30pm. Closed Sun lunch.

Topper's AMERICAN   Neighboring guests first clued us into this spot, raving about the big, delicious steaks and well-poured drinks served up by a gentleman of a certain age in what was essentially a roadside Creole shack. Topper's is indeed a hoot, but someone in the kitchen has a real touch with beef—where else on St. Maarten will you find delicious and tender brisket, served with homemade mashed potatoes and whisky carrots? Other classics include Caesar salad, shrimp cocktail, and meatloaf. The steaks are indeed big and good, and the atmosphere is fun. Best of all, the prices are reasonable for pricey St. Maarten.

113 Welfare Rd., Simpson Bay. ℂ 599/544-3500. www.sxmtoppers.com. Reservations recommended. Main courses $15–$24. AE, MC, V. Mon–Sat 6–10pm.

INEXPENSIVE
Bavaria GERMAN   Sauerbraten, schnitzel, spaetzle, and strudel might seem heavy for the climate, but they go down well with a

frosty draft German beer. Annette Krabbe's little slice of home lures locals in droves for its fine fare at fair prices and cheap cocktails. While the kitchen turns out a proper beef roulade with red cabbage, it also offers "international" selections, from Italian to Indian (surprisingly good chicken curry). There's plenty of oomph in the oompah band (replete with accordion) Wednesday nights.

103 Airport Rd., Simpson Bay. © 599/544-2665. www.bavariarestaurant.com. Main courses $13–$15. MC, V. Daily 5–10pm.

Pizza Galley ⓡ PIZZA   This place gets raves from locals and passing mariners. It's located on the dock at the Lady C Floating Bar. The pizza is thin-crust, with an interesting choice of toppings, from standards such as sausage, pepperoni, and mushrooms to shrimp, roasted peppers, even steak. Homemade desserts include pecan pie and fresh apple/four berry pie.

At the Lady C Floating Bar, Airport Rd., Simpson Bay. © 599/557-7416. Pizza $8, toppings $1–$8. No credit cards. Daily 5–11pm.

Ric's Place AMERICAN/TEX-MEX   The American expat owners wanted "a small neighborhood bar on an island" and this breezy multipurpose hangout is that and more. Everybody comes to Ric's, to paraphrase *Casablanca.* Team pennants (Canadiens, Georgia Bulldogs), games (air hockey, darts, video), and large-screen TVs lure sports buffs. More than a dozen beers, retro cocktails (sidecars, Rusty Nails, coladas like the house BBC—Bailey's and banana), and occasional live bands draw night owls. Come for the "show"—you have the best seat in the house as the Simpson Bay drawbridge rises several times daily to permit passage of mega yachts; be sure to give a self-satisfied toast to the poor saps stuck in bridge traffic. The food is good, cheap, and filling: from burgers with beer-battered onion rings to baby back ribs to burritos. A kids' menu is available

Airport Rd. at drawbridge, Simpson Bay. © 599/545-3630. www.ricsplace-sxm. com. Sandwiches, salads, and main courses $8–$12. No credit cards. Daily 8am–10pm.

2 In French St. Martin

MARIGOT
EXPENSIVE
La Vie en Rose ⓡ FRENCH   The dining room in this balconied second-floor restaurant evokes a tropical version of Paris in the 1920s, thanks to flower boxes, gold gilt mirrors, arches, ceiling fans, candlelight, and time-honored culinary showmanship to match the show-stopping harbor views. The menu is classic French, although

(Tips) Resources for Self-Catering

As a large provisioning hub for passing boats, St. Maarten has plenty of options for visitors with self-catering capabilities, whether a hotel kitchenette or a fully equipped kitchen. You can buy meats, fresh fruits and vegetables, snacks, drinks, and kitchen supplies at **Le Grand Marché,** a full-service grocery chain with three locations on island, including one at Simpson Bay (© **599/545-3055;** www.legrandmarche.net). In Marigot, **Match supermarket,** located in the Howell Center, has a good selection of French foods. The **U.S. Imports Super Marché** (© **590/52-87-14**), a supermarket chain on the French side, has a branch at the drawbridge in Sandy Ground that's open till 10pm (it also has baguettes, pastries, and a cheese selection). You can also find takeout foods at *traiteurs* (take-out/caterers), *pâtisseries* (pastry shops), and *boulangeries* (baked goods). For an excellent selection of wine and spirits, head to **Vinissimo,** at 1 Rue de Low Town, Marigot (© **590/ 877-078**). For fresh fish, head over to the **Simpson Bay Fish Market,** a new open-air seafood market facing the Simpson Bay lagoon, which sells Simpson Bay's fresh catches daily. Finally, the island is home to 130 nationalities, from Latino to Lebanese, Italian to Indian. Don't shy away from the glorified bodegas serving *comida criolla,* Hong Kong Chinese holes-in-the-wall, and shwarma shacks.

Caribbean overtones often creep in. Lunches are relatively simple affairs, with an emphasis on fresh, meal-size salads, simple grills like beefsteak with shallot sauce, brochettes of fresh fish, and pastas. Dinners are more elaborate (attracting a dressier crowd), and might begin with a lobster salad with passion-fruit dressing. Main courses include grilled filet of red snapper simmered in champagne with pumpkin risotto; breast of duck in a foie gras sauce; lobster paired with boneless rabbit in honey-vanilla sauce; and an unusual version of roasted rack of lamb in a mushroom and truffle sauce. Even if you just stop by while shopping, the near-definitive lobster bisque in puff pastry is a must.

Bd. de France at rue de la République, Marigot. © **590/87-54-42.** www.lavieenrose stmartin.com. Reservations recommended. Main courses lunch 10€–18€ ($15–$27), dinner 20€–33€ ($30–$49). AE, DISC, MC, V. Mon–Sat noon–3pm; daily 6:30–10pm.

Le Chanteclair ✿ FRENCH   This simple yet elegant eatery is positioned perfectly on the marina boardwalk. Both decor (from turquoise deck to orange and yellow napery) and owner/chef Cécile Briaud's cuisine are sun-drenched. She brilliantly fuses the warm flavors of Provence with those of the Caribbean and Asia. I can't resist the foie gras sampler: of the four variations, you might luck into sautéed foie gras with roasted mango and curried shallots or duck foie ravioli in chanterelle broth. But I won't quibble if you start with the lobster medallions "stuck in a sandwich" of sweet potatoes and cooked in a tempura, tomato, and ginger, or white and green asparagus in puff pastry. Exceptional main courses include seared yellowtail hamachi tuna marinated with five peppers and quail fillets and duck liver ravioli braised with wild mushrooms. Among the many desserts, the Innommable ("No Name") stands out—pastry bursting with semi-sweet chocolate paired with vanilla ice cream in its own pastry shell swimming in vanilla sauce. The "Chef's Discovery" and "Gastronomic Lobster" menus at 55€ ($83) are comparative bargains with aperitif and four courses.

Marina Port la Royale, Marigot. ✆ **590/87-94-60.** www.lechanteclair.com. Reservations recommended. Main courses 25€–28€ ($38–$42); lobster 46€ ($69). MC, V. Daily 6–10:30pm.

Mario's Bistro ✿✿ FRENCH   The setting defines romantic, with tables staggered along a balcony overlooking Sandy Ground Bridge. The greeting from Martyne Tardif couldn't be warmer. And her husband, Mario, inspires passion with his lovely if now old-fashioned architectural presentations. His inventive cooking is spiced with Asian, Moroccan, and Southwestern accents. Start with tuna tempura with asparagus with a sweet corn and wasabi crème brûlée; roasted quail breast with foie gras, asparagus and shiitake risotto; or gazpacho with artichoke guacamole. For mains, try baked mahimahi with a macadamia-nut crust; grilled jumbo shrimp with Moroccan spiced ratatouille; or sautéed sea scallops with crab mashed potatoes. *Note:* Mario's does not have high chairs or booster seats for kids, although you're welcome to bring your own.

Sandy Ground Bridge, Marigot. ✆ **590/87-06-36.** www.mariosbistro.com. Reservations recommended. Main courses 21€–27€ ($32–$41). DISC, MC, V. Mon–Sat 6:30–10:30pm.

MODERATE
Claude Mini-Club ✿ CREOLE/FRENCH   For more than 3 decades, this has been a long-enduring favorite with in-the-know locals and discerning visitors. The building was constructed to

resemble a tree house around the trunks of old coconut palms and the Haitian decor—straw and shell handicrafts dangling from the beams and marvelous murals of local scenes (islanders liming [chilling out], Carnival, boats, and the marketplace)—captures much of the vibrancy of that island. A big terrace opens onto the sea. Authentic Creole offerings include *lambi* (conch) in zesty tomato stew and *accras* (cod fritters) in shallot sauce, but you can also find entrecôte in green-peppercorn sauce, veal escalope with fresh morels, and such classic desserts as banana flambé and crème brûlée. This place is busiest on Wednesday and Saturday nights, as the restaurant stages the island's best buffets, featuring such crowd pleasers as roast suckling pig, roast beef, quail, chicken, red snapper, and Caribbean lobster, accompanied by bottomless carafes of wine.

Bd. de la Mer, Marigot. 𝒞 590/87-50-69. Reservations required. Main courses 18€–30€ ($27–$45); buffet 42€ ($63). AE, MC, V. Mon–Sat 11am–3pm and 6–10pm. Closed Sept.

Le Plongeoir 𝒜 FRENCH   This nautically themed diner overlooking Marigot Harbor by the Fort St. Louis trail is often overlooked, yet it's a superb choice for lunch. It appears slightly funky—royal blue with crimson awning, portholes, and fishing nets: I half expect the Marseilles merchant marine to enter at any moment. The ever-changing Asian-tinged menu highlights fresh catch. Take in the salt air and boat traffic while you enjoy such starters as Camembert flambéed with Calvados. Entrees are equally simple yet beautifully prepared and presented, from a barely seared "kamikaze" tuna steak to sea scallops bathed with truffle oil to seafood swimming in coconut curry.

Front de Mer, northeast of Le West Indies Mall, Marigot. 𝒞 590/87-84-71. Main courses 12€–20€ ($18–$30). MC, V. Daily 11:30am–10pm.

L'Oizeau Rare 𝒜 FRENCH   Creative French cuisine is served in this blue-and-ivory-colored antique house on a Marigot hillside with a view of three artfully landscaped waterfalls in the garden. The tables are dressed with snowy cloths and Limoges china. At lunch, served on the covered terrace, you can choose from a number of salads and crispy pizzas, as well as fish and meat courses (specials might include tilapia in puff pastry with tomato marmalade or sweet-and-sour duck breast with ginger-garlic/red fruit sauce). Dinner choices include fresh fish, such as snapper or salmon; roasted rack lamb with Provençal herbs; or tagliatelle with shrimp, tomato, garlic, and fresh herbs. There are numerous daily specials and prix-fixe options, and the wine list features plentiful French options at moderate prices. Many guests come here at sundown to enjoy the harbor view over a kir royale and cigar from the extensive selection.

Bd. de France, Marigot. ℂ **590/87-56-38.** Reservations recommended. Main courses lunch 15€–24€ ($23–$36), dinner 18€–25€ ($27–$38). AE, MC, V. Mon–Sat 11:30am–3pm and 6:30–10:30pm. Closed June.

INEXPENSIVE

La Belle Epoque FRENCH/PIZZA   You won't find a better perch to watch the boats in the Marigot marina than this blue-awning boardwalk cafe. After window-shopping in Marigot, stop by for Belgian beers or a glass of proper rosé, grilled Creole specials, pastas, fish, steak, or utterly scrumptious special mini pizzas, with a multitude of toppings. It's open for breakfast, serving omelettes, pastry, and juices.

Marina Port la Royale, Marigot. ℂ **590/87-87-70.** www.belle-epoque-sxm.com. Salads, sandwiches, and main courses 7.50€–19€ ($11–$29). MC, V. Daily 7:30am–11pm; from 5pm on Sun.

GRAND CASE
EXPENSIVE

Le Cottage 𝕽 FRENCH/CREOLE   This perennial favorite in a town loaded with worthy contenders is set in what looks like a private house on the inland side of the main road running through Grand Case. Its atmosphere is at least partly influenced by Burgundy-born sommelier, Stéphane Emorine, who shows a canny ability to recommend the perfect wine by the glass to complement the French-Caribbean cuisine. Stéphane and owner Bruno Lemoine apprenticed with the great Alain Senderens at Lucas-Carton in Paris: Their attention to detail is unmatched, right down to the gray bud vases with fresh blooms. Meals begin dramatically with such dishes as a casserole of crayfish and avocados with a citrus sauce, lobster ravioli infused with ginger and basil, or sautéed foie gras coated lightly with gingerbread and served with apple-almond marmalade. Mains include both rustic *cuisine du terroir* (such as roasted rack of lamb with either rosemary or cream-based *pistou* sauce) and Creole dishes, including mahimahi filet served with a reduction of crayfish. Desserts similarly range from traditional Grand Marnier soufflé to a crystallized eggplant with anise cream and basil sorbet. The four-course lobster dinner is *magnifique*.

97 bd. de Grand Case, Grand Case. ℂ **590/29-03-30.** www.restaurantlecottage. com. Reservations recommended. Main courses 22€–49€ ($33–$74). AE, DC, MC, V. Daily 6–11pm.

Finds Lolos: Local Barbecue Joints

Every Caribbean island has roadside shacks (and mobile vans) serving savory local specialties. These barbecue stands are a St. Martin institution, dishing out big, delicious helpings of barbecued ribs, lobster, chicken or fish grilled on split metal drums, garlic shrimp, goat stew, rice and peas, cod fritters, and johnnycakes—all for around $10, a real bargain on pricey St. Martin. In Grand Case, the two best, **Talk of the Town** (© 590/29-63-89) and **Sky's The Limit** (© 690/35-67-84) have covered seating, a waitstaff, and sea views. In Marigot, there's Derrick Hodge's **Exclusive Bite** (no phone) by the scenic cemetery and **Enoch's** in the open-air Marigot Market (© 590/29-29-88). The Dutch side counters with its own versions. For lunch try **Mark's Place** (no phone) in Philipsburg's Food Center Plaza parking lot; after 6pm head for **Johnny B's Under the Tree** (no phone) on Cay Hill Road in Cole Bay.

Le Pressoir ⊛ FRENCH   This local favorite occupies a charming, 19th-century Creole house painted yellow and blue. The interior delights the eye with blue and white napery, periwinkle shutters, mango walls hung with homey island paintings (many for sale), carved hardwood chairs, and lace doilies as lampshades. The kitchen presents an artful combination of old and new French cuisine, the ultra-fresh products' natural flavors enhanced by imaginative seasoning. Standout standards include lobster ravioli in a passion fruit cream sauce, seafood tagliatelle, grilled sea scallops with foie gras and truffles, and grilled beef tenderloin in a Camembert sauce.

30 bd. de Grand-Case, Grand-Case. © 590/87-76-62. Reservations recommended. Main courses 18€–35€ ($27–$53). AE, MC, V. Daily 6–10:30pm (closed Sun in low season).

Le Ti' Provençal ⊛ FRENCH   At this small beachfront restaurant, award-winning chef Hervé Sageot cooks fish and seafood with Creole flair. The menu changes regularly, but you might start with his warm trunkfish salad prepared Creole style or creamy scallop soup with a dollop of Noilly Prat and a swirl of truffle oil. As a main course, trunkfish (also known as boxfish) is stuffed with herbs and served in a Creole sauce, or you can go for the filet mignon prepared Niçoise style. Sageot does a nice pasta, such as the simple but good linguine with bell pepper, basil, and shrimp.

48 bd. de Grand-Case, Grand-Case. ℂ **590/87-05-65.** Reservations recommended.
Main courses 18€–35€ ($27–$53). MC, V. Mon–Sat noon–2:30pm and 6–10:30pm;
Sun 11am–3pm and 6–10:30pm.

L'Hibiscus 🅡🅡 *(Finds)* FRENCH/CREOLE   Ask other Grand Case
restaurateurs for recommendations and they'll name this unassuming Antillean *boîte.* You know you're in the Caribbean: The tiny cottage is decorated with green trellises, paintings of hibiscus blossoms,
orange-yellow-and-green floral tablecloths, and earthenware pots
and plants dangling from white rafters. Thierry Delaunay and
Franco Burato's original "island-perfumed" cuisine is served on fancy
Faïence (fine pottery). Sterling appetizers range from escargot-pars-
ley samosas with garlic dressing to a heavenly scented fisherman's
soup. Pastas and rice are equally good: try risotto primavera or tagliatelle with scallops and shrimp. For mains, try the red snapper filet
stuffed with tomatoes and black olives. Finish with the assortment of
crèmes brûlées in five tropical flavors (rose, vanilla, banana, mint,
and coffee). Among several worthwhile tasting menus from 29€ to
60€ ($44–$90), my favorite is the "Lobster" (creamy lobster soup,
lobster ravioli, and lobster tail in Colombo sauce). Prices are typical
of Grand Case, except that L'Hibiscus uses a $1 = 1€ rate, a plus for
those with pockets full of dollars.

15 bd. de Grand Case, Grand Case. ℂ **590/29-17-91.** www.hibiscus-restaurant.
com. Reservations recommended. Main courses 16€–33€ ($24–$50). MC, V. Daily
6–11pm. Closed Sept.

MODERATE

Il Nettuno 🅡 ITALIAN   The island's most elaborate Italian
restaurant gracefully handles a cosmopolitan, international crowd.
It was established by a seasoned Italian restaurateur, Raymon Losito,
whose career included a 25-year stint at a French restaurant in
Washington, D.C., where he befriended the Redskins' ex-owner, the
late Jack Kent Cooke. He exported his fanaticism to St Martin: One
wall is devoted to the "home of a Redskins fan" (caps, pennants,
"bears," reserved parking sign). It's a great watering hole, outfitted in
the colors of the Italian flag, and drawing a fervent crowd of fans
for U.S. football games; Raymon hosts splashy parties during the
playoff season. Meals are served on a large, rambling wooden
veranda that the owners bravely refurbish after hurricanes. Specialties include fresh steamed mussels, a classic minestrone, homemade
veal ravioli, linguine with clams, and shrimp *fra diavolo.* The desserts
are superb.

70 bd. de Grand Case, Grand Case. ✆ **590/87-77-38**. www.ilnettuno.com. Reservations recommended. Main courses 17€–28€ ($25–$42). AE, DISC, MC, V. Daily noon–2:30pm and 6–10:30pm. Closed for lunch Apr–Oct; closed Aug 30–Oct 1.

La California *(Kids* FRENCH/ITALIAN   Everything is colorful at this seaside *boîte,* from the decor to the gauzily flowing drapes and unframed paintings on the walls. Be sure to stop by the gallery/boutique featuring hand-tooled leather photo albums, shell artwork, and sculptures. Of course, the finest canvas is free: the ever-changing Atlantic views. The fare is simple but well-executed, with an extensive menu that incorporates seafood, pasta, pizza, crepes, steaks, chicken, and seafood fish stew in a crustacean sauce, tuna steak in a Cajun-Creole sauce, stewed chicken in coconut milk and curry. Don't miss the mussels if they're fresh (usually Thurs–Sat). Kids love the creative pizzas (the Trois Fromages actually features three cheeses: mozzarella, chèvre, and Roquefort); the Pizza Margherita is one of the choices on the Menu Bambino, which comes with an entree, French fries, ice cream, and a little dollop of sweet grenadine or mint syrup over ice tea. Already fairly reasonable, prices are quoted at a 1-to-1 exchange (but double check). The owners also rent two nice beachfront one- and two-bedroom apartments for $900 to $1,100 a week in high season (www.california-st-martin.com).

134 bd. de Grand Case, Grand Case. ✆ **590/87-55-57**. www.california-restaurant. com. Main courses 16€–26€ ($16–$26 with 1-to-1 exchange). AE, MC, V. Daily 11am–10:30pm.

Spiga *(Finds* ITALIAN   The gracious husband-and-wife team of Ciro Russo (a native of Lecco, Italy) and Lara Bergamasco (second-generation St. Maarten restaurant royalty) have crafted the finest Italian restaurant on the island, if not the entire Caribbean. Simple elegance reigns, starting with the charming 1914 Creole home. You can dine inside, where darkly stained wooden doors and windows frame salmon-pink walls, or on the candlelit patio. Many ingredients (oils, cheeses, cured meats) are flown in direct from Italy to ensure freshness and quality. Lara states they want to escape "traditional" Italian fare, yet Ciro prepares a textbook beef carpaccio with white truffle oil. We loved the deeply flavorful tomato and basil lobster bisque and the handmade pappardelle with braised beef sauce. Shrimp are sautéed in a ginger sauce flavored with saffron and served over a sweet pea risotto. The roast pork tenderloin comes wrapped in smoked pancetta and stuffed with mushrooms. Whatever you have, rest assured that Lara will find an appropriate wine pairing. End your enchanted evening with passion fruit parfait with raspberry sauce or a classic tiramisu, washed down with fiery grappa or homemade *limoncello* (lemon liqueur).

4 rte. de l'Espérance, Grand Case. (C) **590/52-47-83.** www.spiga-sxm.com. Reservations recommended. Main courses $17–$25. DISC, MC, V. Daily 6–10:30pm. Closed Tues May–Nov.

Sunset Café ⟨ FRENCH/INTERNATIONAL   This open-air restaurant dramatically straddles the rocky peninsula dividing Grand Case Beach from Petite Plage. Tables are set along a narrow terrace that affords sweeping views of the setting sun, when the water is spotlit for extra effect. It's a great, breezy spot to dine and watch the night waves. Start with the mussels in white wine sauce, locally smoked fish, snails with Roquefort sauce, or a vol-au-vent of shrimp and salmon; fish entrees include Chilean sea bass with almonds, or a beef filet with shallots in red wine with foie gras. Lunch items are simpler, with emphasis on sandwiches, burgers, pastas, salads—and herons dive bombing for their own meal. The wine list is the most favorably priced on the island, and the restaurant often offers a 1-for-1 euro/dollar exchange; call ahead to check. Gracious hosts Pascal and Karen Narm also own the equally fine L'Auberge Gourmande in "downtown."

Grand Case Beach Club, rue de Petit-Plage, Grand Case. (C) **590/87-51-87.** www.sunset-cafe.com. Reservations recommended for weekend dinners in winter. Main courses lunch 10€–22€ ($15–$33), dinner 18€–30€ ($27–$45). AE, MC, V. Daily 7am–midnight.

MONT VERNON
MODERATE

Sol é Luna ⟨⟨ *Finds* FRENCH   This lovely, family-run Creole *caze* is virtually pillowed in luxuriant greenery, with smashing Anse Marcel views. Set back from the road, it can be tricky to find, but the incomparable ambience, service, and food make "Sun and Moon" the perfect place for a romantic dinner. Asian influences and ingredients combine with classic French preparations to create light yet intensely flavored dishes. You might start your meal with rolls of monkfish with pecans and red curry, or homemade crab cakes. Lamb braised for 7 hours melts off the bone and in your mouth, as do lobster ravioli and duck breast served with mango fruit and a Grand Marnier sauce. Delicious desserts like banana crunchy cake with chocolate mousse are followed by a minitasting of artisan rums (plum–passion fruit, vanilla-ginger). The hideaway also offers quite handsomely appointed **studios and suites** from $726 a week (low season) or from $860 a week (high season).

61 Mont Vernon, Cul de Sac above Anse Marcel. ℭ **590/29-08-56.** www.soleluna restaurant.com. Main courses 14€–28€ ($21–$42). MC, V. Daily 6–10pm. Closed mid-June to mid-July and mid-Sept to Oct.

BAIE NETTLE & SANDY GROUND
VERY EXPENSIVE
Le Santal ℞ FRENCH   The approach to this dazzler is through a ramshackle, working-class Marigot suburb, a sharp contrast to the glam interior filled with mirrors, fresh flowers, ornately carved chairs, crystal, Villeroy & Boch china, and Christofle silver. Try to nab one of the coveted oceanfront tables, often occupied by the likes of Robert de Niro, Brooke Shields, Arab sheiks, or minor royalty. Sadly, you will no longer be greeted by owner, Jean Dupont; he passed away in 2005, but his wife and children continue to run the restaurant. The fare, as you may expect, focuses on the classic. The crepe stuffed with lobster meat, mushrooms, and scallions in a white wine crawfish butter sauce is a formidable starter; the grilled whole red snapper flambéed in Pastis with fennel beurre blanc is deboned at your table. Seafood rules the menu, though you can savor superb chateaubriand au poivre flambéed in aged Armagnac and coated with béarnaise. End your evening with crêpes suzette prepared the old-fashioned (some might say stuck-in-the-Eisenhower-era) way, tableside; to me, it's a charming touch. Good news for Yanks: The restaurant offers a 1€ to $1 rate, but call ahead to verify.

40 rue Lady Fish, Sandy Ground. ℭ **590/87-53-48.** www.restaurantlesantal.com. Reservations recommended. Main courses $29–$49 AE, MC, V. Daily 6–10:30pm (lunch by advance reservation for groups of 6 or more).

EXPENSIVE
La Cigale ℞℞ FRENCH   This family-run establishment provides a winning combination of innovative French fare and tropical flair, beachfront setting, and warmth and intimacy. Tucked away behind the Laguna Beach hotel at the end of an alley, congenial Olivier Genet's bistro is worth a potential wrong turn or three to find. He recruited his parents from the Loire Valley to help him run the tiny operation: Mama is the hostess, papa the pastry chef (bravo to the molten chocolate cake soufflé). The setting and ambience are casual, but Chef Stéphane Istel's subtly seasoned food is anything but. Try the *crottin de Chavignol* (goat cheese) *en nougatine* (in filo pastry)

with nuts and honey; seabass filet Provencal style; or duck breast with a pear. One complaint is the comparatively high price of wines. But at least Olivier will ply you with several home-brewed rum *digestifs* and animated anecdotes of his Sancerre upbringing.

101 Laguna Beach, Baie Nettlé. © **590/87-90-23.** www.restaurant-lacigale.com. Reservations required. Main courses 26€–33€ ($39–$50). MC, V. Mon–Sat 6–10:30pm.

5

What to See & Do on St. Maarten/St. Martin

Though St. Maarten/St. Martin is most celebrated for beaches, shops, restaurants, and nightlife, it also packs a number of natural and man-made attractions into its compact terrain. From zoos to zip lines and working farms to forts, the array of diversions here suits history buffs, eco-geeks, and active types alike—and despite the island's reputation as an adult playground, it's a very family-friendly place.

1 Island Layout

St. Maarten/St. Martin is a hilly island; driving around you'll discover numerous lookouts with splendid panoramas of the coast and offshore islets. One main road essentially circumnavigates the island; a detour from Marigot to Cole Bay on the Dutch side hugs the eastern shore of Simpson Bay lagoon and avoids traffic around the airport and bustling Maho area during rush hours.

The island is shaped—very roughly—like a boot. The toe at the western point encompasses the French **Lowlands (Terres Basses),** a tony residential area with several stunning beaches. Following the main road east takes you through **Sandy Ground,** a strip of land crammed with tour-group-style hotels, restaurants, shops, and beach bars. It's bordered on the north by Baie Nettlé and on the south by **Simpson Bay,** the Caribbean's largest enclosed body of water. **Marigot,** the French side's capital, is just over 2km (1¼ miles) to the northeast. Ferries depart its harbor for **Anguilla.** The main route ambles north, with turnoffs west on rutted roads to fine beaches, as well as east to **Pic du Paradis** (the island's highest peak at 424m/ 1,400 ft.) before reaching **Grand Case,** site of the tiny inter-island L'Espérance Airport, and beloved by foodies for its superlative eateries. The highway runs east, with a fork at Mont Vernon. The north turnoff accesses **French Cul-de-Sac** (embarkation point for ferries to the offshore cays) and a side road to Anse Marcel, home of a marina and the Radisson resort. The other turnoff accesses the beautiful

Orient Bay beach, continuing south through the residential **Orléans** quarter, straddling the Dutch border at **Oyster Pond** and its marina.

Dawn Beach, site of increased development (and the Westin resort) is the first major strand on the Dutch side. The main highway turns slightly inland and passes the Great Salt Pond on its way to the Dutch capital, **Philipsburg,** which unfurls along **Great Bay.** The major cruise ships dock here; there are also several marinas offering boat rentals and excursions. **Pointe Blanche** forms the very flat heel. From Philipsburg, the highway parallels the south coast, rising and dipping over Cay and Cole Bay Hills. Traffic here in both directions is often dreadful, especially on weekends: the "Caribbean's longest parking lot," as locals joke. Party central begins at **Simpson Bay,** where the highway officially becomes Airport Road. Marinas, bars, restaurants, timeshare units, casinos, and strip malls line both sides, continuing almost unabated past Princess Juliana International Airport to **Maho Beach,** another nightlife nirvana. The road passes Mullet Bay and the lively **Cupecoy** area in the Dutch Lowlands before hitting the French border.

2 Recommended Tour Operators

Because most activities are geared toward the water (see "Beaches" and "Sports & Other Activities," later in this chapter, for some suggested excursions), taxi drivers (see "Getting There" in chapter 2) are a good choice for tours around the island.

Rendezvous Tours, Marigot (© **590/87-79-22;** www.rendezvous tour.com), caters mostly to huge cruise ship tours, but can be an excellent option for active travelers, with sightseeing via kayak, mountain bike, and your feet.

3 The Main Sights
DUTCH SIDE
Philipsburg ✮, capital of the Dutch side, is named, perhaps surprisingly, for an 18th-century Scottish governor. The town has always enjoyed an uncommonly lovely setting at the headlands of Great Bay, on a spit of land separating the Caribbean from the Great Salt Pond. Its superb, deep natural harbor can accommodate such enormous cruise ships as the Queen Mary II. They disgorge passengers, who descend eagerly if not rapaciously on the casinos and duty-free stores lining the main drag, **Front Street** (see chapter 6). The

Tips Mapping It

For locations of the sights listed in this chapter, please refer to the St. Maarten/St. Martin, Marigot, or Philipsburg maps on p. 46, p. 57, and p. 49, respectively.

hordes tend to obscure the many handsome colonial buildings, including the ornate white 1792 **Courthouse** (still in use) replete with cupola at Wathey Square, which roughly bisects Front Street. A series of hurricanes left Philipsburg somewhat dilapidated: one part lower-rent New Orleans, one part Reno.

Over the last several years, Philipsburg has undergone a beautification project. The face-lift added a delightful beachfront red brick boardwalk (Great Bay Beach Promenade), with newly planted royal palm trees, clock towers, and old-fashioned cast-iron street lamps and benches. The beach side of Front Street is now a pedestrian-friendly place to stroll, goggle at the cruise ships and mega-yachts, walk in the sand, or enjoy the sunset over an umbrella-shaded concoction in one of the many inviting cafes.

The continuing makeover includes a revamped tourist office, marinas, and expanded ferry and cruise dock, and the rejuvenation of Back Street, which now has improved pavement and sidewalks, the underground placement of electrical cables, newly planted trees and shrubs, and new streetlights. Eventually, the beautification will extend to the Great Salt Pond (where locals still fish for mullet), with paving and planting all the way north to the French border.

Fort Amsterdam Built in 1631 on the peninsula between Great and Little bays as the Caribbean's first Dutch bastion, Fort Amsterdam was promptly captured by the Spaniards, who made it their most important garrison outside El Morro in San Juan before abandoning it in 1648. Only one small intact storage building, a few walls, and rusted cannons remain, but it's most noteworthy for its smashing views of Philipsburg. Easiest access is via the Divi Little Bay Beach Resort (guards will let you pass if you tell them you're hiking to the fort).

On the peninsula between Great and Little bays. No phone.

St. Maarten Heritage Museum Documenting island history and culture, the St. Maarten Heritage Museum starts with an impressive collection of indigenous Arawak tools, pottery shards, and *zemis* (spiritual totems) that date back over 2 millennia. The plantation and piracy era yields its own artifacts (including cargo salvaged from an 1801 wreck), period clothes (contrasted with slave beads), and weapons. The environment is represented by exhibits on typical flora, fauna, geology, and coral reefs. The final multimedia display recounts the catastrophic effects of Hurricane Luis in 1995.

7 Front St. *©* **599/542-4917**. Admission $1, free for students and children. Weekdays 10am–4pm; Sat 10am–2pm.

St. Maarten Zoological Park ⟨∗⟩ *Kids*   Just east of Philipsburg, this is the largest park of its kind in the Caribbean. More than 500 animals comprising 80 different species from the Caribbean basin and Amazon rainforest inhabit this safari reserve. There are no cages or bars of any kind. Rather, cannily erected, environmentally conscious "naturalistic" boundaries carefully protect both animals and visitors while duplicating typical habitats. An example is Squirrel Monkey Island: The capuchins and vervets are separated by a moat (replicating the streams that draw them in the wild) stocked with water lilies, turtles, and freshwater fish. Nicely landscaped botanic gardens (with interpretive signs) alternate with various environments from a caiman marsh to a tropical forest to a boulder-strewn savannah. Walkthrough aviaries hold more than 200 birds: macaws, toucans, and the Caribbean's largest display of exotic parrots. Other residents include capybaras, ocelots, peccaries, coatis, baboons, and such highly endangered species as the golden lion tamarin. Fascinating activities range from regularly scheduled zookeeper talks, feedings, and one-on-one close encounters to face-painting competitions, puppet shows, clown acts, and treasure hunts. The zoo even features the island's largest playground (slides and, of course, jungle gym). Kids of all ages will love the Night Safari, held 1 night a week (usually Sat), 7 to 9:30pm: The Monkey Bar is the zoo's souvenir shop.

Arch Rd., Madame Estate. *©* **599/543-2030**. Admission $10, $5 children 3–11. Daily 9am–5pm (9:30am–6pm in summer).

FRENCH SIDE

Marigot, capital of the French side, is one of the Caribbean's more charming towns: gas lamps, sidewalk cafes, and traditional Creole brightly hued, gingerbread-trimmed wood houses ringing a lovely harbor, as well as a separate marina, **Port la Royale.** Aside from drinking in the marine activity (and kirs or rum punches), there are several boutiques and galleries (see chapter 6) worth exploring. The waterfront **Market** is a hub nearly every day for vendors and farmers.

It's busiest early mornings as islanders converge to buy fresh-caught fish, fruits, vegetables, and herbs. A crafts market is there on Wednesdays and Saturdays, but vendors tend to offer many of the same goods: colorful dolls, spices, drums, trinkets, clothing.

A steep trail runs from the harbor-side Sous-Préfecture (by the splashy West Indies Mall) to **Fort Louis.** Better preserved than its Dutch side counterparts (forts Willem and Amsterdam), the 1767 bastion was erected to repel English incursions. Its hilltop situation rewards hikers with sensational 180-degree vistas of Marigot, Simpson Bay lagoon, and most of the French coast, with Anguilla shimmering in the background.

Butterfly Farm *⊛ (Kids)*   More than 100 species of butterflies from around the world (including such rarities as the Central American postman, Malaysian malachite, and Brazilian blue morpho) flit and flutter through this miniature, hot and humid bamboo rainforest replica. The atmosphere is hypnotically calming, between tinkling waterfalls, ponds stocked with splashing koi, passing chickens, and soft classical music. If you arrive early, you might witness butterflies emerging from their chrysalides; wear bright colors or floral scents and they might light on you. Multilingual docents conduct 25-minute hands-on tours following the typical life cycle from egg to caterpillar and on to adulthood. The ramshackle shop sells butterfly earrings, wind chimes, pewter figurines, fridge magnets, and framed mounted sets.

Rte. Le Galion, Quartier d'Orléans. © **590/87-31-21.** www.thebutterflyfarm.com. Admission $14, $7 children 3–12. Daily 9am–3:30pm (last tour starts at 3pm).

Loterie Farm *⊛⊛ (Finds) (Kids)*   Located along the turnoff to Pic du Paradis halfway between Marigot and Grand Case, this splendid sanctuary—by far the greenest spot on island—merits a stop. It was a famed sugar plantation between 1721 and 1848 (the original slave walls still surround the property). In its modern heyday a half-century ago, the Fleming family hosted Fortune 500 elite and celebrities (Benny Goodman, Jasper Johns, Harry Belafonte). But after Hurricane Luis ravaged the property in 1995, it became derelict. Californian B. J. Welch purchased the land in 2003 with the goal of establishing a nature retreat, preserving the island's last remaining virgin rainforest. Literally thousands of plant species including towering mahogany, corossol (soursop), mango, papaw, and guavaberry trees have reclaimed a hillside of rock formations and running streams. Iguanas, parrots, hummingbirds, monkeys, and mongoose run wild. Well-maintained trails zig and zag from the foothills to the

(*Finds* **Dinner in the Treehouse**

Set on a *carbet* (covered wood patio) at Loterie Farm's entrance, the **Hidden Forest Café** (www.loteriefarm.net) serves delicious lunches and dinners Tuesday through Sunday. It sports a funky-chic treehouse look, with photos of dread-locked musicians, a blue-tile bar, oars dangling from the rafters, and hurricane lamps. There's live music several evenings in season (perfect for an aperitif). But this is the domain of Canadian-born, self-taught chef Julia Purkis, who says her surroundings provide inspiration (and, of course, fresh ingredients from the organic gardens and forest). Her sophisticated culinary techniques and presentation (including often-edible floral garnishes) are all the more impressive given the cramped, basic kitchen and frequent power outages. You might start with cumin chicken rolls, mahimahi fingers with red pepper tartar sauce, shrimp spring roll, or brie in puff pastry with mango chutney. Standout main courses include grilled salmon with apple-ginger compote, rare duck breast with banana-mint-tamarind salsa, pan-seared sea scallops with vanilla rum sauce, and Julia's signature curried spinach-stuffed chicken.

top of Pic Paradis, the island's highest point, where a viewing platform offers sweeping 360-degree panoramas. You can trek on your own or take one of the farm's guided tours, from a mild sunset walk to a wild, strenuous eco-challenge. Along the way, enthusiastic guides discourse on local history, geology, wildlife, and bush medicine. The **Fly Zone** (35€/$53) lets you fly over the forest canopy on ropes and cables suspended high in the air. The newest attraction, **Extreme Fly Zone** (55€/$83), gives you even more adrenalin chills with a challenging hike uphill and a thrilling ride on a high-tech zipline down. Kids can fly on slightly lower suspended bridges and swinging rope on the park's the **Ti' Tarzan** (20€/$30) attraction. The **Hidden Forest Café** (see below) is a delightful place to dine; it's open for lunch (noon–3pm) and dinner (6:30–9:30pm) Tuesday through Saturday (open noon–6pm Sun).

Rte. Pic Paradis, Colombier. © **590/87-86-16.** www.loteriefarm.net. Admission 5€ ($6.25). Tues–Sun 9am–6pm.

Musée de Saint-Martin   Subtitled "On the Trail of the Arawaks," this museum details island history and culture going back 2,500 years through the colonial era. The ground floor features rotating arts and crafts exhibits. The second floor is a treasure trove of maps, prints, daguerreotypes, and newspapers spanning the 18th to early 20th centuries. Ask the clerks about guided tours of the island focusing on its cultural heritage, including visiting archaeological digs (some closed to the general public), as well as discussing natural phenomena, such as the island's volcanic origins.

Terres-Basses Rd. ℃ **590/29-48-36.** Admission $5. Weekdays 9am–4pm; Sat 9am–1pm.

The Old House (aka Musée du Rhum)   A restored 18th-century green-and-black sugar plantation greathouse, the Old House has an interior that carefully replicates the life of a typical planter: with period furniture and original family portraits and personal objects preserved for six generations. The museum's complementary second half retraces the history of rum, from the first voyages of Columbus, through the buccaneer days and the rise of the sugar plantocracy, up to the effects of Prohibition. The old posters and print ads are especially delightful; more sobering exhibits cover French West Indies calamities, including the eruption of Martinique's Mont Pelée.

Main Rd. (across the main highway from Mont Vernon Plantation), Cul de Sac. No phone. Admission 5€ ($6.25). Daily 9am–4pm.

Plantation Mont Vernon *(Kids*   Not far from Orient Beach, this restored .8-hectare (2-acre) 1786 plantation provides valuable historic perspective while maintaining the island's agricultural and craft traditions. New buildings in vernacular style cleverly blend with 18th-century structures, including an animal-powered mill and the classic stone-and-exotic-wood manor house with corrugated red tin roof. It's stuffed with antique furnishings, ornaments, and objects. But the highlight is the 1-hour walk-through, self-guided tour (with trilingual audio sets, bilingual interpretive signs, and several interactive elements). The botanical and herb gardens are dotted with displays on such traditional plantings as manioc, corn, tobacco, and spices that perfume the air. Along the route, several buildings act as mini museums on different cash crops. You can visit decantation pools used to process indigo into dye. The coffee museum re-creates the gathering, drying, roasting, and grinding processes. The excellent rum museum not only features old equipment from sugar press to still but bottles and labels from the last 3 centuries. Admission includes audio sets and rum and coffee tastings. The site also contains a kids' playground, a pleasant restaurant (recommended for its Antillean brunch), and a fine gift shop stocking not only jams, rums, and coffee, but local crafts fashioned from mango wood, bamboo, and banana leaves.

2 Main Rd., Cul de Sac. ✆ **590/29-50-62.** www.plantationmontvernon.com. Admission $12 adult, $7 children 3–12. Daily 9am–5pm.

4 Beaches

Coves scissor the island's rugged littoral like a child's whimsical paper cutouts; with 39 beautiful beaches of varying length and hue, it's fairly easy to find a place to park your towel. All are public though access is often via a rutted dirt road and/or through a fancy resort. Beaches on the western leeward half are generally hotter and calmer; those on the eastern windward side are, predictably, breezier with rougher swells (when not reef-protected). *Warning:* If it's too secluded, be careful. It's unwise to carry valuables; robberies have been reported on some remote strips. And never leave valuables in the car.

Wherever you stay, you're never far from the water. Beach samplers can sometimes use the changing facilities at bigger resorts for a small fee. Beach bars often rent chairs and umbrellas for roughly $6 and $3, respectively, but may waive the charge if you order lunch or drinks. Those who prefer topless sunbathing should head for the French side of the island, although the Dutch side is getting more liberal.

DUTCH SIDE

Popular **Cupecoy Beach** ✿ is very close to the Dutch-French border at the island's southwest tip. It's a string of three sand beaches set against a backdrop of caves, rock formations resembling abstract sculpture, and dramatically eroded limestone cliffs that provide morning shade. Locals come around with coolers of cold beer and soda for sale, though you can also pop into two bars with absolutely stunning sunset views. The beach has two parking lots, one near Cupecoy and Sapphire beach clubs, the other a short distance to the west. Parking costs $2. You must descend stone-carved steps to reach the sands. Cupecoy is also the island's major gay beach. Clothing is optional toward the northwest side of the beach. *Warning:* The steep drop-off and high swells make the beach hazardous for young children and weak swimmers; prevailing weather affects not only the surf but also the sands' width.

The next strand down, west of the airport, palm-shaded white-sand **Mullet Bay Beach** beckons. Once it was the most crowded beach on the island, but St. Maarten's largest resort, Mullet Bay, has been shuttered (save for a timeshare section) since Hurricane Luis in

1995, so it's relatively deserted, though locals flock here on weekends. Watersports equipment can be rented at a local kiosk, while a few stands dish out local fare. Local surfers enjoy the wave action and rip currents (never swim alone here!); snorkelers will find several miniature bejeweled reefs around the offshore rocks. Any beachcomber will savor the views of Saba and Statia, as well as the lovely sunsets.

Another lovely spot near the airport, **Maho Beach,** at the Sonesta Maho Beach Hotel and Casino is a classic Caribbean crescent that dances to a reggae beat, with vendors hawking colorful wares and locals inviting you to impromptu beach barbecues. This is one of the island's busiest beaches, buzzing with windsurfers—and buzzed by jumbo jets that nearly decapitate the palm trees. The blasts from 747s and 757s are so powerful they've been known to topple cars: Shield your eyes from the sand storm and hang onto your hats, towels, and partner. Food and drink can be purchased at the hotel, as well as such legendary watering holes as Sunset Beach Bar and Bamboo Bernie's (see chapter 7), where the takeoffs and landings are augmented by other entertainment.

West of Philipsburg before you reach the airport, the 2km-long (1¼-mile) white sands of crescent-shaped **Simpson Bay Beach** ring the lagoon and are set against a backdrop of brightly hued fishing boats, yachts, and town homes that resembles an Impressionist canvas. This beach is ideal for a stroll or a swim (beware the steep dropoff), with calm waters and surprisingly few crowds. Watersports equipment rentals are available, but there are no changing rooms or other facilities, and only a couple of bars. Adjacent **Kim Sha Beach** is often mistakenly considered part of Simpson Bay, though it lies outside the lagoon. It's generally livelier, with local outings, frequent promotions, sand castle competitions, watersports operators, and several eateries within walking distance.

Great Bay Beach ⚓ is best if you're staying along Front Street in Philipsburg. This 2km-long (1¼-mile) beach is sandy and calm; despite bordering the busy capital, it's surprisingly clean: Think of it as St. Maarten's less trendy answer to South Beach in Miami. It's a splendid place to kick back after shopping, admiring the cruise ships from one of many strategic bars along the new boardwalk. On a clear day, you'll have a view of Saba. Immediately to the west, at the foot of Fort Amsterdam, is picturesque **Little Bay Beach,** but it, too, can be overrun with tourists disgorged by the cruise ships. When you tire of the sands here, you can climb up to the site of Fort Amsterdam itself. Built in 1631, it was the first Dutch military outpost in the

Caribbean. The Spanish captured it 2 years later, making it their most important bastion east of Puerto Rico. Only a few of the fort's walls remain, but the view is panoramic. Snorkeling is excellent, and several resorts offer plentiful refreshment and recreation options.

Guana Bay ✯, just north of Philipsburg up Pondfill and Guana Bay roads, is long, wide, windswept, and usually deserted (aside from a few surfer dudes and boogie boardistas hanging ten and hanging out). It's topless; the southern section is often clothing-optional. Baying guard dogs occasionally interrupt the solitude (it's a mini–celebrity enclave), the Atlantic swells can be fierce, and it lacks shade and facilities. But the rugged beauty, seclusion, and smashing St. Barts views compensate.

On the east side of the island, **Dawn Beach** ✯ is noted for its underwater life, with some of the island's most beautiful reefs immediately offshore. Visitors talk ecstatically of its incredible sunrises. Dawn is suitable for swimming and offers year-round activities such as sand-castle-building contests and crab races. There's plenty of wave action for both surfers and windsurfers. Fairly undeveloped until recently, Dawn Beach is now the site of the **Westin Resort.** This, in addition to the expansion of **Oyster Bay Resort,** has diminished its peaceful allure, but the views of St. Barts, remarkable reef, and soft pearly sand remain unchanged. Food and drink come courtesy of **Busby's Beach Bar** (✆ **599/543-6828**), reincarnated come evening as a scintillating Italian restaurant, Daniel's by the Sea; **Ms. B's** (✆ **599/557-7370**); and the Oyster Bay Resort's worthy beachfront bar on the section also called **Oyster Pond Beach,** where bodysurfers take advantage of the rolling waves.

FRENCH SIDE

Baie Longue (Long Bay) ✯✯ on the west coast is one of those beaches that exudes a pull as potent as pheromones: pristine water, sand the hue of antique lace, dunes as curvaceous as Goya's *Naked Maja*. Chic, expensive La Samanna hotel opens onto this beachfront, but it's otherwise blissfully undeveloped and uncrowded, conducive to R&R. Its reef-protected waters are ideal for snorkeling, but beware of the strong undertow and steep drop-off; there was also a little erosion when I visited last, and ongoing construction of exclusive private villas on the resort's southern ledge was something of an eyesore. Baie Longue is to the north of Cupecoy Bay Beach, reached via the Lowlands Road. Don't leave valuables in your car, as break-ins have been reported along this stretch of highway.

Baie aux Prunes (Plum Bay) is a Cheshire grin of ivory sand, stretching luxuriantly around St. Martin's northwest point. This is a sublimely romantic sunset perch (bring your own champagne, as there are no facilities) that also offers good surfing and snorkeling near the rocks. Access it via the Lowlands Road past Baie Longue.

Baie Rouge (Red Beach) 🏖, is caught between two craggy headlands where flocks of gulls and terns descend like clouds upon the cliffs at dusk—hence its western end is dubbed Falaise des Oiseaux (Birds' Bluff). The other side is marked by the Trou du Diable (Devil's Hole), a collapsed cave with two natural arches where the sea churns like a washing machine. You'll find superlative snorkeling here, but beware the powerful undertow. Beachwear becomes increasingly optional as you stroll west, though the modest will find several stands hawking sarongs, shorts, and sunbonnets. Baie Rouge is a charmer, from the serene waters to the views of Anguilla to the *accueil sympa* (cordial welcome) at the two beach bars, **Gus'** (no phone) and **Chez Raymond** (📞 690/30-70-49). The latter cooks up blistering barbecue and delivers a knockout punch with Raymond's Special, a blend of six rums, and rocks with reggae on weekends.

Baie Nettlé (Nettle Bay) unfurls like a plush beige carpet between the Caribbean and Simpson Bay, just west of Marigot. Access is right off the main highway running through Sandy Ground. The area has become increasingly developed in the past decade, with several hotels, apartment complexes, watersports franchises (waterskiing and kiteboarding are quite popular), and tiny beach bars alternating with fancier restaurants. The view on the Caribbean side frames Anguilla, Marigot's harbor to the north, and the ruins of La Belle Creole along the Pointe du Bluff to the south. Among the numerous *pieds dans l'eau* (literally, feet in water) bistros, I love Laurent Maudert's **Ma Ti Beach Bar** (📞 590/87-01-30), where specialties include homemade duck foie gras and calamari "steak" flambéed with Pastis.

Isolated **Anse des Pères (Friar's Bay Beach)** lies at the end of a winding bumpy country road that always has me begging for a chiropractor; its clearly signposted entrance intersects with the main highway between Grand Case and Marigot. Although you certainly won't be alone here, this is a less-visited beach with ample parking. Shelling, snorkeling, and sunset watching are all favored. Two beloved beach bars organize raucous themed bashes. At **Friar's Bay Beach Café** (no phone) you can purchase a provocative, often politically charged painting on display or order Laurent's sublime stuffed mussels. The competitor is **Kali's Beach Bar** (📞 590/49-06-81), a

Moments A Grand Day on the Isle of Pinel 😿😿

Imagine a tropical island movie set. Bathers swim in a gin-clear lagoon fringed by palm trees and St. Martin's curtain of jade mountains. Gentle surf laps a beach dotted with *palapas* and parasols. Tiny fishing boats trawl vividly hued nets in the distance. The scent of barbecued meat and coconut oil commingle with the salt air. Welcome to Îlet Pinel, a tiny islet a few hundred meters—and worlds away—from Orient Beach.

The island has no residents (except wild goats) or electricity—just fine white-sand beaches, idyllic reefs with great snorkeling (especially over the hill on the even more secluded, wind-lashed northeast coast), and waters ideal for bodysurfing. You'll find three delightful beach bistros, each with its own section of beach chairs and umbrellas (20€/$30 for the day) and separated by **Paradise Boutique** (aka Tom's Place), which sells hand-painted pareos, tie-dyed shirts, shell jewelry, and whimsical wind chimes. Right at the dock, **Yellow Beach** (© 690/33-88-33) is a series of thatched wood huts; sample the planters punch with litchi and the Creole specialties (the Salade Royale—crab, lobster, large prawns, corn, peppers, and endive—could serve a whole family). **Karibuni** 😿 (© 690/39-67-00), the country's longest running beach bar, enjoys a lovely setting, its decks looking out over the lagoon. Savor fresh lobster from traps bobbing just offshore, oysters (fresh from Normandy on Wed and Sat), and house-smoked fish or ceviches (the owner catches the wahoo, tuna, and mahimahi himself). The newest restaurant, **Up on the Key** (© 690/77-35-47; www.uponthekey.com), has grilled chicken and ribs, fish, and a warm shrimp salad. At a hut on the beach, you can rent pedal boats, kayaks, and snorkeling gear. Oh, and this is a French beach, after all (owned by the French government), so be prepared to encounter topless bathers of both sexes.

Ferries, costing 5€ ($7.50) per passenger, run from Cul de Sac on St. Martin's northeast coast to Pinel daily on the hour from 9am to 4pm (to 5pm on Sun). Watch for the last return trip at 4:30pm. You can also hop aboard a **Wind Adventures** (formerly CNS Watersports) catamaran from Orient Beach for a "One Day in Pinel" snorkeling safari (© 590/29-41-57; www.wind-adventures.com; 50€/$75 per person for the day for 1, 2, or 3 people).

thatched bamboo hut splashed in Rasta colors, where Kali himself serves some of the island's best barbecue. Kali hosts "full moon parties," featuring reggae bands on the beach along with a bonfire and plenty of drink. *Tip:* Have one of the staff here point you in the direction of relatively undiscovered **Anse Heureuse (Happy Bay)** ✸, a 10-minute walk north through underbrush over a hill from Friar's (pause to drink in the views of Anguilla). It richly deserves the name, thanks to the tranquillity, fine snorkeling, and blinding white sand fringed by swaying palms.

White-sand **Grand Case Beach,** a long narrow ribbon right in the middle of Grand Case, is often crowded, especially on weekends. The waters are very calm, so swimming is excellent and it's a good choice for kids. A small beach, it has its own charm, with none of the carnival-like atmosphere found elsewhere. Unparalleled dining choices along the Caribbean's "Restaurant Row" run from *lolos* (essentially barbecue shacks) to gourmet bistros. For something in between, try the fun and funky **Calmos Café** (see chapter 7).

To the east of Grand Case, follow the winding road up and over Pigeon Pea Hill. The spectacular setting of **Anse Marcel** comes into view. The adjacent **Marina Port de Lonvilliers** offers several restaurants and shops, and the former le Méridien is now a Radisson, with additional recreational and gustatory opportunities. The beach itself is protected, with shallow waters ideal for families. You can swim here or else take a hike for 1½ hours north over a hill and down to one of the island's most pristine beaches, **Baie de Petites Cayes.** This is also the most idyllic spot on St. Martin for a picnic. A ribbon of brilliant white sand beckons, and the waters ripple from sapphire to turquoise. Part of the fun is the hike itself, with panoramic views stretching all the way to Anguilla.

On the east coast, clothing optional **Baie Orientale (Orient Beach)** ✸✸ is a beauty. Its southern end contains the naturist resort, Club Orient: Passing cruise ships actually snap the sexy Gallic 20-somethings molting thong bikinis and *grand-mères* letting it all hang out. But you needn't shed your bathing suit or inhibitions. This buoyant beach jumps with bands and bistros, vendors and swimwear models, and watersports from windsurfing to waterskiing to snorkeling around the pyrotechnically colored offshore reef. Eating, drinking, and people-watching qualify as sports, and many beach bistro/bars offer not only grilled crayfish Creole to Cristal, but also live music, boutiques (with fashion shows), massages, parasailing, jet ski rentals, kiteboard instruction, and more. Of those marketing

---

Fun Fact **A Trip to Tintamarre**

Pinel is just one of several Robinson Crusoe cays cast like dice from a gambler's hot hand off the east coast. You can haggle with fishermen at Cul de Sac, Anse Marcel, and Orient (or take an excursion, usually $55 with drinks and lunch) to go even further afield to wild, 10-sq.-km (4-sq.-mile) **Tintamarre,** patois for "noisy sea" after the nesting birds (and bleating goats). The island features pristine snow-white beaches (including the aptly named Baie Blanche), striking ocher cliffs, and wrecks such as an upright tugboat encrusted with jewel-like coral reefs. You can clamber through the scrub and woodlands, discovering the ruins of a 19th-century stone farmhouse and an airport for regional carriers abandoned half a century ago. But nothing matches slathering yourself with mineral-rich mud from the flats, adding sea water, and baking avocado-colored in the sun: nature's exfoliant. **Wind Adventures** has several different trips to Tintamarre from Orient Bay, including a private snorkeling and eco-tour for two (© 590/29-41-57; www.wind-adventures.com).

---

themselves as "the Five Stars of Orient Bay," **Waïkiki Beach** (© 590/87-43-19) is a favorite of the well-heeled barefoot St. Barts set, who down beluga caviar with Belvedere shots. **Kontiki** (© 590/87-43-27) has two sections: the main eatery and the Tiki Hut, serving a mix of dishes from jerk chicken to paninis to quesadillas to sushi. **Bikini Beach** (© 590/87-43-25), which also stays open for dinner, runs from American-styled hamburgers to Spanish-influenced paella studded with lobster; its Manokini snack bar is cheaper (it stocks fine wraps). Like Kontiki, the live music and DJs (best Tues–Wed and Fri) rock. Don't miss the non-star weekend hot spot, **Boo-Boo-Jam** (© 590/87-03-13), with wild Caribbean music mixes, various sponsored parties; and a Sunday afternoon bash that attracts locals in droves. Remarkably for this adult sandbox, it offers a playground and kid-friendly activities. Another must is **Baywatch** (© 690/66-22-27), Andy and Cheryl Susko's little piece of the Jersey shore (can't beat those hot wings, meatballs, or sausage-and-pepper sandwiches).

Baie de l'Embouchure ⟨⟩, embracing **Le Galion** and **Coconut Grove beaches,** just south of Orient, is part of the St. Martin Réserve Sous-Marine Régionale, established to protect migrant waterfowl habitats and rebuild mangrove swamps. A coral reef encloses the bay: The calm shallow water (you can wade up to 100m/330ft. out) makes it ideal for kids—it's the only beach on the French side where topless sunbathing is discouraged. Yet the steady gusts also make it a windsurfing mecca; **Tropical Wave** (see "Sports & Other Activities," below) is one of the best places to learn. Tiki carvings and blue umbrellas mark the appealing **Le Galion Restaurant** (aka Chez Pat after owner Pat Turner; *©* **590/87-37-25**). Locals love this laid-back spot; many families make charcoal pits in the sand for impromptu barbecues.

5 Sports & Other Activities

If it's aquatic, St. Maarten/St. Martin offers it: from sailing to scuba diving, big game fishing to boogie boarding. It almost seems the island has more marinas per square mile than anywhere else on earth (one even changed its name to Dock Maarten, neatly combining two local economic mainstays—boating and shopping). Land-based excursions are less popular, though hiking and mountain biking can be rewarding.

ORGANIZED TOURS

Every seasoned sea salt worth his or her salt seemingly ends up on St. Maarten at some point, if only to compete in the many renowned regattas. To keep themselves two sheets (or more) to the wind, they charter their boats. Needless to say, the island offers everything from booze cruises to eco-kayaking on all manner of pleasure craft from banana boats to catamarans to dinghies.

   Aqua Mania Adventures offers a plethora of pleasures out of Pelican Marina, Simpson Bay (*©* **599/544-2640;** www.stmaarten-activities.com). In addition to a parasail outfit, a PADI dive shop, ferry service to Saba and St. Barts, and a boutique abounding in beach toys and resort wear its three party-hearty boats patrol the waters several times daily. Two catamarans, *Lambada* and *Tango,* cruise to Anguilla and Prickly Pear for snorkeling and beach barbecues ($85 adults, $40 children 4–12). Or simply opt for sunset sails ($25 including open bar). *Sand Dollar* clings closer to St. Martin with a 3-hour snorkeling excursion to Creole Rock ($45 adults, $25 children 4–12). Kids can take turns piloting the *Calypso* in Simpson's Bay's serene waters ($20), then bombard a small wreck with water balloons. Prizes and bobbing blow-up animals keep things happy. Or the family can frolic just offshore on *Playstation* ($15 for a half-day;

9:30am–4:30pm), a converted colorful "swing, slide, and splash" catamaran that resembles an avant-garde art installation. The platform includes Tarzan swings, several slides, and plenty of room to clamber. Dinner cruises (some aboard, others stopping at restaurants in Marigot's Marina Royale) are generally genial affairs; the return voyage toward St. Maarten's blazing neon skyline is memorable indeed.

The sleek 23m (75-ft.) catamaran **ScoobiTOO** (© **590/52-02-53;** www.scoobidoo.com) departs from Anse Marcel and Grand Case, sailing to Tintamarre, Anguilla, Prickly Pear, St. Barts, sunset cruises, or some combination of the above. The operator's newest boat, **Scoobifree,** is a 60-foot catamaran that specializes in luxury charters and mini cruises. Most outings ($55–$145) include snorkeling equipment, lunch, and open bar. The crew spins arguably the best mix of the charter boats. Two new cruises are "A Taste of Tuesday," a culinary cruise complete with an onboard chef; and "Salsa and Tapas Too," where you can learn a few salsa steps from an onboard dance instructor.

Eagle Tours at Bobby's Marina in Philipsburg (© **599/543-0068** or 599/542-3323; www.sailingsxm.com) offers lagoon sightseeing tours aboard the flatboat *Explorer,* stopping in Marigot for shopping before heading home; mimosas and rum punches flow copiously. But their pride and joy is the 23m (76-ft.), custom-designed *Golden Eagle* catamaran. Originally built for the prestigious Whitbread Around the World Race, it features a 24m-tall (80-ft.) main mast and a 7.2m (24-ft.) sail that took two men 3 weeks to paint by hand. It cruises to various deserted strands and cays for snorkeling and soaking up both tropical ambience and drinks (the pampering service includes a floating bar). The Friday jaunt ($99 per person) sails to Tintamarre and Creole Rock, puts in at Grand Case for lunch, then stops by Baie Longue for a final cooling dip. Transportation to and from your hotel is included.

The 12m (40-ft.) catamaran *Celine* departs Skipjack's dock at Simpson Bay (© **599/545-3961;** www.sailstmaarten.com) for a mellow sunset cruise ($25; with dinner $65). But South African skipper Neil Roebert, who built *Celine* by hand, is most (in)famous for leading a Lagoon Pub Crawl around Simpson Bay, with sons Graham and Johann as occasional accomplices. Neil calls himself the "ultimate designated driver," steering guests toward some of the better local bars. In addition to an open bar aboard, the first drink is free at each stop, along with a signature bite (from filet mignon

---

(Moments) **Come Sail Away**

Ever wonder what racing a swift state-of-the-art yacht is like? The **St. Maarten 12-Metre Challenge** ⋆ in Philipsburg at Bobby's Marina (© **599/542-0045**; www.12metrechallenge. com) gives nautical nuts a chance to crew on one of five famed America's Cup yachts specially designed for the 1987 competition off Fremantle, Australia. The marquee boats include Dennis Conner's champion *Stars & Stripes, True North,* and *Canada II.* Each boat takes nine to 18 competitors (12 and up) for a thrilling 3-hour race ($80–$100 per person). Previous sailing experience isn't required: The captains and mates brief their swabs-for-a-day on the basics, from grinding a winch to tacking. Or you can just drink in the experience along with rum punches, letting everyone else worry about even keels.

---

cubes to mahimahi kabobs). Departures are at 7pm Wednesdays and Thursdays, with Mondays added in high season. The 3-hour bender costs a mere $75. Neil also charters *Celine* for full-day trips to Pinel, Tintamarre, Baie Longue, Friar's Bay, and more; the cost is $1,150 (up to 10 people; $115 each additional person).

STAYING ACTIVE

BOATING   Sea dogs will happily bark (or bite) at **Lagoon Sailboat Rental** in Simpson Bay Lagoon (© **599/557-0714;** www. lagoonsailboatrental.com). You can explore the lagoon and surrounding waters in state-of-the-art 6m (20-ft.) Sunfasts for $150 for a full day ($110 for a half-day). The congenial Cary and company also give a thorough 10-hour course for $200 (minimum two people, maximum three) that can be broken up however you like.

DEEP-SEA FISHING   The island hosts several highly regarded competitions, including May's Marlin Cup and June's Billfish Tournament, that lure an impressive international roster of entrants. The waters teem with tuna, wahoo, snapper, grouper, jack, pompano, yellowtail, marlin, and other big game fish. The crew from **Lee's Roadside Grill** on Welfare Road 84, Simpson Bay (© **599/544-4233;** www.leesfish.com), knows where to catch the big boys, since they supply their own wildly popular seafood haunt. Its 9.3m (31-ft.) Bertram, *Baby Blues,* is available for a minimum of four people (maximum six). Drinks are included in the half-day trip ($200) and lunch and drinks are included in the ¾- and full-day excursions

($250 and $300, respectively). And yes, they'll cook your trophy up at the restaurant.

On the French side, **Big Sailfish Too** (© 690/27-40-90) at Anse Marcel will take four to eight anglers aboard a 32-ft. Hatteras. The crew is knowledgeable, the tackle high quality, and the rum punches strong. Drinks are included for half-day charters ($600; maximum 5 people); add lunch to the full-day trip ($1,100; maximum 5 people).

GOLF   The **Towers at Mullet Bay** (© 599/545-3069; www. towersatmulletbay.com), a timeshare condominium complex on the Dutch side, is where you'll find the island's only golf course. It's a slightly battered, slightly dusty 18-hole Joseph Lee–designed course, whose fate has hung in the balance, based on some ongoing court battles, for years. Mullet Pond and Simpson Bay Lagoon provide both beauty and hazards. Greens fees are $60 for 9 holes or $88 for 18 holes, for players who opt to walk instead of ride. Renting a two-person electric cart will cost an additional $8 to $18 depending on how many holes you play. Club rentals cost $21 for 9 holes or $26 for 18 holes.

HIKING & MOUNTAIN BIKING   Despite its small size, the island offers terrain ranging from limestone plateaus to a central volcanic ridge topped by 445m (1,482-ft.) Pic du Paradis, and ecosystems from semi-desert to tropical rainforest. Birders will sight coots, black-necked stilts, and ospreys nesting amid the swamps and cliffs.

Adrenaline junkies and eco-buffs will feel at home at **TriSport** headquarters on 14B Airport Rd. in Simpson Bay (© 599/545-4384; www.trisportsxm.com). Bikers can rent Trek mountain bikes and hybrids ($17 half-day, $24 full day, $110 per week). TriSports also ventures into the open water with snorkeling/kayaking tours around Anse Guichard's hulking Henry Moore–ish boulders and Caye Verte. The 2½-hour Simpson Bay Lagoon tour ($49) includes instruction and a stop at deserted Grand Îlet, whose mangrove system houses unusual critters from sea cucumbers to upside-down jellies. You can rent kayaks for $15 per hour; a double kayak costs $19/hr.

HORSEBACK RIDING   In its new location in Seaside Nature Park, **Lucky Stables** (© 599/544-5255) offers a romantic Moon-light Champagne ride ($70 per person) including a marshmallow roast or a sunset jaunt (from $45). Guides explain local folklore, fauna, and flora along the picturesque route through the closest thing to wilderness on the Dutch side. In its new location, Lucky

Stables will also be offering carriage rides, snorkeling tours, and a bar on the beach. The highlight is a ride into secluded, stony, unspoiled Cay Bay (aka Cape Bay) as Saba, Statia, St. Kitts, and Nevis drift on the horizon. Suddenly the horses wade into the warm water; your saddle feels like a flotation device as they swim with surprising grace. There's time to go shelling and snorkel in the offshore reef (without your ride, of course). It's also an excellent vantage point for whale-watching in spring and waterfowl sightings year-round. Private lessons are $35 for half-hour. Barring heavy traffic, the stables are 10 minutes from the airport and 15 minutes from Philipsburg.

Its eco-sensitive counterpart on the French side is **Bayside Riding Club,** rue de la Galion, Coconut Grove (© **590/87-36-64;** www. baysideridingclub.com). Prices start at $70 per person for 1-hour group beach rides. Group sunset beach rides are $80 per person. Here too, the highlight is swimming astride your mount in the water. Children can take pony rides for $35 per half-hour.

SCUBA DIVING   Scuba diving is excellent around **St. Martin,** with reef, wreck, night, cave, and drift diving; the depth of dives is 6 to 21m (20–69 ft.). Off the northeastern coast, dive sites include Îlet Pinel and Creole Rock, for shallow diving; Green Cay, a barrier reef; and Tintamarre, for sheltered coves and geologic faults. To the north, Anse Marcel and neighboring Anguilla are good choices. **St. Maarten's** crystal-clear bays and countless coves make for good scuba diving as well as snorkeling. Underwater visibility runs from 23 to 38m (75–125 ft.). The biggest attraction for divers is the 1770 British man-of-war, **HMS *Proselyte,*** which came to a watery grave on a reef 2km (1¼ miles) off Philipsburg in 1801. Other excellent sites include Tugboat Annie, Frenchman's Reef, Lucy's Barge, Pelican Rock, the double pinnacles of One Step Beyond, Moonhole (a large crater with caves and walls of sponges), and the intact fishing vessel Fu Cheng 36m (120 ft.) down.

Memorable sightings amid virtual mountain ranges of coral with crevices, ledges, and drops galore include schools of vibrantly colored fish from grunts to queen angels, sea fans beckoning like come-hither courtesans, stingrays, mantas, moray eels, barracuda, tarpon, banded coral shrimp, Caribbean spiny lobsters, endangered turtles (green, leatherback, hawksbill, loggerhead), and reef and nurse sharks. Most of the big resorts have facilities for scuba diving and can provide information about underwater tours, photography, and night diving.

Scuba Fun Dive Center has offices at Marina Port Lonvilliers, Anse Marcel (© **590/87-36-13;** www.scubafun.com), and Dock Maarten Marina, Great Bay, Pointe Blanche (© **599/542-3966**). Morning and afternoon dives in deep and shallow water, wreck dives, and reef dives cost $45 per dive (certified divers only). A resort course for first-time divers with reasonable swimming skills costs $75 and includes 45 minutes of instruction in a swimming pool and a one-tank shallow dive above a coral reef. Full PADI certification costs $350, an experience that requires 5 days and includes classroom training, sessions with a scuba tank within the safety of a swimming pool, and three open-water dives. Snorkeling trips cost $30 for a half-day, plus $10 for equipment rental.

Dive Safaris, at two locations—at Bobby's Marina, Philipsburg (© **599/542-9001**), and Simpson Bay (© **599/545-2401;** www.divestmaarten.com)—offers competitive rates and a full range of PADI certification courses, including specialty instruction in marine habitats, photography, and wreck diving. Those wanting to get up close and personal with sharks can don chain-mail-like armor to feed the sharks in their "Shark Awareness Dives."

The larger-than-life owner of **Ocean Explorers** at Kim Sha Beach (© **599/544-5252;** www.stmaartendiving.com), LeRoy French, is still diving more than a half-century after he caught the bug (using some of Cousteau's first Aqua Lungs). Starry students in his 40-plus-year career have included Jackson Browne, Matthew McConaughey, and Sandra Bullock. He's been profiled by *Sports Illustrated,* and even the Cousteau team might envy his vivid videos. The personalized touch—he takes a maximum of six divers—costs a bit more ($49–$55 single dive, $100 double; $360 full certification) and means reservations are essential.

SNORKELING 𝒦𝒦 Calm waters ringing shallow reefs and tiny coves make the island a snorkeler's heaven. The waters off northeastern French St. Martin have been classified as a regional underwater nature reserve, **Réserve Sous-Marine Régionale,** which protects the area around Flat Island (also known as Tintamarre), Îlet Pinel, Green Key, and Petite Clef. Equipment can be rented at almost any hotel, and most beaches have watersports kiosks. The waters surrounding the entire Dutch side to a depth of 60m (200 ft.; with designated fishing, scuba, and shipping zones) are protected as the **St. Maarten Marine Park,** which also inaugurated an Artificial Reef program, utilizing special balls to imitate the appearance and function of natural coral reefs. The island's top snorkeling beaches are Mullet Bay, Cay Bay, Little Bay, Dawn Beach, Plum Bay, and Baie Rouge.

One of St. Martin's best sources for snorkeling and other beach diversions is **Carib Watersports** (© **590/87-51-87**), a clothing store, art gallery, and watersports kiosk on the beachfront of the Grand Case Beach Club. Its French and U.S. staff provides information on island activities and rents kayaks and paddleboats for $20 an hour and snorkeling equipment for $10 a day. The main allure, however, are the guided snorkeling trips to St. Martin's teeming offshore reefs, including Creole Rock, an offshore clump of reef-ringed boulders rich in underwater fauna. The 2-hour trips depart daily at 10am, noon, and 2pm; cost is $30 including equipment. Reservations are recommended.

TENNIS   You can try the courts at most of the large resorts, but you must call first for a reservation. Preference, of course, is given to hotel guests.

On the Dutch side, there are four courts at the **Maho Beach Hotel,** Maho Bay (© **599/545-2115**). **Port de Plaisance,** Cole Bay (© **599/544-5222**) has seven courts. **The Pelican,** Simpson Bay (© **599/544-2503**) has four courts, and the **Divi Little Bay Beach Resort,** Little Bay Road (© **599/542-2333**), has one court, but they are for guest play only. On the French side, **Esmeralda Resort,** Orient Bay (© **590/87-36-36**) has two courts.

WATER-SKIING & PARASAILING   Most of French St. Martin's large beachfront hotels maintain facilities for water-skiing and parasailing, often from kiosks that operate on the beach.

Club Caraïbes at the Hôtel Mercure Simson Beach in Nettle Bay (© **690/33-30-01;** www.skicaraibes.net) provides wakeboard and jet ski rentals, as well as water-skiing instruction with Laurent Guy and Brigitte Lethem (the 2004 U.S. Master Champion). You can learn slalom or tricks for 35€ ($53) per set; 5-day intensive water-skiing and wakeboard courses cost 320€ to 660€ ($480–$990).

WINDSURFING & KITEBOARDING   Most windsurfers gravitate to the eastern part of the island, most notably Coconut Grove/Le Galion Beach, Orient Beach, and to a lesser extent, Dawn Beach, all in French St. Martin. The top outfitter here, **Tropical Wave,** Le Galion Beach, Baie de l'Embouchure (© **590/87-37-25;** www.sxm-orientbeach.com/chezpat), capitalizes on the near-ideal combination of wind and calm waters. Pat rents Mistrals for 20€ ($30) an hour, with instruction offered at 30€ ($45) an hour, and 45€ ($68) for a 2-hour beginner course. They also rent snorkeling gear, pedal boats, and kayaks (tours can be arranged).

Wind-Adventures (formerly Club Nathalie Simon) on Orient Beach (© **590/29-41-57;** www.wind-adventures.com) is one of the Caribbean's premier windsurfing schools. Lessons cost 40€ ($60) per hour, 55€ ($83) for 1½ hours. Kite trips for the experienced to Green Cay start at 95€ ($143). CNS also rents windsurfers and Hobie Cats from 35€ ($53) per hour, and offers both safaris and instruction (with excellent multilesson discounts). Equipment is state-of-the-art. Wind Adventures also offers kitesurfing, kayaks, island excursions, eco-tours, and a number of kids' activities.

6

Shopping on
St. Maarten/St. Martin

The island teems with duty-free bargains in just about everything from linen to liquor, china to cameras, with prices as much as 25% to 40% lower than those in the U.S. and Canada (the gains, of course, somewhat offset by the dollar's slide against the euro). There's an energizing hubbub in **Philipsburg** every morning as cruise-ship passengers scatter eagerly in search of latter-day treasure: The goods displayed in the windows along Front Street are a mind-boggling display of conspicuous consumption, with an emphasis on high-end (gold, diamond, and platinum) jewelry and designer watches. Philipsburg's inviting French counterpart **Marigot** boasts smart boutiques with striped awnings and wrought-iron balconies that recall the Riviera, and galleries showcasing local artists' work. Philipsburg encourages you to "shop till you drop." Marigot murmurs seductively, "relax, the shops will still be open in an hour or two": It's the perfect place to savor the salt air, watch the ferries load for Anguilla, and enjoy a steaming cup of café au lait.

1 The Shopping Scene

Not only is Dutch St. Maarten a free port, but it has no local sales taxes. Prices are sometimes lower here than anywhere else in the Caribbean, except possibly St. Thomas. Many well-known shops from Curaçao have branches here.

Except for the boutiques at resort hotels, the main shopping area is in the center of **Philipsburg.** Most of the leading shops—from Tiffany to Tommy Hilfiger—line **Voorstraat (Front Street),** which stretches for about 2km (1¼ miles). The **Sint Rose Shopping Mall,** on the boardwalk on Front Street, has such big names as Cartier, Lalique, and Façonnable.

Just off Front Street, **Old Street** lives up to its name, with adorable 19th-century houses that today contain specialty stores. More shops and souvenir kiosks sit along the little lanes, known as *steegjes,* that connect Front Street with **Achterstraat (Back Street),** another shoppers' haven.

Maho Plaza (surrounding the glitzy Sonesta Maho Beach Resort) is another area for name-brand offerings (and outlets), including branches of Front Street stalwarts.

In general, the prices marked on the merchandise are firm, though at some small, personally run shops, where the owner is on-site, some bargaining might be in order.

Many day-trippers head to Marigot from the Dutch side just to browse the French-inspired boutiques and shopping arcades. Since St. Martin is also a duty-free port, you'll find some good buys here as well, even at the ultraluxe boutiques along **rue de la République, rue du Général de Gaulle,** and **rue de la Liberté** (think New York's Madison Ave. or Paris's av. Montaigne). French luxury items such as Christofle tableware, Vuitton bags, Cartier accessories, and Chanel perfume are understandably emphasized.

The waterfront **Le West Indies Mall** (© **590/51-04-19**) is an ornate stone-wood-and-concrete structure with arches, skylights, curved staircases, and gazebos galore. But it does concentrate 22 big-name boutiques, from Escada to Lacoste, their wares brightly lit and displayed. You'll also find a branch of the venerable gourmet shop Hédiard (established in Paris in 1854), where you can purchase champagne, caviar, and foie gras; its aromatic tea room is a delightful stop for fresh pastries. Smaller but equally prestigious complexes include **Galerie Périgourdine** and **Plaza Caraïbes** (Cartier and Hermès outposts).

At Marigot's harbor side, there's a lively **morning market** on Wednesday and Saturday with vendors selling spices, fruit, shells, and handicrafts. There's a cookie-cutter quality to the crafts, with many of the vendors offering the same goods, but it's a good spot to pick up some spices.

At bustling **Marina Port la Royale,** mornings are even more active: Schooners unload produce from the neighboring islands, boats board guests for picnics on deserted beaches, and a dozen different little restaurants ready for the lunch crowd. Marina Royale is peppered with boutiques and galleries selling everything from lingerie to liqueurs.

Several clothing boutiques and galleries fight for scraps of space between the bistros along the main drag of St. Martin's "second" city, Grand Case, nicknamed "Caribbean Restaurant Row." They keep unusual hours: Most are shuttered during the day, but fling their doors open come evening for pre- and post-dinner strollers.

Tips **Mapping It**

For locations of the shopping establishments listed in this chapter, please refer to the St. Maarten/St. Martin, Marigot, or Philipsburg maps on p. 46, p. 57, and p. 49, respectively.

Prices are often quoted in U.S. dollars, and salespeople frequently speak English. Credit cards and traveler's checks are generally accepted. When cruise ships are in port on Sundays and holidays, some of the larger shops stay open.

2 Shopping A to Z

CLOTHING *&*

DUTCH SIDE

Del Sol St-Maarten This shop sells men's and women's sportswear. Embedded in the mostly black-and-white designs are organic crystals that react to ultraviolet light, which transforms the fabric into a rainbow of colors. Step back into the shadows, and your T-shirt will revert to its original black-and-white design. The same technology is applied to yo-yos, which shimmer psychedelically when you rock the baby or walk the dog. 23 Front St., Philipsburg. (C) 599/542-8784.

Rima Beachworld Rima hawks essentially any beach accessory you might need, from peasant skirts to pareos, bonnets to bags, and much, much more, all bedecked in luscious tropical colors. Nisbeth (Pondfill) Rd. just north of Philipsburg. (C) 599/542-1424. www.rimabeachworld.com.

FRENCH SIDE

Act III Act III prides itself on its designer evening gowns and chic cocktail dresses. If you've been invited to a reception aboard a private yacht, this is the place to outfit yourself. Designers include Christian Lacroix, Cavalli, Armani, Lanvin, Versace, and Gaultier. The bilingual staff is accommodating, tactful, and charming. 3 rue du Général de Gaulle, Marigot. (C) 590/29-28-43.

Desmo This Florence-based style guru understands the wisdom of that fabulous *Steel Magnolias* line, "The only thing that separates us from the animals is our ability to accessorize." Whether it be shoes, purses, scarves, or belts, Desmo features Italian designers—Dibrera, Perla-Azzurra, Francesco Biasia—who take that quote as their mantra. 15 Marina Royale, Marigot. (C) 590/87-84-62.

Havane Boutique   This boutique is a hyper-stylish clothing store for men and women, selling designer clothes from Armani to Zegna. 50 Marina Royale, Marigot. (⦿ 590/87-70-39.

Jessy'K   This children's clothing store sells good-quality kids' brands, such as Petit Bateau, Kenzo, and Elle, at reasonable prices. If you live in a cold climate, look for good deals on European-made winter jackets. 46 Marina Royale, Marigot. (⦿ 590/87-58-75.

L'Atelier ✿   L'Atelier showcases clothing and accessories (shoes, belts, and bags) from well-known European designers, with the store stocked with the latest Paris fashions. 28 Marina Royale, Marigot. (⦿ 590/87-13-71.

Longchamp   A branch of the famed family-run, trendsetting Parisian boutique, Longchamp specializes in exquisitely hand-crafted leather goods, as well as nylon totes in edible colors like blueberry, lime, and mango. Plaza Caraïbes, rue Général de Gaulle. (⦿ 590/87-92-76. www.longchamp.com.

Max Mara   This, the first Caribbean franchise for the Italian Maramotti empire, carries every line from the more casual, lower-priced SportMax and Weekend to the dressy Pianoforte. 6 rue du Président Kennedy, Marigot. (⦿ 590/52-99-75.

Serge Blanco "15" Boutique   Although a relatively unknown name in North America, in France Blanco is revered as one of the most successful rugby players of all time. His menswear is sporty, fun, and elegant. Clothes include polo shirts, shorts, shoes, and truly wonderful latex jackets. Marina Royale, Marigot. (⦿ 590/29-65-49.

Vie Privée   Care for a python to curl around your waist? This shop offers belts in leather and various exotic skins from ostrich to crocodile with elaborate buckles. It also sells bags and luggage. Marina Royale, Marigot. (⦿ 590/87-80-69.

CONTEMPORARY ART ✿✿

The island's charming local scenes and resplendent light have inspired such renowned artists as Romare Bearden over the years. I generally find the galleries more sophisticated on the French side; curious shoppers can also visit various ateliers.

DUTCH SIDE

Greenwich Galleries ✿   This is the Dutch side's oldest and most urbane art gallery, with Bajan pottery in sea greens and blues, replicas of Taïno artifacts from the Dominican Republic, and the largest selection of Caribbean art on the island. 35 Front St. (⦿ 599/542-3842.

Planet Paradise   Also known as Island Arts of That Yoda Guy, this is the playpen of the wildly creative Nick Maley, an artist/SFX designer who was instrumental in fashioning *Star Wars*'s resident gnomic gnome and contributed to other blockbusters from *Superman* to *Highlander*. John Williams's iconic theme music wafts through the air as you examine rare Lucasfilm prints, posters signed by the director himself, and Nick's own island-themed artworks. If you're lucky, he'll be around, relating cinematic anecdotes ("I spent my first career making 53 movies, my second making piña coladas," he quips). He's slowly creating a museum in back holding his own considerable collection of film memorabilia, including casts of various stars' faces, set schematics, original drawings, and items such as a *Daily Planet* front page. There's a second location at 106 Old St. 19A Front St. ℂ 599/542-4009. www.yodaguy.com.

FRENCH SIDE

Alexandre Minguet 🐾   Yet another highly regarded French expat, Minguet's fluid canvases are influenced by the rich colors of Matisse with the bold, contrasting lines of Dufy. He also exhibits other Caribbean painters of note. Rambaud Hill between Marigot and Grand Case. ℂ 590/87-76-06. www.minguet.com.

Antoine Chapon   Andrew Wyeth lauds this Bordeaux-born painter's ethereal watercolors of serene marine scenes. His prints are pretty (and quite inexpensive), but the comparatively flat medium lacks the elusive, watery quality of his paintings. Terrasses de Cul de Sac. ℂ 590/87-40-87. www.chaponartgallery.com.

Atelier des Tropismes   With a studio in back, Atelier des Tropismes is run by three artists. Patrick Poivre de la Fréta studied in Paris with Salvador Dalí and creates playful, witty still life paintings, genre scenes in feverish Fauvist hues, and *objets* like screens. Paul Elliott Thuleau faithfully reproduces architectural facades in superrealist fashion with luminous hues. Nathalie Lepine's portraits of women, some sturdy like Léger or de Lempincka, others attenuated like Modigliani or Giacometti, are contemplative. Other local artists are represented here. 107 Boulevard de Grand Case, Grand Case. ℂ 590/29-10-60.

Dona Bryhiel *Finds*   Provence native Dona Bryhiel focuses on the curvaceous, even zaftig feminine form as a visual metaphor for the island and vice versa; she also produces splendid light-suffused paintings of Provence. You'll also find hand-painted T-shirts, beach towels, and textiles; stunning jewelry incorporating local materials from shells to banana wood; and the delicate enameled ceramics of fellow Provençal, Martine Azéma. 9 Residence Lou Castel, Oyster Pond. ℂ 590/87-43-93. www.donabryhiel.com.

Francis Eck An Alsatian expat inspired rather like Rothko and Gottlieb by the purity of Asian art, Francis Eck commands fabulous prices for his intense abstract genre scenes, landscapes, and seascapes. Their jazzy riffs of primary color and bold brush work (combined with knife and trowel) enable him "to explore the intersection of figurative and abstract." The atelier is open by appointment only. 48 rue du Soleil Levant, Concordia outside Marigot. ℂ 590/87-12-32. www.francis-eck.com.

Gingerbread Gallery ✿ Gingerbread Gallery exhibits vivid, powerful Haitian art, including works by such modern masters as Françoise Jean and Profil Jonas. 14 Marina Royale, Marigot. ℂ 590/87-73-21. www.gingerbread-gallery.com.

NOCOart Studio ✿ NOCOart was founded in 2004 by sisters Norma and Corinne Trimborn, whose work couldn't be more different. Norma's paintings are figurative with abstract expressionist elements. Corinne's unsettling neo-surrealist melting and disfigured faces and strong striking color fields suggest the essential duality of the female experience. 39 Falaise des Oiseaux, Terres Basses near Plum Bay. ℂ 590/87-55-29. www.nocoart.com.

Roland Richardson Paintings and Prints ✿ Known for luminous landscapes, portraits, and still lifes, Roland Richardson's clearest influence is the 19th-century Barbizon School of Impressionists. A native of St. Martin and one of the Caribbean's premier artists, he works in numerous media: oil, watercolors, pastels, charcoal, even batik and stained glass. You can often find him working *en plein air* to capture Nature's fleeting colors and forms as rapidly as possible. His work has been exhibited in nearly 100 one-man and group shows in museums and galleries around the world. Celebrity collectors have ranged from Martha Graham to Jackie Kennedy Onassis, Harry Belafonte to Ivan Lendl, the Getty family to Queen Beatrix of the Netherlands. He and wife Laura are gracious hosts in their carefully restored landmark West Indian home with concealed courtyard garden and gallery dating back to the 1700s. Richardson is also the resident artist at **La Samanna resort,** where he has a changing collection of works. 6 rue de la République, Marigot. ℂ 590/87-84-08. www.rolandrichardson.com.

HANDICRAFTS & GIFTS 🎁🎁
DUTCH SIDE
Blooming Baskets by Lisa   Blooming Baskets showcases the talents of two sisters from Harrisburg, Pennsylvania. The baskets are actually straw-and-raffia handbags in various sizes adorned with silk flowers duplicating not just island blossoms but a virtual botanical garden, from irises to sunflowers. Their hand-mixed dyes, inspirations of the moment, ensure no two bags are ever quite alike. 21 Maho Marketplace, Sonesta Maho Resort, Maho Beach. 📞 599/545-2270. www. bloomingbasketsbylisa.com.

Dutch Delft Blue Gallery 🎁   The authentic source for hand-painted Delftware, visitors find the four primary types here: Delft Imari, Delft Green & Gold, traditional Delft Blue, and Delft Polychrome (including the Animal series modeled after antique Dutch tiles). 37 Front St., Philipsburg. 📞 599/542-5204.

Lalique   It is surprising that this store is found in Philipsburg, not Marigot. The fabulous and fabulously priced art glass and stemware (as well as authentic jewelry) should tempt any collector. 13 Sint Rose Arcade, Front St., Philipsburg. 📞 599/542-0763.

Linen Galore 🎁   The beautiful tablecloths, napery, placemats, towels, fine lace, and runners are carefully sourced from Europe (Belgian tapestries, Battenburg lace) and Turkey. Holland House Hotel. 97 Front St., Philipsburg. 📞 599/542-2533.

Shipwreck Shops   With 14 stores scattered throughout the island (one location on the French side: Le West Indies Mall, Marigot), this place offers one-stop souvenir shopping, from handmade hammocks to herbs, batik sarongs to bronze geckos. 42 Front St., Philipsburg. 📞 599/542-2962.

FRENCH SIDE
Amahoro Afro-Caribbean Art & Craft Gallery   This gallery showcases the island's African heritage with assorted tribal masks, wall hangings, fertility icons, and eye-catching jewelry. Le West Indies Mall, Front de Mer, Marigot. 📞 590/29-51-16.

Blue Lime Gallery 🎁 *Finds*   This shop showcases the handmade pottery of Cécile Petrelluzzi, the potter who formerly sold her works out of her studio, the Perfect Ti' Pot, at the foot of the Hotel L'Esplanade. She displays her own ceramics, which deftly balance art and function, alongside the work of other local artists. 101 Boulevard de Grand Case, Grand Case. 📞 690/61-90-48.

Laguna Blue Laguna Blue sells Italian arts and objects, such as sublime Murano glass, ornate Venetian masks, and an alluring array of ornaments and knickknacks in whimsical shapes. Marina Royale, Marigot. © 590/29-68-83.

Les Exotiques *⚘* This is the workshop and showroom of Marie Moine, a ceramicist who fires charming local scenes onto plates: Creole houses, birds flying over Monet-like ponds, tiny Antillean figures in traditional dress. 76 rue de la Flibuste, Oyster Pond. © 590/29-53-76. www.ceramexotic.com.

JEWELRY *⚘⚘*

Front Street seems like one jeweler after another (not unlike New York's West 47th St. Diamond Exchange), all selling loose stones as well as designer items. Marigot counters with its selection of luxury brands, particularly in watches. Many stores operate branches on both sides of the island. *Note:* Beware of unscrupulous hucksters selling loose "gems" like emeralds and diamonds on the street.

DUTCH SIDE

Colombian Emeralds International This is yet another branch in the Caribbean-wide chain that sells unmounted emeralds from Colombia at heavily discounted prices, as well as jewelry fashioned from other precious stones. Old Street Shopping Center. © 599/542-3933.

Hans Meevis Jewelry Hans Meevis is a master goldsmith who works brilliantly in miniature. He loves using inlays, such as larimar in ebony, or fashioning mosaics of tiny gems. Signature items include dolphin rings and pendants and remarkable keepsake blued titanium disks with intricate relief of the island in burnished white gold—right down to salt ponds and isthmuses. But Hans is also happy to customize all manner of decorative pieces (including bric-a-brac) on-site. 65 Airport Blvd., Simpson Bay. © 599/522-4433. www.meevis.com.

Little Switzerland This is part of a chain scattered throughout the Caribbean, whose top-of-the-line famous-name imports (watches, china, crystal, and jewelry from the likes of Tiffany) sport equally lovely price tags. 52 Front St. © 599/542-2523.

Touch of Gold This store actually sells liquor and various luxury items as well as baubles. Sapphires, rubies, diamonds, emeralds, tanzanite, and more are prettily mounted on platinum and gold. Brand-name watches include Daniel Mink, Skagen, and Christian Bernard; top-flight jewelry designers range from Louis Feraud to Susy Mor. 38 Front St. © 599/542-4120.

Zhaveri Jewelers   Zhaveri carries the spectrum of certified loose gems, as well as genuine cultured pearls, brand-name watches, and handsomely designed necklaces, rings, bracelets, and brooches. 53A and 103 Front St. ℂ 599/542-5176. www.zhaveri.com.

FRENCH SIDE

Artistic Jewelers   This store carries extravagantly designed and priced jewelry and watches, ranging from frankly garish to utterly ravishing. Featured individual designers and brands include David Yurman, Mikimoto, Fabergé, Scott Kay, Van Cleef & Arpels, Piguet, and Girard-Perregaux. Visitors to the Philipsburg store, 61 Front St. (ℂ 599/542-3456), find even more inventory. 8 rue du Général de Gaulle. ℂ 590/52-24-80. www.artisticjewelers.com.

Carat   This is one of several upscale jewelers along this street, featuring a smaller but still select variety of watches from Baume & Mercier to Breitling, not to mention sparkling bracelets, chokers, and pendants. 16 rue de la République. ℂ 590/87-73-40.

Goldfinger   Goldfinger is the island's official Rolex agent. But timepiece fanatics will find it's the ticket for designs by Tag Heur to Tissot. Other high-ticket items include designer jewelry, art glass (Kosta Boda, Orrefors, Waterford), tableware (Christofle, Daum), and porcelain (Herend, Lladró). They seem to open a new store annually: You can also stop by Rue de la République (ℂ 590/87-55-70), Marina Royale (ℂ 590/87-59-96), and Philipsburg at 79 Front St. (ℂ 599/542-4661). Le West Indies Mall on the waterfront. ℂ 590/87-00-11.

LIQUORS, CANDIES & CIGARS ☞

In addition to the usual upmarket single malt and stogie culprits (remember that Cubanos are illegal in the U.S.), the island produces its own concoctions noteworthy for their attractive packaging. Though the base rums are imported from Guadeloupe, local distillers blend or infuse them creatively. Look for Rum Jumbie, whose flavored varieties include coconut, mango, vanilla, and pineapple. But its trademark is Guavaberry liqueur (incorporating citrus, spices, and passion fruit), sold in a sculpted brown figurine bottle that resembles a cross between Harry Belafonte in his Calypso days and Aunt Jemima.

DUTCH SIDE

Antillean Liquors   This store has a complete assortment of liquor and liqueurs (including guavaberry), cigarettes, and cigars. Prices are generally lower than in other stores on the island, and the selection is larger. Queen Juliana Airport. © **599/545-4267**.

Belgian Chocolate Shop ⨂ All ages will savor the delicious chocolates here, with such specialties as Grand Marnier butter-cream truffles. It should come as no surprise that it's always bustling, especially when cruise ships are berthed at the nearby piers. 109 Old St. © **599/542-8863**.

Cigar Emporium This place claims to stock the Caribbean's largest selection of Cuban cigars under one roof, and the walk-in humidor is certainly impressive. The smoking lounge is often filled with would-be CEOs practicing one-upmanship, puffing out their chests while puffing on Partagas. The shop also carries countless cigar and pipe accessories, cutters, and cases (but sadly, no classic smoking jackets!). 66 Front St. © **599/542-2787**. www.cigaremporium.biz.

Guavaberry Emporium Guavaberry Emporium sells the rare "island folk liqueur" of St. Maarten, which for centuries was made only in private homes. Sold in square bottles, this rum-based liqueur is flavored with guavaberries, grown on the hills in the center of the island and harvested once a year near Christmas. (Don't confuse the yellow guavaberries with guavas—they're quite different.) The liqueur has a fruity, woody, smoky, bittersweet tang. Some people prefer it blended with coconut as a guavaberry colada or splashed in a glass of icy champagne. You can sample the line of liqueurs, including wild lime and mango, and frozen libations (free recipes available) at the counter. The charming Creole cottage also contains exotic natural perfumes and hot sauces (like habanero-lime or creole chipotle). The elegant hand-crafted specialty bottles and hand-carved wooden boxes make especially nice gifts. 8–10 Front St. © **599/542-2965**. www.guavaberry.com.

La Casa del Habano This highly regarded chain, with outposts from Cancún to Kuala Lumpur, has its own walk-in humidor and a men's club–like lounge (ah, the aroma of leather, tobacco, and fresh Cuban coffee!) behind a waterfall, respite from the cruise crowds. The selection is nearly as comprehensive, and there's a branch in Marigot, 71 Marina Port La Royale (© **590/87-58-94**). 24 Front St. © **599/543-1001**.

FRENCH SIDE
Le Goût du Vin This is one of the island's top sources for wines (as well as brandies and rare aged rums). The inventory of 300,000 bottles showcases the best of France, but thoughtfully includes

intriguing offerings from around the globe. If you're around the first Friday of the month, stop by for free tastings at 6pm. The head sommelier, Martial Jammes, offers suggestions with a soupçon of wit. Rue de l'Anguille. ℂ 590/87-25-03.

Ma Doudou ℛ *Finds*   Ma Doudou occupies a tiny shack virtually obscured by overgrown foliage in the town of Cul-de-Sac. Call ahead unless you're in the neighborhood, as it keeps irregular hours. Ma Doudou means "my darling" in Creole patois. Darling certainly describes the collectible hand-painted bottles garnished with madras clippings. The products—rum-filled candies, spices, jams, and 20 flavored rums (including one starring an enormous embalmed centipede that reputedly possesses aphrodisiacal properties)—practically overflow the shelves in the cramped space. The owners often throw in a free bottle with a minimum purchase. ℂ 590/87-30-43.

Vinissimo ℛ   This wine boutique, which also has locations in Anguilla and St. Barts, is one of the island's top places to buy wines from around the world. 1 Rue de Low Town, Marigot. ℂ 590/87-70-78. www.stmaarten.org/shops/vinissimo.html.

PERFUMES & COSMETICS

Lipstick   This is a Caribbean chain noted for its top-notch selection of scents and cosmetics, from Clarins to Clinique, Chanel to Shalimar. Stylists here do makeovers, touch-ups, skin care sessions, and even facials utilizing primarily Dior products. There's a Dutch side branch at 31 Front St. (ℂ **599/542-6051**). Rue de Président Kennedy, Philipsburg. ℂ 590/87-73-24.

Pharmacie Centrale ℛ   Browsing in French pharmacies is a delicious shopping experience in itself. The French are famous for the quality of their skincare creams and potions, and even basic toiletries—deodorants, toothpastes—have been fashioned with typical French flair and care. Here you can find highly touted (and hard to find in the States) French brands at duty-free (and tax-free) prices. 10 Rue du Général de Gaulle, Marigot. ℂ 590/51-09-37.

7

St. Maarten/
St. Martin After Dark

It's been said that the French/Dutch border was established by an 18th-century drinking contest. How fitting, then, that St. Maarten/St. Martin arguably contains more bars per capita than any other Caribbean island. Or maybe it just seems that way, given the myriad sunset booze cruises to toast the legendary elusive green flash (no, not a superhero but an atmospheric phenomenon caused by prismatic refraction of the sun's rays—or one margarita too many). Bars come in all shapes and sizes, from rickety rum shops to salvaged scows to neon-streaked nightclubs. And of course, after gamboling on the beaches, you can gamble in the Dutch side's casinos. Whether you seek a quiet sunset cocktail or after-hours boogieing, St. Maarten/St. Martin delivers.

Best of all, there's rarely a cover charge or minimum purchase, save at the occasional velvet-rope scene on St. Maarten (definitely the party-heartier side of the island—at times the Dutch side resembles perpetual spring break). Free entertainment abounds. Most restaurants (notably at Simpson Bay; see chapter 4) and beach bars (especially on Orient Bay; see chapter 5) host rocking live bands at least once a week, not to mention joyous happy hours. Hotels sponsor beachside barbecues with string bands.

Then there are the regular community jump-ups. Friday nights, the Philipsburg boardwalk along Front Street percolates with activity, as does Marigot's waterfront market Wednesdays and Sundays in season. Tuesdays from January to May, the "Mardi de Grand Case" (aka Harmony Night) explodes with color and sound: brass or steel drum bands, dancers, street performers, local crafts booths, and mouth- (and eye-) watering barbecue. The late-night nexus of Maho Village is transformed weekends by scantily clad acrobats, fire-eaters, and belly dancers. Come join the friendly, fun-loving locals in celebrating the sun, the sea, and the gentle breezes.

1 Clubs & Lounges

Both sides of the island provide the endorphin rush of dancing to a great DJ's mix. The action usually starts at 10pm (though the beach-front discos throw afternoon theme parties).

DUTCH SIDE

Bliss 🔄 Conveniently located within walking distance of the Maho "strip," Bliss defines incendiary Miami Beach–style disco chic. Every afternoon features a different theme or promotion, usually revolving around the pool (4–6pm happy hours are ideal for sunset-watching and include half-price bottles). On Wednesdays ladies get free massages, world-renowned guest DJs spin on weekends, and Sounds of Sunday is the liquid brunch du jour. But Thursdays (two-for-one drinks all night) are really hip and happening, with singles looking to generate heat. Try a "Blisstini"—designer martinis flavored with espresso, watermelon, passion peach, and more. The heated pool has a swim-up bar.

Kuta Beach The open-air dance club sister of mega-lounge Bamboo Bernie's (see "Classic Hangouts," below), it attracts an even sexier bunch than Bliss to such popular events as "Cult Movie Classic on the Beach" (*M.A.S.H.* to *The Matrix*). Sunday's barbecue/beach competition (volleyball, *pétanque,* board games) also lures an elegantly rowdy crowd. Frequent beauty pageants and bathing suit contests add still more spice. In between, sleek bodies gyrate to local, French, and Spanish DJs, or recline on rattan beds in the sand. Tribal Vibe Thursday and Fusion Friday are the big nights, when lasers strobe over the Balinese artifacts and flowing crimson sheets. 2 Beacon Hill Rd., behind Caravanserai. ☎ **599/526-1331.**

Mambo Dance Club This place could generously be termed cozy. The laser-swept dance floor takes up half the space; the bar and a small seating area seem almost after-thoughts. Tuesdays (two-for-one happy hours) and Hot Fridays with DJ Silk are the big nights, when sultry *señoritas* squeeze themselves into dresses until they can barely breathe. Salsa, soul, soca, and merengue comprise the musical menu. Maho Village upstairs. ☎ **599/556-5174.**

Q-Club This is the island's loudest and dressiest (though not necessarily most fashionable) dance club—reflected by the higher cover charge. The closest thing to a big city disco, it features several bars, multilevel dance floors, wraparound catwalks, and nooks and crannies aplenty. The back-to-the-future decor (think *The Jetsons*)—tables

> **_Tips_ Mapping It**
>
> For locations of nightlife options listed in this chapter, please
> refer to the St. Maarten/St. Martin, Marigot, or Philipsburg
> maps on p. 46, p. 57, and p. 49, respectively.

lit from beneath; streamlined Deco touches; raised seating areas with
silvery or slate-blue semi-circular banquettes divided by geometric
floating walls; floral, chessboard, and Miró-inspired patterns—ranks
among the Caribbean's most cosmopolitan looks. The vast space pul-
sates not only with deep house, techno, and jungle trip-hop mixes
(courtesy of state-of-the-art sound system and an impressive roster of
local and international spin gurus), but a color wheel of fiber-optic
lighting and videos. It's jammed and jamming weekends with strap-
ping guys and strapless gals. Casino Royale, Sonesta Maho Beach Resort.
© 599/524-0071. www.qclubdisco.com.

FRENCH SIDE
Club One Formerly known as In's Club/L'Alibi, this _boîte_ lies
among the hotbed of cool joints peppering the marina that bop until
dawn. The two main DJs, Léo and Antoine, have developed quite a
following, especially for their sizzling House mixes. Saturday nights
are ladies' nights. Alberge de la Mer, Marina Royale, Marigot. © 590/27-13-11.

StarBar This club attracts Gallic youth (and a smattering of
celebs) for funky house and techno music. My favorite night is Saturday, when slinky live acts such as Hanna Haïs (a bossa nova/soul
genius) perform, and "Vertigo 38" with DJ Tarzan (Léo) and Nério
turns the animals loose in the jungle. The tiny club is gussied up to
match the showgirls _manquées_ in spangled stilettos, leopard and
zebra skins, plumed headdresses, feather boas, and scarlet Fu
Manchu nails. No wallflowers or shrinking violets: Everyone's a star
among this exhibitionist crowd begging for reality-TV cameras. Nettle Bay. © 590/29-65-22.

2 Beach Bars & Classic Hangouts
BEACH BARS & SHACKS
For many people, the best hangs on the island are those barefoot
beach shacks right on the beach, where you can sit under a palm
tree or a shady awning, listening to music, sipping a drink, and dining on fresh grilled fish or ribs. Some, like the Sunset Bar, have gone

on to semi-fame (or semi-notoriety), but others have remained bless-edly low-tech and laidback. Here are a few we recommend.

DUTCH SIDE

At **Dawn Beach, Mr. Busby's Beach Bar** (*C* 599/543-6828), is a favorite place to kick back and even take a dip in the sea during the day; it turns into Daniel's by the Sea at night. **Beau Beaus's at Oyster Bay** (*C* 599/543-6040) is the Oyster Bay Beach Resort's beach-front bar, which offers tropical drinks, music, and food.

FRENCH SIDE

At **Baie Rouge (Red Beach)** you have two beach bars to sample: **Gus'** (no phone) and **Chez Raymond** (*C* 690/30-70-49). The latter cooks up blistering barbecue and delivers a knockout punch with Raymond's Special, a blend of six rums; hear reggae on weekends. On **Baie Nettlé (Nettle Bay),** Laurent Maudert's **Ma Ti Beach Bar** (*C* 590/87-01-30) and **Layla's** (*C* 590/51-00-93) are lively beach bars with French and Creole specialties, respectively.

On isolated **Anse des Pères (Friar's Bay Beach), Friar's Bay Beach Café** (no phone) sells Laurent's sublime stuffed mussels. The competitor is **Kali's Beach Bar** (*C* 590/49-06-81), a thatched bamboo hut splashed in Rasta colors, where Kali serves some of the island's best barbecue. Kali hosts "full moon parties," featuring reggae bands on the beach, a bonfire, and plenty of drinks.

Happening (and clothing-optional) **Baie Orientale (Orient Beach)** has full-service beach bars that offer not only food, but also beach chairs and umbrellas, live music, boutiques, massages, parasailing, jet ski rentals, kiteboard instruction, and more. **Waïkiki Beach** (*C* 590/87-43-19; www.waikikibeachsxm.com) has fabulous parties and beach lounges, plus a restaurant and snack bar—on New Year's eve, it features one of the biggest fireworks displays in the Caribbean. **Kontiki** (*C* 590/87-43-27) has two sections: the main eatery and the Tiki Hut, serving a mix of dishes from jerk chicken to sushi; it's famous for its Sunday-night parties. **Kakao beach bar** (*C* 590/87-43-26; www.kakaobeachsxm.com) is an all-pupose beach bar that has watersports rentals, beach chairs and umbrellas, a boutique selling Kakao-labeled T-shirts, towels, and more, and a menu of grilled meats, pizzas, and fresh lobster. **Bikini Beach** (*C* 590/87-43-25; www.sxm-orientbeach.com/bikinibeach) is a beachside tapas bar and grill that also sells fresh fruit smoothies (along with more hardcore drinks). It has a full watersports facility, a boutique, and even a children's playground.

At **Baie de l'Embouchure,** embracing **Le Galion** and **Coconut Grove beaches,** tiki carvings and blue umbrellas mark the appealing **Le Galion Restaurant** (aka Chez Pat after owner Pat Turner; ✆ 590/ 87-37-25; www.sxm-orientbeach.com/chezpat). Locals love this laid-back spot; many families make charcoal pits in the sand for impromptu barbecues.

CLASSIC HANGOUTS
DUTCH SIDE

Axum Art Café ✦   Axum was the coronation place of Christian Ethiopian kings in the 4th century A.D., and the alleged home of the Ark of the Covenant. The minimalist decor (sponge-painted apricot walls, artfully rust-colored furnishings) reinforces the vaguely revolutionist air, as nihilist neo-Goths, dashiki-ed ethnographers, and disaffected European philosophy majors articulately deconstruct their contempt between puffs and riffs. With provocative art exhibits, reggae and jazz parties, poetry recitals, storytelling, open-mic nights, and more, it's actually quite fun, and that *could* be the next Sartre or Miles Davis brooding one table over. It even has limited e-mail, scanning, and printing. Upstairs 7-L Front St. ✆ 599/542-0547.

Bamboo Bernies ✦   In its new location at Sonesta Maho Beach Resort, Bernies remains an updated homage to the Trader Vic's tiki bar: a United Nations riot of Buddhas, African masks, Chinese paper lanterns, totem poles, Indian tapestries, torches, painted wood barrels, and transparent glowing tiki gods. The menu—and clientele—is almost as eclectic, from the island's best sushi (try the Tiki Roll—salmon, tuna, and yellowtail topped with salmon roe and spicy eel sauce) to house-smoked hickory barbecue. The new **Buddha Lounge,** as the owners say, "may very well be the only place in St. Maarten where one can relax, chill out, and actually have a conversation and hear the other person while conversing." It serves food and drinks into the wee hours. Sonesta Maho Beach Resort, Rhine Rd. ✆ 599/545-3622. www.bamboobernies.net.

Buccaneer Beach Bar   Head here any time of day or night for a sublimely mellow setting and kick back over pizzas or burgers and knockout rum punches (or try the BBC: Bailey's Banana Colada, with Bailey's, fresh banana, rum, and cream of coconut). The triple B is less frenzied than other sunset-watching perches, though daily special $1 shooters, from Kamikazes to Green-Eyed Blondes (melon, Irish cream, and crème de banane liqueurs) ensure some excitement. Kim Sha Beach behind Atrium Resort. ✆ 599/544-5876. www.buccaneerbar.com.

The Greenhouse ☞   This breezy, plant-filled, open-air eatery with marina views is a favorite among locals and island regulars who know the food is great value, especially the certified Angus steaks, poultry (luscious mango chicken), and such seafood specials as baked stuffed swordfish. They swarm the place during happy hours (4:30–7pm), downing two-for-one drinks and discounted appetizers from conch fritters to jalapeño poppers. Wednesday's Crab-a-ganza and Friday's Lobster Mania sate anyone's crustacean cravings. The big screen broadcasts major sporting events and pool tables and video games keep things lively. It's *the* place on Tuesday: The entire island shows up for a dance party as DJs rock the house and from 9:30pm on all the drinks are two for one. Bobby's Marina, Front St. ℂ 599/542-2941. www.thegreenhouserestaurant.com.

Lady C **Floating Bar**   Although the rickety 1938 craft barely seems seaworthy, *Lady C* cruises Simpson Bay lagoon Wednesday and Sunday afternoons. The deceptively decorous-sounding *Lady Carola* remains berthed otherwise. Theme nights include Two for Tuesdays (from 10pm), Wacky Wednesdays with DJ Don Marco, Thirsty Thursdays ("really, really big drinks" after 10pm), and Rock the Rock Fridays and Saturdays. It's the kind of spot that posts Wall of Shame photos of inebriated customers (all in good fun) and hosts Playboy Bunny dress-up and body-painting parties. Pizza Galley is located here, serving surprisingly excellent pies (see chapter 4). Airport Rd. ℂ **599/544-4710.** www.ladycfloatingbar.com.

Sunset Beach Bar ☞   License plates, baseball caps, Christmas lights, and patrons' business cards seem to be all that holds this sprawling gazebo together. Just another bar, save for its utterly unique location: on the beach—and 15m (50 ft.) from the main airport runway (so close that the planes' exhaust perfumes the air, while management broadcasts radio transmissions between the pilots and air traffic controllers). Don't panic if you see the flight crews knocking them back (they're usually on layover). The ultimate all-purpose, something-for-everyone, anything-goes venue, Sunset offers decent pub grub, a huge screen for sporting events, a tiny dance floor swept by laser lights, live music daily from acoustic guitar to hardcore reggae, sunset variety shows featuring high school marching bands and the Island Heat dancers, and DJs after 10pm. It's noisy, crowded, silly—and beers that not so long ago were $6 are now $10—but where else can you get buzzed by 757s and kamikazes? 2 Beacon Hill Rd. ℂ **599/545-3998.** www.sunsetbeachbar.com.

Taloula Mango's Caribbean Café Facing Great Bay Beach, Taloula Mango's offers magnificent views of the harbor. The handsome colonial room (with ceiling fans and plantation shutters) is a fine place to sample creative cocktails and delicious pub grub (burgers, pizza, tapas, salads) as well as island specialties, such as fish prepared Creole style and Caribbean conch and dumplings. Weekends welcome sensational jazz, blues, and funk artists such as saxophonist Sapphron Obois. On the Boardwalk, Great Bay Beach, Front St., Philipsburg. © 599/542-1645. www.taloulamangos.com.

FRENCH SIDE

Bali Bar 🏵 A bohemian crowd bellies up to Bali's bar for glorious global tapas—grilled chorizo, stuffed mussels, shrimp tempura, tuna curry samosa, fajitas, and fried calamari—costing 4€ to 6€ ($6–$9) each. Plush decor accentuates the lounge's sensuous ambience: mauve drapes, mango walls, Indian embroidered silk wall hangings, Warhol-inspired Pop Art prints, and carved teak chairs. Smoky soca and jazz chanteuses occasionally animate the proceedings. Marina Royale, Marigot. © 590/51-13-16.

Calmos Café 🏵 This place defines the laidback beach shack ethos (a sign near the entrance warns NO SNOBS). Calmos Café is splashed in sunset colors, with lots of chaises on the sand; at a little front library, you can borrow beach reading. Young slicksters come to flirt, gossip, and drink (terrific frozen concoctions and homemade infused rums—try the banana). In winter, there's sometimes live jazz or blues to accompany the sublime, affordable food. 40 bd. de Grand Case. © 590/ 29-01-85.

The Tree Lounge 🏵 This lounge high up in the trees at Loterie Farm is a very pleasant place to relax over a drink and some delicious tapas with fellow grownups. It's perched atop the farm's original 19th-century milk shed. It's a switch from the beach-bar scene—you'll be nestled in greenery. 49 blvd. de Grand Case (not on seaside). © 590/87-86-16.

3 Live Music

DUTCH SIDE

Cheri's Café 🏵 American expat Cheri Batson opened this cherished institution in 1988. The rare tourist trap that even appeals to locals, this great place to meet people is outfitted in an irrepressible color scheme of scarlet, hot pink, and white. Everybody from rock bands to movie stars, casino high rollers to beach bums makes a pit stop at this open-air pavilion. The surprisingly good, relatively cheap food (think burgers, steaks, pastas, and fresh fish) is a bonus, but most come for flirting and dancing to an assortment of live acts 6 nights a week. Don't miss such regulars as Sweet Chocolate Band, if only to watch the guys don wigs and falsies. Rhine Rd. #45, Maho Village, Maho. ℂ **599/545-3361.** www.cheriscafe.com.

Pineapple Pete ℛ   Pete co-opts most of an alley between the lagoon and the main drag. T-shirts dangle from the rafters in the main room (with five pool tables and dart boards), where yachters, local businesspeople, and timeshare owners marinate and get tight. The fairly priced fare is quite good—signature dishes include crab-stuffed shrimp, lobster thermidor, and dark rum crème brûlée. Infectious, if ear-splitting, live music keeps things rocking half the week, including live classic rock, pop, and blues Wednesdays through Sundays with local stalwart Ronny Santana. Airport Rd., Simpson Bay. ℂ **599/544-6030.** www.pineapplepete.com.

Red Piano Bar   This joint attracts 40-something singles looking for romance and couples looking to rekindle sparks. The grand piano is indeed quite red, and patrons are often red-faced from the killer cocktails, which help lubricate the lousier acts, death-by-karaoke, or both. The performers, professional or otherwise, are variable (one recently forgot the lyrics to "Memory"—ouch), but the place is comparatively refined and quiet. Pelican Resort, Billy Folly Rd. ℂ **599/544-6008.**

Sopranos Piano Bar   Mobbed by 30-somethings in the mood for romance, the piano bar (replete with small area for old-fashioned touch dancing) delivers a soigné ambience without thematic overkill (other than the signature Bada Bing merchandise for sale). The photos of musicians posed as Mafiosi and giant poster of James Gandolfini aka Tony Soprano glaring down at the grand piano (or maybe at the singers) are witty; the dim lighting, intimate dark wood banquettes, and red-and-black color scheme set the right tone. Sit back and enjoy the good martinis, superb cognac selection, and fine collection of Cuban cigars. Sonesta Maho Beach Resort & Casino. ℂ **599/522-7088.** www.sopranospianobar.com/stmaarten.

FRENCH SIDE

Blue Martini   Although it doesn't have beach access, this place more than compensates for it with an enchanting garden, the perfect place to savor specialty cocktails, intriguing international beers like Abbé Leffe on tap, and tasty tapas. It shakes and stirs things up with live bands Tuesdays and Thursday through Saturday at 7pm. 63 blvd. de Grand Case, Grand Case. ℂ **590/29-27-93.** www.bluemartinisxm.com.

Gecko Café Although nominally an Italian eatery, Gecko Café serves tapas and emulates Japanese decorative simplicity right down to tatami mats and low tables on the polished wood floor. It's an ideal place to zone out, except perhaps at sunset, when an invigorating mix of yachters and local yupsters cruise by for happy hours and late-night live acoustic jams Thursday through Saturday. Marina Royale. ℂ **590/52-21-25.**

La Chapelle ☞ This bar is where savvy locals head when they tire of the nonstop action at the "sand" bars on Orient Beach—but still want to drink, dine, dance, or shoot pool and the breeze in congenial surroundings. Orient Village. ℂ **590/52-38-90.**

4 For Adults Only

It's impossible to ignore the more titillating aspect to nightlife, especially on St. Maarten, where the international lineup of exotic dancers entertain each evening.

DUTCH SIDE
Golden Eyes Calling itself a topless "ultra-lounge" with "American management and European dancers," Golden Eyes gives the Platinum Room a run for its (and your) money. In an effort to be inclusive, it welcomes couples and women. Theme nights include Monday amateur wet T-shirt contests and Tuesday costume nights with DJ, lingerie, and pajama party, and two-for-one drink specials. Specialty acts are a tad hard core. The club itself is handsomely appointed and the balcony offers lovely marina views. 12 Airport Rd., Simpson Bay. ℂ **599/527-1079.** www.goldeneyesclub.com.

Platinum Room The gold standard of gentlemen's clubs, this place cultivates an air of class: neo-colonial arches and colonnades, inlaid woods, knockoffs of Michelangelo's David and Grecian urns, sequined curtains, and cheery turquoise banquettes. It crowds up quickly, with everyone from suits to bikers to cyber-geeks, and stays open till 5am. Maho Village. ℂ **599/557-0055.** www.theplatinumroom.com.

FRENCH SIDE
Crazy Paradise Le Crazy is the only official adult entertainment venue on the French side. The "cabaret" gives way to a nightclub after 9pm. The stage juts out in phallic fashion, and the walls are adorned with Georgia O'Keeffe–meets–old *National Geographic* paintings of sultry beauties in silhouette. And yes, some of the ladies dress up as naughty French maids. 21 rue Victor Maurasse. ℂ **690/88-96-98.**

St. Maarten's Red-Lights

The Dutch are notoriously liberal and have cultivated a permissive attitude regarding prostitution on St. Maarten. This review is neither endorsement nor encouragement; it merely offers some enlightenment on a major element of St. Maarten nightlife. Brothels operate around the island and must purchase a permit and supply affidavits on their employees (mostly Dominican, Venezuelan, Colombian, Guyanese, and Jamaican immigrants who must submit to monthly medical checkups). Several brothels are situated just outside Philipsburg (if this is your thing, ask the security guards at your hotel for advice on where to go).

It all started with the aptly named **Seaman's Club** (79 Sucker Garden Rd.; ✆ **599/542-2978**). It was founded in the 1940s to service Japanese tuna fishermen who'd been to sea for months at a time. These single men needed a place to carouse and the government didn't want them hassling local girls, so a tradition was born.

Note: One big difference from Amsterdam's red-light district is that possession of marijuana is not tolerated here. An infraction could lead to stiff fines or even imprisonment.

5 Casinos

Gaming is currently only legal on the Dutch side. For all its self-promotion about a Caribbean Vegas, the scene is closer to Laughlin or Biloxi. Regardless, the 14 casinos offer free live theater, with everyone from blue-haired fanny packers to dreadlocked Rastas robotically feeding the maw of the machines. If you indulge, just remember there's no such thing as a sure system (or, Lord help us, ESP)—and the odds always favor the house, especially in games like Keno. Hours vary, but most casinos are open from 1pm to 6am.

Atlantis World Casino ⟨ⲅ⟩   This is St. Maarten's most Vegas-style venue, if only for adopting that destination's gourmet aspirations. The owner/developer cleverly attracted top restaurateurs by offering competitive rents. The interior is fairly posh if you don't look too closely: mirrored ceilings, Christmas lights, faux plants, lipstick red accents, and murals and frescoes, mostly depicting cherubs cavorting in azure skies or surreal encounters between Renaissance figures and islanders. Atlantis features all the major table games, as well as more than 500 slot and video poker machines. It tends to attract a more mature, settled crowd: guys chomping on cigars and tan women who look like aging Lakers Girls, as well as junior corporate sharks in the Texas Hold 'Em poker room. Rhine Road 106, Cupecoy. ℂ 599/545-4601. www.atlantisworld.com.

Casino Royale ℛ   St. Maarten's largest, glitziest, and supposedly ritziest gaming emporium, Casino Royale's splashy exterior of illuminated fountains and its huge multihued neon sign spitting lasers almost approximates the gaudy best (and worst) of Vegas. Despite the upscale pretensions, most people ignore the rarely enforced dress code (no shorts or tank tops). The casino offers games from blackjack to baccarat and more than 400 slot machines. The 800-seat **Showroom Royale** is the island's largest, most technologically sophisticated theater; its glittery shows change every few months, but generally follow the same pattern. Like a poor man's *Ed Sullivan Show/Star Search,* the evening might include acrobatics, jugglers tossing bowling pins and bad jokes with equal aplomb, and/or magicians with the usual large-scale tricks up their sleeves (including dismemberment and disappearing tigers). Upstairs is the island's loudest dance spot, the **Q-Club** (see "The Club Scene," earlier in this chapter). Sonesta Maho Beach Resort. ℂ 599/545-2590 or 599/544-2115. www.mahobeach.com.

Coliseum Casino   Sadly, this tri-level, ancient Rome–themed establishment, doesn't approach the garish yet playfully camp excess—or style—of Caesars Palace (Nero undoubtedly would have fed the designers to the lions, though he'd appreciate the smoky ambience). Still, it supposedly offers the highest table limits, as well as free limousine pickups for high rollers, and loud entertainment. 74 Front St. ℂ 599/543-2101.

Hollywood Casino   Although it regrettably lacks deliciously cheesy theming, Hollywood Casino does make some half-hearted stabs: "Oscar" door handles, movie stills (*Pulp Fiction* and *Planet of the Apes*), fake stars in the ceiling, klieg lights, Rodin-like statues, and a wall devoted to Marilyn Monroe. It offers a panoramic view of the bay, roulette, blackjack, stud-poker, Let It Ride, progressive jackpot bingo, 150 slot machines, bingo, and a high-tech Sports Book with nine screens broadcasting major events via satellite, plus nightly dancing on the Pelican Reef Terrace and island shows featuring Caribbean bands. Pelican Resort, 37 Billy Folly Rd., Simpson Bay. ℂ 599/544-2503 or 599/544-4463. http://mostelegant.com/hollywood.

Jump Up Casino   A Carnival-themed casino, it has several ornate costumes on display. Live late weekend shows (11pm–2am) showcasing the island's hottest bands (Playstation, Jump Up Stars, Explosion, Impact) are the best reason to visit. Emmaplein 1, end of Front St. ℂ 599/542-0862. www.jumpupcasino.com.

Princess Casino ✪   This place wins the prize for overall elegance, as evidenced by the dressier crowd and handsome neoclassical design (columns, arches, domes, and frescoes galore). Princess has more than 650 one-armed bandits and 20 table games from craps to blackjack. Dining options include the newly located Peg Leg Pub, a fine buffet, and a sushi bar. The live shows are spectacularly mounted (by island standards). House lounge lizard extraordinaire, the Teddy Pendergrass/Marvin Gaye clone, Melvin Hodge, croons soulfully in between patter. Port de Plaisance Resort, Cole Bay. ℂ 599/544-4311. www.princesscasinosxm.com.

Rouge et Noir   This joint is all red and black inside, just like a roulette wheel, with a vaguely futuristic design. It offers slot machines, roulette, blackjack, bingo, and Antillean and 3-card poker. 66 Front St. ℂ 599/542-3222 or 599/542-2952. www.casinorougeetnoir.com.

8

Anguilla

by Alexis Lipsitz Flippin & Sherry Marker

Once upon a time Anguilla was one of the Caribbean's best-kept secrets. Then, in the 1980s, this small, serene, secluded island embarked on a careful plan of marketing itself as a top-end destination with a handful of resorts. Quite deliberately, Anguilla (rhymes with "vanilla") turned its back on the package tours, the casinos and cruise ships, the glitzy shopping and nightlife of neighboring St. Martin.

Just like Anguilla itself, the island's first resorts were (and remain) small gems, serene and secluded. It wasn't until 1995 that Anguilla's Wallblake Airport was expanded to take medium-size commercial jets. Even now, however, there are days when more private than commercial jets land at Wallblake. Last year, when I stopped at Wallblake to check the arrival time of the American Eagle flight from San Juan, I noticed a sleek little jet purring for takeoff near the terminal. When I returned 4 hours later, the jet was still there. When I asked someone whether the mini-jet had a problem, he laughed. The jet's owner, he told me, had phoned after lunch to say he felt like a swim and nap before departure.

Even though Anguilla is clearly one of the Caribbean's most chic destinations, the island has somehow remained laidback and unaffected. If Anguilla has a secret today, it is that in addition to the island's justly famous first-class resorts and restaurants, it also has a number of (relatively) affordable small inns and villas. Stay at one of Anguilla's more modest places and you'll still have those famous beaches to enjoy. The beaches here are public, and although some resorts make non-guests park some distance away from their manicured beaches, many of the best beaches are ones you'll discover yourself. The budget-minded will also find plenty of dining choices that don't cost an arm and a leg. Simply head to one of Anguilla's many locally popular beach bars and cafes, or perhaps get takeout from the Fat Cat Gourmet for a beach picnic (see "Resources for Self-Catering," later).

Anguilla: A Love Affair

The first time we went to Anguilla, in 1989, my husband and I were fleeing Puerto Rico after two waterless and powerless weeks following Hurricane Hugo. When Anne Edwards of Sydans Villas met us at the airport and asked if we had some bottled water, I thought, *What have I gotten into! Have I fled an island disaster only to land on an island where you're expected to have your own water?* (Turns out, in those days some people *did* bring bottled water with them to Anguilla. The local water has a sea-tang, and bottled water was still expensive in those days on Anguilla.) When we arrived that first time, there were no lights between the airport and Sandy Ground. Really. I had no idea where we were going or if there was any *there* there. We woke up in the morning to find a small goat staring at us through the screen door and nibbling my towel, which I had left as an inadvertent snack on a chair outside the room. And, I admit, this may not sound like an intro to why I have been going back to Anguilla (and Anne Edwards' Sydans) for 20 years, but it sure turned out that way.

—*Sherry Marker*

If you're looking to rest, unwind, and be pampered without pomp or snobbery, then this is the place for you. Prepare yourself for two guaranteed pleasures: the breathtaking beauty of the island's 30-odd beaches and the amazing hospitality of Anguilla's 12,000 inhabitants. Most Anguillians are of Afro-Caribbean descent; many Anguillians, especially those from the village of Island Harbour, have Irish as well as Afro-Caribbean ancestors. Almost all will greet you with at least a nod, and often a reassuring "okay." If you walk into a shop in Anguilla and ask where something is, you'll be told—but locals will be surprised that you didn't say "Good Day" before you got down to business.

While it's true that Anguilla's scant rainfall and unproductive limestone and coral soil support mainly low foliage, sparse scrub vegetation, and droll red-topped Turk's head cactuses, the island will delight you with the lilies and flowering shrubs that blossom after rainfalls. For years, the island's largely inhospitable soil forced many Anguillian men to leave the island to find work in shipping, fishing, and trade. The women stayed home and tended to their families and

A Little History

In 1980 Anguilla gained its independence from an awkward federation with St. Kitts and Nevis and has since been a self-governing British Dependent Territory. The British government is represented by the Governor, who is responsible for a good deal, including foreign policy. There is an elected House of Assembly and the chief Anguillian elected official is the Chief Minister. Public holidays, including Anguilla Day (May 30), the Queen's Birthday (June 18), and Separation Day (December 19) honor both Anguilla's ties to Britain and its independence from St. Kitts and Nevis. Most government offices are in the Valley, Anguilla's capital, where most of the island's banks, groceries, and shops are also located. While you're in the Valley, be sure to drive up Crocus Hill and see some of the island's oldest and most charming Caribbean gingerbread cottages.

their vital kitchen gardens. Today, many islanders work in the tourist and hospitality industries; the economy is so sound that off-islanders come here in search of work, often in the booming building industry.

In the last few years, Anguilla has seen more development than in the last several decades: the **Temenos** resort (scheduled to be fully open in 2009) has the island's first 18-hole golf course, while the homey old **Rendezvous Bay Hotel** hopes to reinvent itself as an upmarket hotel and condo complex. Across the island, multi-story villas are going up on once-isolated hillsides. The one thing that hasn't changed is the truth of Anguilla's slogan: "TRANQUILLITY WRAPPED IN BLUE."

1 Essentials

VISITOR INFORMATION

The **Anguilla Tourist Board,** Coronation Avenue, the Valley, Anguilla, B.W.I. (© **264/497-2759** or 877/4-ANGUILLA; fax 264/497-2710; www.anguilla-vacation.com), is open Monday to Friday from 8am to 5pm.

In the United States, contact Ms. Marie Walker, 246 Central Ave., White Plains, NY 10606 (© **914/287-2400;** fax 914/287-2404), or log onto www.anguilla-vacation.com. For U.S. travelers who need quick answers to questions about Anguilla, contact the toll-free **Anguilla Hotline** (© **800/418-4620**).

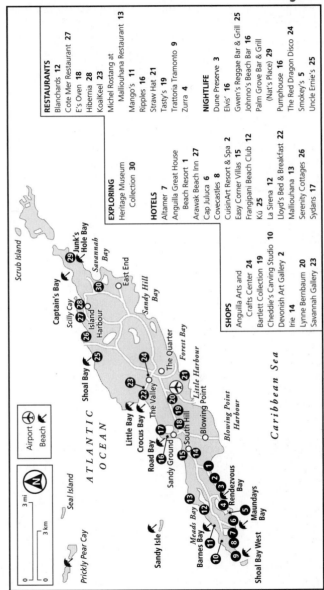

Anguilla

RESTAURANTS

Blanchards **12**
Cote Mer Restaurant **27**
E's Oven **28**
Hibernia **28**
KoalKeel **23**
Michel Rostang at
  Malliouhana Restaurant **13**
Mango's **11**
Ripples **16**
Straw Hat **21**
Tasty's **19**
Trattoria Tramonto **9**
Zurra **4**

NIGHTLIFE

Dune Preserve **3**
Elvis' **16**
Gwen's Reggae Bar & Grill **25**
Johnno's Beach Bar **16**
Palm Grove Bar & Grill
  (Nat's Place) **29**
Pumphouse **16**
The Red Dragon Disco **24**
Smokey's **5**
Uncle Ernie's **25**

EXPLORING

Heritage Museum
  Collection **30**

HOTELS

Altamer **7**
Anguilla Great House
  Beach Resort **1**
Arawak Beach Inn **27**
Cap Juluca **6**
Covecastles **8**
CuisinArt Resort & Spa **2**
Easy Corner Villas **15**
Frangipani Beach Club **12**
Kú **25**
La Sirena **12**
Lloyd's Bed & Breakfast **22**
Malliouhana **13**
Serenity Cottages **26**
Sydans **17**

SHOPS

Anguilla Arts and
  Crafts Center **24**
Bartlett Collection **19**
Cheddie's Carving Studio **10**
Devonish Art Gallery **2**
Irie **14**
Lynne Bernbaum **20**
Savannah Gallery **23**

Scrub Island

Seal Island

Prickly Pear Cay

Captain's Bay

Junk's **29**
Hole Bay

*Savannah
Bay*

East End

Island **30**
Harbour

*Sandy Hill
Bay*

Scilly Cay **27 28**

Shoal Bay **26 25**

24

The Quarter

Forest Bay

Little Bay **23 22**
Crocus Bay **19**
The Valley **18**

Road Bay **16**

Sandy Ground **15**
South Hill **14**

20 21

Little Harbour

Blowing Point

*Blowing Point
Harbour*

*ATLANTIC
OCEAN*

Caribbean Sea

Rendezvous **1 2 3**
Bay **4**

Maundays **5**
Bay **6**

Meads Bay **13 12**

Barnes Bay **11 9 8 7 6**

10

Shoal Bay West

Sandy Isle

Airport ✈
Beach ⚑

N

0 ___ 3 mi
0 ___ 3 km

131

In the United Kingdom, contact the **Anguilla Tourist Board,** 7A Crealock St., London SW182BS (② 208/871-0012).

In the Valley, the **Drugstore** (② 264/497-2738), the **Anguilla Arts and Crafts Center** (② 264/497-2200), and the **National Trust Office** (② 264/497-5297; www.axanationaltrust.org) stock books on Anguilla, including guides to the local flora and fauna, and Brenda Carty and Colville Petty's *Anguilla, an Introduction and Guide,* which is usually also available at Mr. Petty's **Heritage Collection Museum** 🅀 in the island's East End (see "Exploring Anguilla," later).

USEFUL WEBSITES   In addition to the websites above, other helpful Internet sites include the **Anguilla government** (www. gov.ai), **Anguilla Hotel and Tourism Association** (www.ahta.ai), and the *Anguillian* newspaper (www.anguillian.com). The **Anguilla Guide** (www.anguillaguide.com) and the **Anguilla Forum** (www. anguillaforum.com) are very helpful, and the message boards contain good travel tips.

GETTING THERE

BY PLANE   More than 50 flights into Anguilla's Wallblake Airport are scheduled each week, not counting various charter flights. There are no nonstop flights from mainland North America, however, so visitors usually transfer through San Juan, Puerto Rico, or the Princess Juliana International Airport, St. Martin's main airport, on nearby Dutch St. Maarten. There is also service from Antigua and St. Thomas.

Keep in mind that the last ferry from St. Martin to Anguilla leaves around 7pm; if you have a late-arriving flight, you may quite literally miss the boat. You can do one of two things: You can spend the night in St. Maarten/St. Martin or arrange a charter plane flight (see below) into Anguilla.

American Eagle (② 800/433-7300 in the U.S. and Canada; www.aa.com), the commuter partner of American Airlines, has several nonstop daily flights to Anguilla's Wallblake Airport from American's San Juan hub. In the offseason flights are reduced to one daily during the week and two on weekends. Flights leave at different times based on the seasons and carry around 40 passengers.

Winair (Windward Islands Airways International; ② 888/255-6889 in the U.S. and Canada; www.fly-winair.com) has daily flights to Anguilla from Dutch St. Maarten and Antigua.

LIAT (② 868/624-4727 in the U.S. and Canada, or 264/497-5002; www.liatairline.com), which in 2007 merged with the now-defunct Caribbean Star, offers daily flights from Antigua and St. Thomas.

For the ultimate in convenience (and prices to match), you can charter a private plane to take you from St. Maarten/St. Martin or other nearby islands directly to Anguilla; **Trans Anguilla Airways** (© 264/497-8690; www.transanguilla.com) and **Island Charters** (© 264/497-4064) charter planes to and from Anguilla.

BY FERRY   Public ferries run between the ports of Marigot Bay, St. Martin, and Blowing Point, Anguilla (© 264/497-6070), every 30 minutes. The trip takes 20 to 25 minutes, making day trips a snap. Usually, the first ferry leaves St. Martin at 8am and the last at 7pm; from Blowing Point, the first ferry leaves at 7:30am and the last at 6:15pm. The one-way fare is $15 ($10 children 2–18) plus a $3 departure tax. No reservations are necessary; schedules and fares are subject to change. Ferries vary in size, and none takes passenger vehicles. While you're waiting at Blowing Point, you might want to try **Big Jim's** (no phone), one of several *very* casual places serving up scrumptious barbecued chicken and baby back ribs (as well as island stews such as goat water and bull-foot soup).

An extremely convenient option is to take one of the **privately run charter boats and ferries** that deliver passengers between Anguilla and the airport in St. Maarten. Anguilla-based charter boats will pick you up at the Princess Juliana airport in St. Maarten and carry you and your luggage to Blowing Point or a hotel on the south side of Anguilla. These boats are more expensive than the public ferries, but let you avoid having to travel to the ferry port in Marigot by taxi (a 10- to 15-min. trip)—a smart option for travelers with a lot of luggage. Plus, the privately run boats are smaller and have fewer passengers and can even arrange full-boat charters for groups or families. Keep in mind that these boats do not run as frequently as the government-run ferry, but most do include ground transportation. Check out the *M.V. Shauna VI* (© 264/476-6534 in Anguilla; 599/580-6275 on St. Maarten; myshauna6@hotmail.com; $35 one way adults, $20 children 2–12) or **Funtime** (© 264/497-6812 or 264/235-8106; http://funtimeai.com; $70 one way).

Many hotels also offer private boat charters between the ferry dock at Blowing Point, Anguilla, and the airport in St. Maarten, with door-to-door ground transportation included.

GETTING AROUND
BY RENTAL CAR   To explore the island in any depth, I highly recommend you rent a car, though be prepared for some badly paved roads. Four-wheel-drive vehicles are a real bonus for exploring the

Favorite Festivals

Anguilla's most colorful annual festival is **Carnival,** held jointly under the auspices of the Ministries of Culture and Tourism. The festival begins on the Thursday before the first Monday in August and lasts 10 days. The festival also features spectacular parades with floats, elaborately costumed dancers, terrific bands, and lots of competitions, including the very popular Miss Anguilla contest. Carnival harks back to Emancipation Day, or "August Monday," in 1834, when enslaved Africans all throughout the British colonies were freed. **Boat races** are Anguilla's national sport, and the distinctive swift, high-masted, brightly painted open boats stage a number of exciting races during Carnival. In early May, the **Anguilla Regatta** (www.anguillaregatta.com) features competitive races over a three-day weekend, with free entertainment and barbecues every night. Anguilla's other major festivals are the 4-day late-March **Moonsplash Music Festival** (www.bankiebanx.net/moonsplash), founded by Anguilla's best-known musician, Bankie Banx, and **Tranquility Jazz Festival** (www.anguillajazz.org), held in the second week of November; artists featured at the 2008 festival included jazz vocalists Cassandra Wilson and Diane Schuur.

island's unpaved and pitted back roads, but not necessary elsewhere. Car hire agencies on the island can issue the mandatory Anguillian driver's license, which is valid for 3 months. You can also get a license at police headquarters in the island's administrative center, the Valley, and at ports of entry. You'll need to present a valid driver's license from your home country and pay a one-time fee of $20. *Remember:* Drive on the left side of the road!

Most visitors take a taxi from the airport to their hotel and arrange, at no extra charge, for a rental agency to deliver a car there the following day. All rental companies offer small discounts for rentals of 7 days or more. Car hire is not cheap on Anguilla, and begins at about $40 a day, plus insurance and taxes, which can be steep.

Avis, which is represented by **Apex** in the Valley (*✆* **800/331-1212** in the U.S. and Canada, or 264/497-2642; www.avis.com; avisaxa@anguillanet.com), offers regular cars and some four-wheel-drive vehicles as does **Hertz**'s representative, **Triple K Car Rental,**

Airport Road (© **800/654-3131** in the U.S. and Canada, or 264/
497-2934; www.hertz.com; hertzatriplek@anguillanet.com). Local
firms include **Connor's Car Rental,** c/o Maurice Connor, South
Hill (© **264/497-6433**), **Island Car Rentals,** Airport Road (© **264/
497-2723;** islandcar@anguillanet.com), and **Carib Rent A Car**
(© **264/498-6020;** caribcarrental@anguillanet.com).

Note: It's worth pricing a car rental with one of the larger agencies
and then checking with your hotel to see what price they can get for
you. Many hotels and inns on Anguilla rent all their customers' cars
from one or more small local agencies. Your car may not be as new
and shiny as some of the other rentals available, but your savings
may be considerable.

BY TAXI   Taxi fares are posted at Walblake Airport, at the Blowing
Point ferry, and in most taxis. In January 2008, typical fixed taxi
fares were about $20 from the airport and Blowing Point to Cap
Juluca, $15 to the Anguilla Great House, and $16 to Malliouhana.
Most rides take 15 to 20 minutes. If you like your driver, ask for his
card and cell phone number for future rides. You can also get a cab
through the **Airport Taxi Stand** at © **264/497-5054** or **Blowing
Point Ferry Taxi Stand** at © **264/497-6089.** A $2 surcharge goes
into effect between 6pm and 6am.

Taxi drivers also make great tour guides; check out "Exploring
Anguilla," later in this chapter.

FAST FACTS: Anguilla

Banks   Banks with ATMs are open Monday to Thursday 8am to
3pm, Friday 8am to 5pm. Several banks, including **Scotiabank,**
the Valley, Fairplay Commercial Complex (© **264/497-3333**),
and **First Caribbean,** the Valley (© **264/497-2301**), have ATMs
that are usually accessible after hours.

Currency   The **Eastern Caribbean dollar (EC$)** is the official
currency of Anguilla, although U.S. dollars are the actual
"coin of the realm." The exchange rate is permanently fixed
at about EC$2.70 to each $1 (EC$1=37¢). Rates in this chapter
are quoted in U.S. dollars unless indicated otherwise. That
said, it's a good idea to have some EC$ for use in smaller shops
and restaurants that do much of their business in EC$.

Documents   All visitors must have an onward or return ticket.
U.S., British, and Canadian citizens must have a valid passport.

Electricity The electricity is 110-volt AC (60 cycles), so no transformers or adapters are necessary to use U.S. appliances.

Hospitals For medical services, consult the **Princess Alexandra Hospital,** Stoney Ground (© **264/497-2551**). Many of the larger hotels have a physician on call.

Language English.

Liquor Laws Beer, wine, and liquor are sold 7 days a week during regular business hours. It's legal to have an open container on the beach.

Pharmacies The **Health Authority** at the Princess Alexandra Hospital, Stoney Ground (© **264/497-2551**) is open weekdays 8am to 5pm and Saturday 10am to noon. The **Paramount Pharmacy** has branches at Water Swamp (© **264/497-2366**) and South Hill (© **264/498-2366**).

Police You can reach the police at their headquarters in the Valley (© **264/497-2333**) or the substation at Sandy Ground (© **264/497-2354**). In an emergency, dial © **911.**

Post Office The main post office is on Wallblake Road, the Valley (© **264/497-5453** or 264/497-2528). Collectors consider Anguilla's stamps valuable, and the post office also operates a philatelic bureau and shop with T-shirts and cards showing commemorative stamps, open Monday to Friday from 8am to 4:45pm. Airmail postcards and letters cost EC$1.50 (55¢) to the U.S., Canada, and the United Kingdom. As of January 2009, Anguilla will have its first postal code: AI-2640. So if you're sending a letter to Anguilla from another country, you'll place the new postal code after "Anguilla" and before "British West Indies" (or "BWI").

Safety Anguilla is one of the safest destinations in the Caribbean, but you should still take standard precautions. Although crime is rare here, secure your valuables; never leave them in a parked car or unguarded on the beach.

Taxes The government collects a 10% tax on rooms. Effective January 2008, all visitors traveling through the seaports are required to pay an embarkation tax of $20 per adult, and $10 for children 12–18 (children under 12 free).

Telephone Telephone, cable, and Telex services are offered by **Cable & Wireless Ltd.,** Wallblake Road, the Valley (© **264/497-3100**), open Monday to Friday 8am to 5pm. To call the United States from Anguilla, dial **1,** the area code, and the seven-digit number. **Digicel** (*(C)* **264/498-3444**), with its main office by the Public Library in the Valley, usually has better rates for renting or buying a cell phone than Cable and Wireless.

Time Anguilla is on Atlantic Standard Time year-round, which means it's usually 1 hour ahead of the U.S. East Coast—except when the U.S. is on daylight saving time, when the clocks are the same.

Weather The hottest months in Anguilla are July to October; the coolest, December to February. The mean monthly temperature is about 80°F (27°C). Rain is most heavy in the winter, but few days are without sunshine.

2 Accommodations

For the next few years, expect to see construction going on at several prime spots on the island. The ambitious re-creation of the homey old **Rendezvous Bay Hotel** into a mega resort/hotel/condo complex is under way (although some say the project is stalled); for information, see www.rendezvousbay.com. At Meads Bay the **Viceroy Resort** (www.viceroyanguilla.com) is going up. When it opens in 2010, the **Fairmont Anguilla** (www.fairmontanguilla.com), on the island's south coast, will feature a hotel; an 18-hole championship golf course; and Fairmont Residences, a collection of condominiums, villas, and estate homes. At the west end of the island, the St. Regis **Temenos** hotel, villa, and condo complex (www.temenosanguilla.com) is still under construction. However, the **Greg Norman–designed golf course** is open (Bill Clinton played here in 2007), as is **Zurra,** the snazzy new golf course-front restaurant run by Anguilla's best-known restaurateurs, Bob and Melinda Blanchard, proprietors of Blanchards (see later).

Keep in mind that "villa" is used on Anguilla to mean either a separate unit *or* a self-contained unit in a building with several other self-contained units. That's a big difference, so be sure which kind of villa your rental is before you send off your deposit!

VERY EXPENSIVE

If your idea of a Caribbean getaway includes being cared for by a personal butler and staff of eight, you may want to make one of architect Myron Goldfinger's three villas at **Altamer** *(F)(F)* (Shoal Bay

West, the Valley; (©) **264/498-4000;** www.altamer.com) your "private palace," just as its website suggests. The five- to six-bedroom villas go for prices that nudge upward towards a whopping $50,000 a week in high season, but tumble to a mere $27,500 to $30,000 off season. The furnishings suggest casual luxury, with floating stairways, cantilevered walls, and dramatic floor-to-ceiling windows. Creature comforts at all the villas include a private swimming pool, an elaborate game room (with pool table), and entertainment center (including a home theater).

Cap Juluca ✸✸✸ At press time, Cap Juluca was changing owners, but it's hard to believe that the high standards of this ultra-classy 28-year-old resort will be diminished one whit. This is the premier property on the island, and its name appears over and over again at or near the top of everyone's list of the Caribbean's best hotels. Encircling Maundays Bay's lovely white-sand beach and nestled in luxuriantly landscaped 179-acre grounds, the resort entertains moguls, celebrities, and a clientele that returns year after year. Hand-holding honeymooners criss-cross the beach day in and day out. What do they all come for? Laid-back luxury and utter seclusion.

While Altamer and Covecastles practically knock you over with their edgy, in-your-face architecture, Cap Juluca's low-lying structures blend harmoniously with the landscaped palms and lush vegetation; of course, having one of the best beaches on the island as a sparkling frontispiece doesn't hurt. The architectural style is quasi-Moorish, with sun-blasted exteriors, white domes, arched doorways, and walled courtyards. Rooms and villas are spacious, with luxurious beds, tile floors, Oriental rugs, and colonial-style louvered doors opening onto patios, many with pathways leading directly to the sea. A number of villas have private plunge pools. Butler service is available with private-pool suite and villa bookings. The bathrooms are enormous and sheathed in marble, with fabulous Bulgari toiletries. The spa offers traditional treatments as well as alternative holistic treatments. The resort has three restaurants, all with amazing sea views. **Pimm's** offers classic dining, and **George's** is a sunny beachfront spot that's open for breakfast and lunch and dinner drinks (and the weekly alfresco barbecue). As part of the new ownership revitalization project, **Kemia** is being replaced by a pan-Asian restaurant overseen by René Bajeux, former Executive Chef of the Four Seasons Maui and the Four Seasons Beverly Hills. Another serious plus: service that is unobtrusively excellent, without a smidgen of attitude. Cap Juluca's congenial staff (most of them locals who have worked here for years) gets consistently high marks from guests; in fact, after the 2008 sale, the former owner showed his appreciation for the resort's 400 employees by splitting a cool million bucks among them.

Maundays Bay (P.O. Box 240), Anguilla, B.W.I. © **888/858-5822** in the U.S., or 264/497-6666. Fax 264/497-6617. www.capjuluca.com. 71 units. Winter/spring $825–$1,500 double, from $1,670–$3,815 suite; off season $535–$795 double, from $1,145–$2,410 suite. Rates include continental breakfast. AE, MC, V. **Amenities:** 3 restaurants; 2 bars; outdoor pool; driving range; 3 tennis courts; croquet; fitness center; yoga and tai chi; spa; kayaks; sailing; snorkeling; water-skiing; windsurfing; bicycles; children's programs (in summer only); rental cars; business center; room service (7:30am–10:30pm); massage; babysitting; laundry service; dry cleaning; boutique and sundries shop' nature trails; island excursions. *In room:* A/C, ceiling fan, dataport, Wi-Fi, minibar, hair dryer, safe.

Covecastles 𝒦𝒦   Nothing else on Anguilla looks like architect Myron Goldfinger's Covecastles: This cluster of post-modernist buildings has sleek white exteriors interrupted by smooth curves, jagged triangles, and cylinders—*Architectural Digest* has featured the resort not once but twice. Rumor has it that Bill, Hill, and Chelsea have stayed here. The resort sits on a spectacular stretch of beach on Shoal Bay West, and each unit has sea views; many have private pools. The large bedrooms have twin or king-size beds with hand-embroidered linens and equally sizable, stylish bathrooms. Interiors have cathedral ceilings; louvered doors and enormous picture windows crafted from Brazilian walnut; terra-cotta tiles; comfortably oversize rattan and wicker furniture; a fully equipped, state-of-the-art kitchen; and even a hammock or two.

The resort's French chef, Dominique Thevenet, will prepare pretty much whatever you want in Covecastles' central dining room (open to the public) overlooking the beach or, with some advance notice, in your own quarters.

Shoal Bay West (P.O. Box 248), Anguilla, B.W.I. © **800/223-1108** in the U.S., or 264/497-6801. Fax 264/497-6051. www.covecastles.com. 15 units. Winter $895–$4,500; off season $595–$2,395; extra bed $75. AE, MC, V. Closed mid-Aug to mid-Oct. **Amenities:** Restaurant; tennis court; aerobics; deep-sea fishing; glass-bottom boat excursions; kayaks; snorkeling; Sunfish sailboats; windsurfing; bicycles; car rental; secretarial service; room service; massage; babysitting; laundry service. *In room:* A/C, ceiling fan, TV, dataport, Wi-Fi, full kitchen, beverage maker, hair dryer, iron, safe.

CuisinArt Resort & Spa 𝒦𝒦𝒦 *(Kids)*   Pillowed in the sand dunes that line a gorgeous stretch of Rendezvous Bay beach, CuisinArt's whitewashed villas seem transplanted from some sunny Greek isle. This beautifully landscaped resort has a wonderful infinity pool that flows all the way to the beach—its long stretches of shallow water are perfect for toddling kids. CuisinArt has a happy, supremely comfortable vibe, with roosters crowing in the morning and baby chicks skittering in the underbrush and a palm-fringed patio that faces the gleaming pool. The place must be doing something right: CuisinArt is the number-one resort on Anguilla for travelers on TripAdvisor.com. And, yes, it is owned by CuisinArt (of blender fame), and yes, it takes its food seriously, with Anguilla's first hydroponic farm (see "Down on the [Hydroponic] Farm," below), a "kitchen stadium" offering cooking classes and demos, and an herb garden. In fact, if CuisinArt has a secret, it's that the twice-weekly **barbecue buffets** ✦✦ are the best on the island, laden with grilled lobster, spit-roasted chicken, ribs, homemade desserts, as well as delicious sides and salads made with hydroponic-farm-fresh produce.

The rooms are sun-splashed and cheery, with comfy wicker and dark wood furniture and bright Haitian paintings on the walls. Bathrooms are luxuriously spacious, with lots of marble and fluffy towels. Patios have spectacular ocean views.

In 2007, CuisinArt added **Chef's Table**—twice a week six-course dinners featuring local produce and inventive menus—to its usual offerings at the **Santorini Restaurant.** Another restaurant, the **Mediterraneo,** serves up more casual fare, with great breakfasts that include delicious corn pancakes and fresh fruit smoothies. At press time, the **Venus Spa** was being greatly expanded and will feature 16 treatment rooms, a Thalasso pool of heated seawater, and an oceanfront relaxation room. CuisinArt frequently has excellent on-and-off season specials with seriously reduced rates; it also offers full and modified meal plans.

Rendezvous Bay (P.O. Box 2000), Anguilla, B.W.I. ⓒ **800/943-3210** or 264/498-2000. Fax 264/498-2010. www.cuisinartresort.com. 93 units. Winter $705 double, $875–$1,500 suite; off season from $400 double, from $500 suite. Rates include continental breakfast. AE, MC, V. Closed Sept–Oct. **Amenities:** 3 restaurants; 3 bars; outdoor pool; 3 tennis courts; bocce court; croquet; billiards room; fitness center; spa; Jacuzzi; deep-sea fishing; kayaks; sailing; scuba diving; snorkeling; windsurfing; mountain bikes; children's playground; salon; limited room service; babysitting; laundry service; dry cleaning; nonsmoking rooms; horseback riding; rooms for those w/limited mobility; sundries shop; boutique. *In room:* A/C, TV, Bose Wave music system, dataport, Wi-Fi, minibar, hair dryer, iron, safe.

Malliouhana ✦✦✦ *(Kids)* Decisions, decisions: How to chose between Cap Juluca and Malliouhana? Well, if you want to walk out your door and saunter across the beach into the water, head for Cap Juluca. If you want to relax in an understated-chic room or villa

Down on the (Hydroponic) Farm

It's the world's only hydroponic farm in a greenhouse setting, where hundreds of ripe red tomatoes, foot-long cucumbers, dewy lettuces, and fragrant herbs ripen spectacularly in a giant greenhouse with little more than water and a sprinkling of plant nutrients. There's no soil, no weeds, no bugs. To help feed guests and staff in a country where the soil is non-arable and most of the fresh produce must be flown in, Cuisin Art hired plant scientist and horticulturist Dr. Howard Resh, Ph.D., to devise a greenhouse that could produce vegetables year-round and withstand strong winds. Today the farm supplies both resort restaurants and the employee cafeteria, with an average harvest of 128 heads of lettuce a day. Tours of the hydroponic farm are very popular; call ℂ **264/498-2000** to join one of the regularly scheduled tours with Dr. Resh, who is passionate about every aspect of the farm. You'll get to sample some of the incredibly sweet cherry tomatoes right off the vine.

tucked into the lush gardens of a cliffside resort overlooking the sea, and meander down a path to the beach, Malliouhana is the place for you. Situated on a rocky bluff between two crescent beaches, Malliouhana's 10 hectares (25 acres) are lushly landscaped with terraces, banks of flowers, pools, tiled walkways, and fountains. All rooms have either sea or garden views—sometimes both. As for the **Michel Rostang at Malliouhana** restaurant, it garnered the top spot on *Condé Nast Traveler's* Gold List in 2008 as the best hotel for food in the Caribbean (see "Dining," later). The 15,000-square-foot full-service spa is highly professional and popular with repeat clients from the local and expat communities here, as well as Malliouhana's own guests. Many of the spacious, casually elegant rooms have four-poster beds; a number have their own verandas and mini-gardens. If you're traveling with a child, this is a kid-friendly oasis, complete with a terrific supervised playground with a faux pirate ship; nonguests can use the playground for $25 per person per day.

Meads Bay (P.O. Box 173, the Valley), Anguilla, B.W.I. ℂ **800/835-0796** in the U.S., or 264/497-6111. Fax 264/497-6011. www.malliouhana.com. 55 units. Winter $850–$1,110 double, $1,200–$3,400 suite; off season $375–$595 double, from $585–$2,145 suite. AE, MC, V. Closed Sept–Oct. **Amenities:** 2 restaurants; 2 bars; 3 outdoor pools; 4 tennis courts; basketball court; gym; spa; Jacuzzi; boat trips; fishing; sailing; snorkeling; water-skiing; windsurfing; children's playground; 24-hr.

concierge; salon; room service (7:30am–10:30pm); massage (spa only); babysitting; laundry service; dry cleaning; library; TV room; boutique; tennis shop; sundries and souvenir shop. *In room:* A/C, ceiling fan, dataport, minibar, hair dryer, safe.

EXPENSIVE

Frangipani Beach Resort 🐟🐟   Set directly on a lovely Meads Bay beach, this appealing pink-hued resort has upgraded its rooms and public spaces to stay competitive in an increasingly competitive market. The Spanish Mediterranean–style buildings feature one-, two-, and three-bedroom configurations. The one-bedroom suites are the best, with gleaming stainless-steel kitchens, ocean views, and spacious living quarters. (All junior suites, one-bedroom suites, and two-bedroom suites have full kitchens and washer/dryers.) It has a nice big infinity pool and an on-site restaurant and bar, **Meads Bay Beachfront Grill,** which serves local specialties and grilled seafood. Note that construction of the Viceroy resort next door may be ongoing during your visit; ask for a room away from the building noise.

Meads Bay (P.O. Box 1655), Anguilla, B.W.I. 📞 **866/780-5165** or 264/497-6442. Fax 264/497-6442. www.frangipaniresort.com. 18 units. Winter $350–$475 double, $675–$1,500 suite, $685–$1,800 penthouse; offseason $250–$350 double, $450–$1,175 suite, $500–$1,300 penthouse. Rates include continental breakfast. AE, MC, V. Closed Sept 2–Nov 1. **Amenities:** Restaurant; bar; pool; tennis court; kayaks; Hobie cats; babysitting. *In room:* A/C, ceiling fans, TV/DVD, CD player, Internet access, hair dryer (in some), safe, robes.

Kú 🐟 *Value*   Unlike Anguilla's resorts that hide themselves away in acres of landscaped privacy, Kú is in the heart of things at very popular Shoal Bay. Kú opened in 2005 after completely renovating the nondescript five-building condo complex that had been here since the 1980s. The result: an easy barefoot back-and-forth walk from the island's most famous beach to good-value quarters on stratospherically priced Anguilla. Each suite has a living/dining room with a full kitchen, good-size bedroom and bathroom, and an oceanfront terrace or ocean-view balcony. The suites are decorated in a minimalist style, with lots of bright white offset by colorful throw cushions; glass, chrome, and wicker tables and chairs; and pale pastel walls. Some reports indicate the rooms are in need of a little refreshment. Kú's 23m-long (75-ft.) beach bar and pool is a daylong gathering place for guests, who range in age from thirty-something to long-standing AARP members. Uncle Ernie's, one of Anguilla's best-known beach bars and grills, is just next door, as is the Shoal Bay Scuba Center. Other restaurants and bars are strung out for a good mile or so along the beach, which is increasingly chock-a-block with rental umbrellas, beach chairs, and day-trippers from St. Martin. In short, Shoal Bay is Anguilla's only seriously crowded beach and Kú is a great place for action and nonstop people watching—but not necessarily for blissed-out Caribbean tranquility.

Shoal Bay East (P.O. Box 51, the Valley), Anguilla, B.W.I. © **800/869-5827** or 264/ 497-2011. Fax 264/497-3355. www.ku-anguilla.com. 27 units. Winter $320–$450 double; off season $180–$240 double. Meal Plan (breakfast, lunch & dinner) $105 a day. Extra person $50 ($30 off season). AE, MC, V. **Amenities:** Restaurant; bar; outdoor pool; gym; spa; dive shop; snorkeling. *In room:* A/C, ceiling fan, TV/DVD, Internet access, kitchen, safe.

La Sirena ⭐ *Value*   Built in 1989, this formerly Swiss-owned resort, separated from the beach by a nicely landscaped garden, still draws a good deal of its clientele from Switzerland and Germany. Many guests are snorkelers; La Sirena offers dive packages with **Anguillian Divers** (www.anguilliandivers.com). Some critics have called the units, redecorated in 2007, hip and stylish. I'd go for sedate and comfy: Most, in three two-story bougainvillea-draped wings, have dark wood or rattan and wicker furniture, rugs with interesting abstract patterns, king-size beds, and bathrooms with tub/shower combinations. Ground-floor rooms have a veranda, while upper-story rooms have balconies. One real drawback in Anguilla's hot climate: The rooms have minibars, but only the villas have fridges in which to store cold drinks and snacks. The **Mahi-Mahi** restaurant honors its Swiss heritage with a weekly fondue night; it also has a Thai night and a Caribbean barbeque night. The off-season packages offer exceptional value.

Meads Bay (P.O. Box 200), Anguilla, B.W.I. © **800/331-9358** in the U.S., or 264/ 497-6827. Fax 264/497-6829. www.sirenaresort.com. 26 units, 6 villas. Winter $290–$350 double, $400–$480 suite, $500–$600 villa; off season $145–$190 double, $220–$250 suite, $230–$360 villa. Modified American Plan (breakfast and dinner) $55 per person. AE, MC, V. **Amenities:** Restaurant; bar; 2 outdoor pools; dive center; snorkeling; windsurfing; car rental; limited room service; massage; babysitting; laundry service. *In room:* A/C (in some), ceiling fan, TV/DVD, dataport, minibar, hair dryer, safe.

MODERATE
Anguilla Great House Beach Resort ⭐ *Value*   This old-time, low-key resort sits on perhaps the most glorious beach on an island that has plenty of great beaches. This particular stretch of sand has what many do not: a sweetly shaded grove of palm trees, under which you can park yourself in a beach chair for hours of breezy bliss. You may be joined by a handful of guests and a couple of playful dogs—but otherwise you will have this paradise pretty much to

yourself. Unfortunately, that may be because the resort is not so great these days, with unkempt lawns and rooms that are in need of refurbishment. Worse, you can sit on your back porch and gaze out upon a yard filled with hotel detritus. Some of the staff, too, seems to have given up. On the plus side, the pool is nicely maintained, and the gingerbread-trimmed cottages are just steps from the perfect sands of Rendezvous Bay. Many (especially 111–125) boast water views from their back and front porches—ask for one of these. Rooms in each cottage are cheek-by-jowl, but guests here seem respectful of their neighbors' close proximity. Most rooms have pitched ceilings and bright local artworks, and the shower-only bathrooms are clean and well-kept. At press time, a promising new chef from Guadeloupe was cooking in the alfresco restaurant, **Old Carib,** serving food that was much better than expected: great onion soup, shrimp in garlic butter and wine, and Creole ratatouille. If you'd like a self-catering unit, and don't mind being a few minutes from the beach, ask about the rates for nearby **Kerwin Kottages**—four self-catering one-, two-, and three-bedroom units that enjoy hotel privileges and represent excellent value.

Rendezvous Bay, Anguilla, B.W.I. ℂ **264/497-6061.** Fax 264/497-6019. www.anguillagreathouse.com. 35 units. Winter $310–$350 double; off season $210–$250 double. AE, MC, V. **Amenities:** Restaurant; bar; outdoor pool; fishing; kayaks; snorkeling; Sunfish sailboats; windsurfing; limited room service; laundry service; nonsmoking rooms. *In room:* A/C, ceiling fan, TV, fridge, hair dryer, iron/ironing board.

Arawak Beach Inn (Value This funky, *very* casual hotel offers good value (on pricey Anguilla) for the laid-back traveler. Accommodations consist of studios and one-bedroom suites (some with kitchenettes) in weathered shingle-roofed, sorbet-hued, octagonal-shaped buildings; those on the upper floors have wrap-around balconies with great views of the sea. The eclectic decor runs from Spartan white with splashes of color to more classic four-poster rattan beds and dark wood furniture. Each lodging has a smallish shower-only bathroom and private balcony or terrace. Air-conditioning, high-speed Internet access, and cable TV are available in deluxe units. Swimmers can head for the virtually private little Arawak Cove, 2 minutes' walk behind the resort, which has its own small pool; Shoal Bay's phenomenal beach is a 10-minute drive away. The **Arawak Café,** which merges with the hotel bar and Wi-Fi accessible lobby, has great pizzas and Continental/Caribbean dishes. Innkeeper Maria Hawkins has lots of information on what to see and do on Anguilla. If one room is not enough for your needs, ask about the substantial discount available when a family needs a second room.

Island Harbour (P.O. Box 1403, the Valley), Anguilla, B.W.I. ✆ 877/427-2925 or 264/497-4888. Fax 264/497-4889. www.arawakbeach.com. 17 units. Winter $225–$275 double; off season $120–$185 double. Extra person $35. Children under 12 stay free in parent's room. MC, V. **Amenities:** Restaurant; beach bar; outdoor pool; canoeing; windsurfing; bike rental; car rental; limited room service; babysitting; laundry service. *In room:* Ceiling fan, TV (in some), Wi-Fi (in some), fridge, hair dryer (in some), safe, no phone.

Serenity Cottage ✮ *Finds*   With a great location at the quiet end of Shoal Bay Beach, Serenity is one place that lives up to its name. The crowds at Uncle Ernie's and Kú are a brisk 15-minute stroll away along the beach. Anguillian owner Kenneth Rogers keeps his eye on every detail here, and it all runs very smoothly. The two cottages are surrounded by lovingly tended flowers and trees (at least one unit's shower has a glass wall brushed by palm fronds). Thanks to the layout, most rooms can be rented as a studio for one or (as lockouts) as suites with full kitchens for two to four. The furnishings are a bit on the understated side, with a good deal of dark wood furniture and some busily patterned fabrics, but the views from the rooms and their balconies through the gardens to the sea are marvelous. Every time I stop by here, I notice relaxed guests chatting at the bar in the restaurant, which functions as a meeting place and is open to the breezes. Serenity also has a toes-in-the-sand beach bar and restaurant, and Gwen's Reggae Grill is just steps away down the beach. One thing to keep in mind: There are coral reefs in the sea here, and the waters can be rough; a short walk will take you past the reefs to Shoal's usually calmer waters.

Shoal Bay East (P.O. Box 309, the Valley), Anguilla, B.W.I. ✆ 264/497-3328. Fax 264/497-3867. www.serenity.ai. 10 units. Winter $275 studio, $385 1-bedroom suite, $495 2-bedroom suite; offseason $175 studio, $250 1-bedroom suite, $325 2-bedroom suite. MC, V. **Amenities:** Two restaurants; beach bar; car rental; limited room service; babysitting; laundry service. *In room:* Ceiling fan, TV, Wi-Fi (in some), fridge, hair dryer (in some), safe.

INEXPENSIVE
Easy Corner Villas ✮ *Value*   On a bluff overlooking Sandy Ground (aka Road Bay), this place is a good 15-minute drive from the best beaches, so you'll definitely want a car. No problem: The owner is Anguillian Maurice Connor, the same entrepreneur who rents many of the cars on the island. Note that ongoing construction down the hill may—or may not, the odds are not in yet—obstruct the view from some units down to Sandy Ground and the sea. Easy Corner's one-, two-, and three-bedroom apartments (known as villas) are set on modestly landscaped grounds with beach views from

most of their private porches. Each comes equipped with kitchen facilities, an airy combination living/dining room, good storage space, and simple furnishings. Some guests have complained about the size of the bathrooms here—but I'm not sure why, especially at these prices. Maid service is available for an extra charge, except on Sunday.

South Hill (P.O. Box 65, the Valley), Anguilla, B.W.I. © **264/497-6433**. Fax 264/ 497-6410. www.easycornervilla.com. 12 units. Winter $160 1-bedroom villa, $195 2-bedroom villa, $240 3-bedroom villa; off season $125 1-bedroom villa, $155 2-bedroom villa, $195 3-bedroom villa. AE, MC, V. **Amenities:** Car rental; laundry service. *In room:* A/C, ceiling fan, TV, kitchen, beverage maker, hair dryer.

Lloyd's Bed and Breakfast ✦ *Value* The island's oldest inn opened in 1959 on the crest of Crocus Hill in the Valley. This family-owned inn is the sort of place that makes you feel at home the moment you walk through the door and a long-time member of the staff greets you with a courteous, "May I help you?" The bright yellow exterior, with lime green shutters and a wide, inviting veranda, is exuberantly Caribbean. Inside, the rooms have filmy curtains at the windows, hand-crocheted bedspreads, and traditional ceiling fans (as well as A/C). Lloyd's main room—part dining room, part lounge—with its traditional wood and cane furniture, old prints, and small library, is the perfect place for island travelers (many are repeat guests here) to trade tall tales. There's only one drawback here: Lloyd's is not on a beach. Still, there's an excellent beach down the hill at Crocus Bay, and since nothing is very far away on Anguilla, the island's other beaches are just a short drive away. A full breakfast and the hotel taxes are included in the price, which makes Lloyd's one of the most charming bargains in the Caribbean.

Crocus Hill (P.O. Box 52, the Valley), Anguilla, B.W.I. © **264/497-2351**. Fax 264/ 497-3028. www.lloyds.ai. 9 units. $105 double; $135 double with terrace. MC, V. **Amenities:** Restaurant (breakfast only), bar, car rental. *In room:* A/C, ceiling fan, TV.

Sydans ✦ *Value* Anguillian Anne Edwards is the tirelessly helpful proprietor of Sydans, a hospitable family-run inn that overlooks Sandy Ground's large salt pond and is only steps from the sea. Some guests from the States and Europe have been coming here every year for 20 years; others use this as a long-term home-away-from-home. All rooms have kitchens (some stoves have burners, but not ovens), bathrooms with tub/shower combinations, and homey bed- and sitting rooms. The second-floor units overlooking the salt pond are a birder's delight, with spottings of pelicans, cranes, herons, and seasonal birds; ground-floor rooms open into a central courtyard, lack the pond view, and are less quiet. Sydans is very much part of the Sandy Ground neighborhood: You'll hear roosters at sunrise, see the school bus drop off neighborhood children in the afternoon, and know when Johnno's or the Pumphouse has live music until the wee hours. Things are casual here (water outages are not unknown), but if you ask Ms. Edwards for an extra reading lamp or towels, they'll be in your room by the time you're back from the beach.

Sandy Ground, Anguilla, B.W.I. (C) 264/497-3180 or 264/235-7740. www.inna.ai/sydans. From $100 double. MC, V. **Amenities:** Shop, garden. *In room:* A/C, ceiling fan, TV, kitchen.

3 Dining

You won't want to miss the all-you-can-eat **barbecue buffets** at **CuisinArt Resort & Spa** ((C) 264/498-2000; www.cuisinartresort.com), the best buffets on the island, with grilled lobster, chicken, and ribs; homemade desserts; and delicious sides and salads made with hydroponic-farm-fresh produce; a string band provides the entertainment. We'd also like to mention the terrific breakfasts (truly farm-fresh eggs) at the pleasantly old-fashioned **Old House,** George Hill, the Valley ((C) 264/497-2228); on Sundays, it serves a traditional Anguillian breakfast with salt fish and all the trimmings. *Note:* At many restaurants, prices for fish, lobster, and crayfish rise and fall depending on availability.

VERY EXPENSIVE

Michel Rostang at Malliouhana Restaurant ✦✦✦ CLASSIC MEDITERRANEAN   In January 2008 Malliouhana was awarded the best hotel for food in the Caribbean on *Condé Nast Traveler's* Gold List. The French Mediterranean menu is infused with Caribbean flavors and served in an elegant dining room dramatically situated in an open-sided pavilion on a rocky promontory over the sea. It's supervised by the Parisian two-star Michelin chef Michel Rostang and prepared by resident resort chef Alain Laurent and a staff of almost 30; the wine cellar has some 25,000 bottles.

The hors d'oeuvres selection is the most extensive on the island, including fresh Anguillian lobster prepared in various ways. Laurent's seasonally changing menu might offer roast breast of *poulet de Bresse* (chicken) basted with honey and cider or braised local mahimahi with sweet potato purée. Dessert might be an old-fashioned slice of French-style apple tart or homemade ice cream and sorbet.

Meads Bay. (C) 264/497-6111. Reservations required. Main courses $40–$50. AE, MC, V. Daily 7–11:30am, 12:30–3pm, and 7:30–10:30pm.

Tips Resources for Self-Catering

Anguilla is pricey enough as it is without having to pay marked-up hotel prices for basics like milk, soft drinks, snacks, and beer. For groceries, drinks, and kitchen staples, stock up at **Albert's Supermarket** (© 264/497-2240), in the Valley, a large, full-service grocery store. In Anguilla's West End, you can get a full complement of groceries and other sundries at **Foods Ninety-Five** (© 264/497-6196), just after the entrance to Cap Juluca. **Ashley & Sons** (© 264/497-2641; www.ashley andsons.com), in the South Valley, has a wide selection of beverages, snacks, fruit, and toiletries. Monday through Saturday, don't miss stopping at the **Fat Cat Gourmet** (© 264/497-2307; www.fatcat.ai) by Albert's supermarket in the Valley; hands down, this place has the tastiest take-out goodies (from entire meals to cakes) on Anguilla. When I leave Anguilla, I try to have a veggie wrap, some spicy seafood pastries, and a couple of brownies to comfort me on the trip home. This is also a great place to pick up snacks for a picnic on the beach.

EXPENSIVE

Blanchards ⭑⭑⭑ INTERNATIONAL   In 1994, when Anguilla was just beginning to attract high-spending foodies, Bob and Melinda Blanchard opened a restaurant that was at the end of a dirt track to the sea. It was rumored to be elegantly casual and said to serve fresh and inventive haute cuisine. Frankly, many wondered how long Blanchard's would survive. Since then, this place with indoor-outdoor dining on the beach (now reached by a good road) has become the island's one must-do place to eat for many foodies. It's not uncommon to see dinner guests arrive here clutching copies of the Blanchards' book *A Trip to the Beach,* a charming account of how they created their restaurant. Now Blanchards' only problem is how to live up to its reputation. No problem: The crackerjack staff keeps the engine humming night after night.

Behind tall teal shutters (which are opened to the sea breezes), diners enjoy sophisticated but not fussy food with a spirited Caribbean flair. Among the perpetual favorites are sublime lobster-and-shrimp cakes—worth the trip alone. The specialty is the Caribbean sampler: oven-crisped mahimahi with coconut, lime, and ginger; roasted Anguilla lobster with honey glaze; and jerk chicken with cinnamon-rum bananas. For a real island dessert, opt for the cracked coconut with coconut ice cream accompanied by a rum-custard sauce in a chocolate-crusted shell. You can buy one of the Blanchards' newest tomes on the way out; oh, and those are son Jesse's colorful paintings on the walls.

Meads Bay. © **264/497-6100.** www.blanchardsrestaurant.com. Reservations required. Main courses $38–$58. AE, MC, V. Mon–Sat 6:30–10pm. Closed Sept 1 to Nov 1 and Sun and Mon in off season.

Hibernia *★★ Finds* FRENCH/INDOCHINESE   Anguillian residents since 1987, Chef Raoul Rodriguez and his wife, hostess Mary Pat O'Hanlon, have converted a traditional West Indian cottage at the east end of Anguilla into an inventive restaurant decorated with French-and Indonesian-inspired *objets d'art* collected from their annual world travels. The food here is equally international, with touches of the West Indies, Thailand, and France. This is a place where it's tempting to make a meal of starters, perhaps the Asian mushroom soup, and then the Caribbean smoked fish selection (a house specialty), with an order of the house-smoked tuna, mahimahi, and kingfish with ginger and horseradish, and an order of tomatoes stuffed with different cheeses. Main courses include grilled beef tenderloin served with—are you ready?—a crème brulée of foie gras, port sauce, and potato gratin; lighter options include a wide variety of seafood with Thai touches. Save room for the ice cream, including mint, mango, green tea, and tamarind—all homemade, of course. Be sure to make a reservation: There are only 11 tables.

Island Harbour. © **264/497-4290.** www.hiberniarestaurant.com. Reservations required. Main courses $30–$44. MC, V. Tues–Sat noon–2pm and 7–9pm; Sun 7–9pm; closed Mon and Tues in low season. Closed Aug–Sept.

KoalKeel *★★* ISLAND/ASIAN   This handsome restaurant is housed in one of the island's most historic stone houses, a former sugar plantation "Great House" from the 1790s. (Across the road you can see the oldest dwelling on the island, originally a building sheltering slaves.) When you come here, be sure to ask to see the 200-year-old oven and the rooms with lovely wooden architectural detail. Executive chef Gwendolyn Smith prepares an eclectic menu of local specialties with Asian-inspired flavors and techniques, including island pea soup and dumplings, Tandoori rock lobster, and "rice paper" snapper with Chinese vegetables in a lemon-soya sauce. Oenophiles will appreciate the 15,000-bottle wine cellar; there's also a lounge for aged rums and cigars. Pastries here are terrific; be sure to stop by the KoalKeel Patisserie one morning between 6 and 9am to get some of the French bread, croissants, or other treats available for takeout.

The Valley. ℂ 264/497-2930. www.koalkeel.com. Reservations required. Main courses $24–$37 (lobster priced by pound; special-order slow roast chicken $75). AE, MC, V. Mon–Sat 6:30–9pm.

Mango's ✿✿ CARIBBEAN/NEW WORLD

This pavilion a few steps from the edge of the sea, on the northwestern part of the island, fulfills anyone's fantasies of a relaxed but classy beachfront eatery; its doors open to the breezes and its walls are brightened by local murals. All the breads and desserts, including ice cream and sorbet, are made fresh daily on the premises. You might start with Barnes Bay lobster cakes and homemade tomato tartar sauce, or creamy conch chowder flavored with smoked bacon and chockfull of onions and potatoes. Grilled local crayfish is splashed with lime, curry, and coconut; chicken is barbecued with rum; and snapper filet is marinated in a soy-sesame-tahini mix, but the simple grilled fish with lemon-and-herb butter shines. If you want to dine with (or without) music, find out whether live music is planned during your visit.

Seaside Grill, Barnes Bay. ℂ 264/497-6479. Reservations required for dinner. Main courses $26–$45. AE, MC, V. Wed–Mon 6:30–9pm. Closed Aug–Oct.

Straw Hat ✿✿ ASIAN/CARIBBEAN

The island's only restaurant built not just near, not just by, but *over* the sea, the Straw Hat has a panoramic setting and vistas across to French St. Martin. Perched on wooden pilings driven deep into the sea bed, this place is about as pretty a spot as you'll find. We've had great meals here and some not-so-great ones. Some dishes, like the jerk pork tenderloin and curried goat, are traditional island favorites; others are more eclectic, like the seared Anguillian red snapper with a lime, ginger, and saffron sauce or the pan-roasted duck breast with passionfruit demi-glace. The garlic-mashed potatoes are terrific. A cilantro, lime, and pecan pesto pasta can be served with your choice of grilled chicken, tuna, or red snapper. For dessert, order the chocolate lava cake with lavender crème Anglaise or ginger crème brûlée.

Forest Bay. ℂ 264/497-8300. www.strawhat.com. Reservations recommended. Main courses $25–$44. AE, DC, MC, V. Mon–Sat 6:30–9:30pm; closed Sun and Mon in low season. Closed Sept–Oct.

Trattoria Tramonto ✿✿ (Kids) NORTHERN ITALIAN

This favorite of many, serving great Italian food, is on the West End tip of the island. There's even a Bellini, to make Italy lovers remember the ones they drank at Harry's Bar in Venice. The chef takes special care with his appetizers, including a *zuppa di pesce* (fish soup with porcini mushrooms) and spicy hot penne with a garlic, tomato, and red-pepper sauce. The house specialty is a sublime lobster-filled ravioli. Rumor has it that Denzel Washington enjoyed his meal, and that Robert De Niro was pretty happy, too. So are kids, who are treated like celebs here.

Shoal Bay West. © **264/497-8819.** www.trattoriatramonto.com. Reservations required. Main courses lunch $10–$30, dinner $25–$40. MC, V. Tues–Sun noon–3pm and 6:30–9pm. Closed Sept–Oct.

Zurra 🐾🐾 *Kids* MEDITERRANEAN/CARIBBEAN   The newest restaurant from the Blanchards is an instant classic, looking like a whitewashed Greek villa on the outside and blasted with sunny colors on the inside. The setting is gorgeous, overlooking the Greg Norman golf course at Temenos, and the seating is elegantly casual and supremely comfortable. The spacing is generous; tables are not bunched together, so you really feel like you occupy a special place in the Zurra universe. Service is exemplary. You might want to start with the insouciantly named lobster shooter, fat pieces of lobster with tomato-sherry sauce. The iced shellfish platter comes with lobster, shrimp, crayfish, clams, and oysters. The menu is loaded with local fish flavored with innovative Mediterranean sauces and plenty of U.S.D.A prime cuts of meat to satisfy the hungry-man golfers who stop in. This place has very charming ways of making children feel welcome, such as cookie dough cut out in the shapes of fish or boats. Before the meal begins, kids are given the cookie dough to decorate with colorful sprinkles—then into the oven they go and at the end of the meal, *voila!:* before them, their own personally decorated cookie.

Temenos Golf Club, Rendezvous Bay. © **264/222-8300.** www.zurrarestaurant.com. Reservations recommended. Main courses $33–$49. AE, MC, V. Daily noon–3pm and 6:30–9:15pm. Closed Sept–Oct.

MODERATE

Cote Mer Restaurant 🐾🐾 FRENCH/CREOLE   As soon as I got back to Anguilla in January 2008, I started hearing good things about a new restaurant tucked into a palm grove on the beach at Island Harbour. If there's such a thing as rustic elegance, Cote Mer embodies it. This indoor-outdoor place is almost absurdly picturesque, with a traditional Anguillian open-sided boat, fringed by seagrapes, beached beside the entrance. Just reading the menu is a

Sun, Sand, Music & Barbecue

Anguilla has a number of teriffic casual beach bar/restaurants, most of which have live music at least once a week. You can have a light meal and a drink for around $20. These places are about as casual as casual can be, but remember, this is modest Anguilla; if you've been swimming, cover up before you sit down to eat. At Upper Shoal Bay, check out **Gwen's Reggae Bar & Grill** (© **264/497-2120**), which features Gwen Webster's barbecue daily into the early evening; on Sunday it showcases live reggae performances. I love Gwen's barbecued chicken and her special slaw. The palm grove here is one of the few naturally shady seaside spots on the island, and it comes with hammocks. At the more populated end of Shoal, island institution **Uncle Ernie's** (© **264/497-3907**) is open from morning 'til at least sunset most evenings, serving up generous plates of chicken and ribs, fresh fish, fries, slaw and cold Red Stripe beer. Uncle Ernie died in 2007, but a wonderful photograph of him watches over the action here. At the west end of the island, a sign points off the main road down a bumpy road to Nat Richardson's **Palm Grove Bar & Grill** (© **264/497-4224**) at Junk's Hole. Islanders and visitors flock here for what many think are Anguilla's most succulent grilled lobsters and lightest johnny cakes. Bring your swimming gear and snorkel until your lobster comes off the grill. Over at Sandy Ground, another island favorite, **Johnno's** (© **264/497-2728**; closed Mon), has live music most Wednesday evenings (reggae and soca) and Sunday afternoons (jazz). Burgers and grills are available all day, or you can just order a rum punch, plop down at one of the picnic tables on the beach, and watch the spectacular Sandy Ground sunset. A few minutes' stroll down the beach is the new guy in town, **Elvis'** (© **264/461-0101**), which opened in 2007 and is giving Johnno's

pleasure: there's local crayfish—but here served in a decidedly French champagne sauce. The wide variety of sauces on the menu are so tempting that I've had a fantasy of having a perfectly sautéed grouper or red snapper served up with an medley of sauces (garlic cream sauce, garlic Pernod butter sauce, lemon butter, and leek cream some sunset competition. Elvis' bar occupies an Anguillian boat beached on the sand, with tables and chairs nearby. There's great rum punch and nibbles (sometimes barbeque) and live music several times a week. Half-way between Johnno's and Elvis, overlooking the Salt Pond, the **Pump-house** (✆ **264/497-5154;** www.pumphouse-anguilla.com; closed Sun) has rafter-shaking live music almost every night, the best cheeseburgers on the island, crisp Caesar salads, and dynamite rum punches. As you may soon find out, one Pumphouse rum punch is equivalent to at least two anywhere else! This former rock-salt factory, with some of its original machinery still in place, is the funkiest (what is that pair of downhill skis doing leaning against a ship's figurehead?) bar on the island—unless that award should go to Bankie Banx's **Dune Preserve** (✆ **264/497-2660;** www.dune preserve.com) at Rendezvous Bay, with its own salvaged boats and the island's most seriously relaxed musician. Reggae star Bankie Banx is usually in attendance and joins in the live music performances here several times a week. In 2008, Bankie added a seaside restaurant presided over by Dale Carty, chef extraordinaire at Tasty's, serving light lunches (try the zippy marinated conch and snapper salad), dune burgers, and onion rings, and—in honor of Bankie's vegetarianism—a veggie *plat du jour* that you order by asking the waiter "What's Bankie Eating Today?" Heading from Bankie's toward the east end of the island, keep an eye out for the small sign that points from the main road to **Smokey's** (✆ **264/497-6582**) at Cove Bay. Delicious crayfish, lobster (and lobster rolls), ribs, spicy wings, and curried chicken or goat are served up most days.

sauce). But I'd want to save room for dessert, perhaps just one perfect crème caramel.

Cote Mer, Island Harbour. ✆ **264/498-2683.** www.cotemer-anguilla.com. Main courses $15–$35. MC, V. Mon–Sat noon–3pm and 7–10pm Wed night. Closed Sun).

⌒ *Tips* **Roadside Eats**

Especially on the weekends, you'll notice a number of **roadside food stalls** in the Valley near the outdoor People's Market (a great place to get fresh fruit and veggies) and around the roundabout by the school and library. Out on the island, you may see other food stalls, often doing barbeque in grills fashioned out of oil drums. This is a great way to sample such local delicacies as bull foot soup, pigtail soup, goat water, roti, and fungi. Keep an eye out for **Hungry's,** the mobile food van that is usually parked near the Post Office in the Valley. You can eat yourself silly on sandwiches, wraps, curries, or stews, usually for a good deal less than $10.

Tasty's ⓕⓕ CARIBBEAN/AMERICAN   Set inside a Creole cottage painted in teals, blues, and lavenders is Dale Carty's uplifting hymn to the local cuisine. It's located on the right as you head through South Hill along the main road toward the East End. On the walls are colorful island murals by artist Susan Croft as well as framed magazine articles about Carty (*Bon Appetit,* no less). Trained in international cuisine in the kitchen in Malliouhana, the award-winning chef also has a hand in the new restaurant at Bankie Banx's Dune Preserve. The food is consistently, well, *tasty:* Pumpkin soup is delicious, the fish are always fresh, and the pasta dishes are varied. I highly recommend the seafood salad. Tasty's shrimp are sautéed in coconut curry sauce and served with a sweet potato puree. This is a great place for Sunday morning breakfast brunch ($20 a person), with an all-you-can-eat menu that includes a fruit bowl, boiled or fried eggs, saltfish and eggplant, pancakes, French toast, johnny-cakes, meat, flying fish, and sausages. You're not on the sea—you're on a main road with views of passing traffic, in fact—but the bright pastels of the interior remind you that you are in the Caribbean.

South Hill. ⓒ 264/497-2737. www.tastysrestaurant.com. Dinner reservations recommended. Main courses $18–$30. AE, MC, V. Tues–Sun 7:30am–3pm and 7–10pm.

INEXPENSIVE

E's Oven ⓕ *Finds* CARIBBEAN/INTERNATIONAL   Darting from beach to beach, it's easy to neglect some of Anguilla's inland restaurants. This place at South Hill (by the big curve in the main road) is very popular with locals, and when you eat here, you'll know why. The coconut-flavored pumpkin soup and garlic-crusted crayfish tails are yummy, and the seafood pasta is one of the main reasons some friends of mine say they keep coming back to Anguilla! The dining room is simple, with tables and chairs, nothing fancy, but perfectly pleasant.

South Hill. ☎ 264/498-8258. Main courses $10–$20. MC, V. Wed–Mon 11am–midnight.

Ripples ★★ *Value* CARIBBEAN/INTERNATIONAL   This is where the island's British community heads to watch cricket on the flatscreen TV and American expats congregate for Super Bowl Sunday. Set in a restored clapboard house, Ripples has a raised deck, comfy wicker chairs, a casual West Indian decor, and a nightly crowd of regulars and drop-ins (including Brad Pitt and Jennifer Aniston the night before they announced their separation). You can get anything from a burger to fresh local fish—mahimahi, snapper, tuna, and grouper—prepared any way you like. Specialties include puffy brie in beer batter, traditional fish 'n chips, and cottage pie. The weekly early-bird special offering a choice of three entrees (usually one veggie, one seafood, and one traditional English roast) for $15 is one of the island's best bargains. The bar scene gets increasingly lively as the night wears on, especially when yachties come ashore to unwind. No matter how late it gets, owner Jacquie Ruan and her staff make everyone feel at home.

Sandy Ground. ☎ 264/497-3380. Dinner reservations recommended. Main courses $15–$25. MC, V. Daily noon–midnight.

4 Beaches

Superb beaches are what put Anguilla on the tourist map. There are dozens of them, plus another handful on offshore islets, like Sandy Isle and Prickly Pear. I love Anguilla's limestone and scrub interior, its roaming goats, salt ponds teeming with birds, and the wildflowers that spring up after the rains. Still, let's face it, it's the beaches that bring us here. Miles and miles of pristine, powdery-soft sands open onto crystal-clear waters. As new roads are built, fewer beaches are reached via the bone-jarring dirt paths that make some of us nostalgic for the old days of, well, 10 or 20 years ago. For now, keep in mind that all beaches—even those of the fanciest resorts—are open to the public. That said, many locals and old-timers are increasingly unhappy at how many beaches are becoming the *de facto* preserve of new resorts.

Most of the best beaches (Barnes, Maundays, Meads, Rendezvous Bay, Shoal Bay West) are on the west end of the island, site of the most expensive hotels. **Rendezvous Bay** ☆☆☆ is still the best of the west end bunch, a long, curving ribbon of satiny, pale gold sand that stretches along the bay for 4km (2½ miles). This may change once (some say *if*) the much-ballyhooed Rendezvous Bay resort complex gets off the ground. For now, you will probably have to enter the beach from the public access near the Anguilla Great House or Bankie Banx's Dune Preserve—and pray that future construction does not ruin this beach forever.

In the northeast, 3km (2-mile) **Shoal Bay** ☆☆☆ is Anguilla's most popular beach, a Caribbean classic, with silver-white, powder-soft sands and a backdrop of sea-grapes. This beach is often called Shoal Bay East to distinguish it from Shoal Bay West (see below). The waters are luminous, brilliantly blue, and populated by enough fish to make most casual snorkelers happy. At noon the sands are blindingly white, but at sunrise and sunset they turn a pink to rival any beach in Bermuda. Rental umbrellas, beach chairs, and other equipment are available just behind Uncle Ernie's at the long-established, amazingly helpful **Skyline Beach Rentals** (② 264/497-8644) from brothers Calvin, Raymond, and Solomon. And, no trip to Anguilla is really complete without at least one order of ribs (washed down with a Ting or a Red Stripe) at Uncle Ernie's.

Shoal Bay West ☆ has pristine white sands tinged with pink opening onto the southwest coast. Visitors find deluxe accommodations, including Covecastles, and superior snorkeling at its western tip. Adjoining it is 1.5km-long (1-mile), white-sand **Maundays Bay** ☆☆, site of Cap Juluca and justifiably one of the island's most popular shorelines, with gentle surf for good snorkeling and swimming. Though the waters are luminescent and usually calm, sometimes the wind blows enough to attract windsurfers and sailboats. Most days, you see St. Martin across the way; some days, you see the pointy peak of Saba in the distance.

Sandy Isle, on the northwest coast, is a tiny islet with a few palms surrounded by a coral reef, a beach bar and restaurant, and a place to rent snorkeling gear and buy underwater cameras. During the high season, a speedboat from **Sandy Ground** (which has its own long sand beach) brings visitors back and forth to Sandy Isle almost hourly from around 9am to 4pm.

The northwest coast has a number of other beaches worth seeking out, notably the glittering white stretch of **Barnes Bay** beneath a

Moments Grilled Lobster on a Remote Cay

At Island Harbour, just go out on the pier and wave your arms (or dial © **264/497-5123**) and a boatman will pick you up and transport you across the water to **Scilly Cay,** pronounced "silly key." You wouldn't really call this place an island; it's more like a spit of sand 150m (500 ft.) off the coast of the main island's northeastern shore. At Eudoxie and Sandra Wallace's **Gorgeous Scilly Cay,** a glorified tiki hut, you can select a fabulous fresh spiny lobster or crayfish (you can also opt for chicken or veggies). What you chose is grilled while you wait, marinated in a sauce of honey-laced orange juice, orange marmalade, roasted peanuts, virgin olive oil, curry, and tarragon. You can scuba around the nearby reefs or just relax and watch the pelicans dive for fish. Lunch is daily Tuesday to Sunday from noon to 3pm, with live music Wednesdays and Sundays. This is a place to laze away the day; by the time you leave, you may have spent $100 per person—but what a day.

bullying bluff. You can admire the offshore islands silhouetted against the horizon or join the windsurfers and snorkelers.

Little Bay Beach ⊕ is at the foot of Anguilla's steepest cliffs. The sands are not the characteristic Anguillian white but, well, *sandy.* That said, none of us who have been there, including serious birdwatchers, snorkelers, and scuba divers, seems to mind. (We do mind when day-trippers from St. Martin come over and occupy the beach.) You can get a boat here most days from about 9am to 4pm from Crocus Bay for around $10 round trip. You can also climb down (and back up) the cliff at Little Bay, holding onto a knotted rope that is bolted into the cliff; I have done this, and do not recommend it for anyone who, like me, has trouble with heights (and is suspicious of the strength of a knotted rope).

Sandy Ground (aka **Road Bay**), also on the northwest coast, paints an idyllic old-time Caribbean scene, right down to meandering goats, spectacular sunsets, and clear blue waters, often dotted with yachts coming from St. Martin and beyond. You can watch fishermen and lobstermen set out in fishing boats as brightly colored as children's finger paints. **Johnno's** is arguably the archetypal beach bar, serving burgers and grilled fish and rocking at night. Indeed, many of the weathered wooden Antillean houses around here shaded

by turpentine trees and oleander hold casual bars, making Sandy
Ground Party Central on Friday nights. **Island Harbor** is still a
working fishing port, with island-made boats bobbing by the pier.
For centuries Anguillians have set out from these shores to haul in
spiny lobster, which are still cooked up here at **Smitty's** (© 264/
497-4300). It was Smitty who set up generators and started the tradition of live music and grilled lobster at his toes-in-the-water
restaurant here back in the 1970s before Anguilla had electricity.
Islanders of a certain age remember walking for hours to get to
Smitty's on the weekend to hear the music—and then walking back
home after dark by the light of the moon.

Savannah Bay (aka Junk's Hole) ⦚ offers a long stretch of
uncrowded white sand and offshore reefs full of eels, squid, and
manta rays. The one big attraction here is Nat Richardson's **Palm
Grove Bar & Grill** (seemingly the only building for miles), with its
perfectly boiled or grilled lobster, crayfish, or shrimp. Chances are
you'll have **Captain's Bay** ⦚ all to yourself. Here's why: There's no
shade and the undertow is very dangerous. The rock formations are
starkly beautiful, but this is a spot for a stroll, *not* a swim.

5 Sports & Other Outdoor Pursuits

CRUISES & BOATING At Sandy Ground, **Sandy Island Enter-
prises** (© 264/476-6534), **Island Yacht Charters** (© 264/497-
3744), and **Gotcha! Garfield's Sea Tours** (© 264/235-7902) all
rent boats and arrange fishing excursions. They can advise you on
the best beaches for a quiet swim, or where the fish are.

FISHING Your hotel can arrange for you to cast your line with a
local guide, but you should bring your own tackle. Agree on the cost
before setting out, however, to avoid the "misunderstandings" that
are commonly reported.

GOLF The 18-hole, par-72 Greg Norman–designed **Temenos
Golf Course,** between Long and Rendezvous bays (© 264/497-
7000), has a 111-hectare (274-acre) site that by 2008 will include a
luxury spa and residential complex (the first three villas are utterly
splendid and stratospherically priced). Bill Clinton has already
played here, and so can you, for green fees of around $400. Check
with your hotel desk or the tourist office for the latest details on this
development.

HORSEBACK RIDING First-time and advanced riders can go
horseback riding on the beach or "through the bush" with **Seaside**

Stables, located at Paradise Drive (next to Paradise Cove in western Anguilla), Cove Bay (© **264/235-3667;** www.seaside-stables.com). Rates for beach rides are $60 per hour/person; half-hour pony rides to the beach $35; moonlight rides $85; rides including a swim on horseback $80/hour. Call for current ride times.

SCUBA DIVING & SNORKELING   Most of the coastline is fringed by coral reefs, and the crystalline waters are rich in marine life, with sunken coral gardens, brilliantly colored fish, caves, mini-walls, greenback turtles, and stingrays. Conditions for scuba diving and snorkeling are ideal (check out www.scuba.ai for some helpful information). Over the years, the government of Anguilla has artificially enlarged the existing reef system, a first for the Caribbean. Battered and outmoded ships, deliberately sunk in carefully designated places, act as nurseries for fish and lobster populations and provide new dive sites. At **Stoney Ground Marine Park,** off the northeast coast, you can explore the ruins of a Spanish galleon that sank in the 1772. Offshore cays **(Anguillita, Prickley Pear, Sandy Isle, Scrub)** offer pristine conditions.

At Sandy Ground, ask around for PADI-trained **Douglas Carty** (© **264/235-8438** or 264/497-4567; dougcarty@antuillanet.com), who has been taking visitors on scuba excursions for many years; single tank dive costs from $50. At Meads Bay, **Anguillian Divers** (© **264/497-4750;** axadiver@caribcable.com), is a one-stop dive shop that answers most diving needs. PADI instructors are on hand, with a two-tank dive costing $70, plus another $10 for equipment. Another good choice is **Shoal Bay Scuba & Water Sports** (© **264/497-4101;** mjb@anguillanet.com), with a custom-built, state-of-the-art boat. A two-tank dive costs $80, plus $10 for equipment. They also provide windsurfer rentals and lessons. Both offer packages of three to five dives at deep discounts.

Several places, such as long-established **Skyline Beach Rentals** (© **264/497-8644**) at Shoal Bay, rent snorkeling gear, if your hotel doesn't provide it. The snorkeling's great at Shoal Bay, Maundays Bay, Barnes Bay, Little Bay, and Road Bay.

TENNIS   Once it's completed, the state-of-the-art **Anguilla Tennis Academy** (www.anguillatennis.com) will feature a pro shop, locker rooms, gym, and six lighted courts modeled after those at the U.S. Open facility in Flushing Meadows, New York. You can get lessons, hit with the pros, or have your racket strung. Most of the resorts have their own tennis courts (see "Accommodations," earlier

---

Anguilla's (Second) National Sport

If it weren't for boat racing, **cricket** would be Anguilla's national sport. Anguillians take cricket very seriously, following the success of local teams whether they play on or off the island. If you're lucky, you can catch a game at the **Ronald Webster Park** in the Valley; the island's best-known player is Omari Banx, a son of musician Bankie Banx.

---

in this chapter). **Malliouhana,** Meads Bay (© 264/497-6111), has a pro shop and four championship Laykold tennis courts. All courts are lit for night games.

6 Exploring Anguilla

The best way to get an overview of the island (if you don't have local friends) is on a **taxi tour.** In about 2 hours, a local driver (all of them are guides) will show you everything for around $60 (tip expected). The driver will also arrange to let you off at your favorite beach after a look around, and then pick you up and return you to your hotel or the airport. I highly recommend **Accelyn Connor** (© 264/497-0515 or 264/235-8931; premiertaxiandtour@hotmail.com), whose personable and informative tours make him a sought-after guide. His Premier Property Tour includes drinks (including beer), snacks, and admission to the museum ($140 for first 4 people; $20 each additional person).

It's easy to combine a great lunch at the Palm Grove Bar & Grill at Junk's Hole with a visit to the **Heritage Museum Collection** ✸, East End at Pond Ground (© 264/497-4092), open Monday to Saturday 10am to 5pm, charging $5 admission ($3 children 11 and under). The modest look of the museum belies the range of fascinating artifacts inside, which include Arawak Indian tools, slave shackles, and household items belonging to 19th-century settlers. If Mr. Colville Petty, who founded the museum, is here when you visit, you will have an especially memorable visit—he collected many of these artifacts himself and was awarded an OBE from Queen Elizabeth II.

Ask locally whether former chief minister Sir Emile Gumbs, an Anguilla National Trust volunteer, has resumed his delightful **eco-tours** (© 264/497-2711) spiked with wonderful, often wry historical and political anecdotes every Tuesday morning at 10am. Tours explore the Sandy Ground area, with stops at the recently restored 1900 "Manse," Old Salt Factory, and pink-tinged Salt Pond ("salting" was once Anguilla's economic mainstay) to view migratory fowl from pintails to peregrines. A $10 contribution for the Anguilla National Trust is usual.

7 Shopping

For serious shopping (Gucci, Louis Vuitton, and the like), take the ferry (see earlier in this chapter) and visit the shops in Marigot on French St. Martin. St. Martin is also a good place to stock up on French wines and cheeses if you're planning a long stay on Anguilla.

Clothes are not cheap on Anguilla, and the hotel boutiques do not go out of their way to stock bargains. If you need an extra bathing suit, or some beach gear, try **Irie** (© 264/498-6526) on the cliff-side road at South Hill. Even if you don't buy anything, you'll get a fantastic view down to Sandy Ground.

Anguilla has a thriving local arts and crafts scene. In the Valley, the **Anguilla Arts and Crafts Center** (© 264/497-2200) has paintings and ceramics by local artists, as well as embroidery and some lovely cloth dolls. For a good selection of paintings by Anguillian and Caribbean artists, try the **Savannah Gallery** ⋒, Coronation Street, Lower Valley (© 264/497-2263; www.savannahgallery.com), on the road to Crocus Bay. **Devonish Art Gallery** ⋒, in its new, larger location in Long Bay opposite CuisinArt Road (© 264/497-2949), features the work of Courtney Devonish, the well-known Anguillian potter and sculptor, as well as a good collection of paintings from local artists. **Cheddie's Carving Studio,** West End Road, the Cove (© 264/497-2949; www.cheddieonline.com), is the domain of self-taught Cheddie Richardson, who sculpts intricate, whimsical figures from driftwood, stone, and coral. By the roundabout at South Hill, **Bartlett Collections** has island crafts (as well as terrific smoothies at the outdoor café).

As you explore the island, you'll notice a surprising number of small art galleries. That's because Anguilla has a number of talented resident artists from around the world. One of the best is American **Lynne Bernbaum** (© 264/497-5211; www.lbernbaum.ai), whose George Hill studio features her bold images of Anguilla, the Caribbean, and France. In addition to paintings, Ms. Bernbaum sells prints of her works, including some very Anguillian cactuses and goats.

8 Anguilla After Dark

Nightlife aimed at visitors to Anguilla centers mainly on the various hotels, especially in winter when they host barbecues, West Indian parties, and singers and other musicians. The hotels hire calypso combo groups and string bands, both local and imported. For more impromptu, local music, ask around when you get to Anguilla. Also remember the island's wonderful beach bars and grills, which serve great food and drink and feature live music at least one day a week. For a rundown on the perpetual favorites, see "Sun, Sand, Music & Barbecue," earlier in this chapter.

You might also check out another weekend hot spot, the **Red Dragon Disco,** the Valley (© **264/497-2687**), where dancers gyrate to the latest recorded music. And try to find out where and when popular steel pan musician **Dumpa** is playing when you're on Anguilla; you'll be glad you did.

Keep in mind that Anguilla has no casinos or other gambling spots—the local Church Council, which has its say in matters such as this, ensures that the island stays that way. If you feel the need for some casino action, St. Maarten and its 14 sizzling casinos are just a 20-minute ferry ride (and a short cab ride from there) away.

9

St. Barthélemy

St. Barts: Two words practically synonymous with glitz, glamour, and gorgeous beaches. This is the French Riviera in the Caribbean, as eternally chic as a little black dress and every bit as pricey. St. Barts has its historic sites and thrilling aquatic activities, but visitors go for pampering without pomp, inimitable French flair, world-class beaches, and the promise of eternal sun and blue skies (it rarely rains). It's a place where mega-yachts preen for other mega-yachts, where the well-heeled come to chase eternal youth under the tropical sun. Yet despite its reputation as a playground for the rich, casual dress—sandals, sarongs, tousled hair, bangles, little else—prevails, though the sandals are likely Manolo and the bangles 24-karat gold.

New friends call this tiny island "St. Barts," while old-time visitors prefer "St. Barths," short for St. Barthélemy (San Bar-te-le-*mee*), named by its discoverer Columbus in 1493. With its arid climate and poor rocky soil ill-suited to sugar production, St. Barts never developed a slave-based agro-economy. Most longtime residents are descendants of Breton and Norman fisherfolk, intermingled with Swedes (whose colonial influence lingers in place names), as evidenced by their fair skin, blond hair, and blue eyes. The year-round population of about 8,500 occupies just 21 sq. km (8¼ sq. miles), but the distances seem longer because of the folds and creases of the hilly topography and the hairpin-turn roads.

Despite an influx of young French arrivals, the old ways endure. Many locals still speak 18th-century Norman, Breton, or Poitevin dialect. In little **Corossol,** you might glimpse wizened *grand-mères* wearing the traditional starched white bonnets known as *quichenottes* (a corruption of "kiss-me-not"), which discouraged the close attentions of English or Swedish men on the island. The bonneted women can also be spotted at local celebrations, particularly on August 25, **St. Louis's Day.** Many of these women are camera-shy, but they offer their homemade baskets and hats for sale to visitors.

For a long time, the island was a paradise for a handful of millionaires, such as David Rockefeller, who had a hideaway on the northwest shore, and Edmond de Rothschild, whose compound graces the "other end" of the island. Development was inevitable, but perhaps conscious that the in crowd is always decamping for other hot spots, the island diligently maintains its quaintness, natural warmth, and quiet exclusivity. It has almost an old-fashioned storybook quality, with gaily painted gingerbread houses tucked into hillsides and flower boxes spilling over with colorful blooms. Picturesque Swedish cemeteries are ringed by white picket fences. Cruise ships are discouraged and there are no sterile high-rises or all-inclusives. Indeed, new hotels are restricted to 12 rooms maximum (the largest by far offers only 68). Nevertheless, the A-List, who need only be identified by first name (Brad, Beyoncé, Tom, Harrison), still makes a beeline to its golden coves—or to clamber aboard the superyachts bobbing just offshore. In February, the island guest list reads like a roster from *Lifestyles of the Rich and Famous,* seeking discrete privacy and refuge from personal trainers and stalking paparazzi (the latter often unsuccessfully).

1 Essentials

VISITOR INFORMATION

For information before you go, contact the **French Government Tourist Office** (*©* **202/659-7779;** www.franceguide.com). There are offices at 444 Madison Ave., New York, NY 10022 (*©* **212/745-0960**); 9454 Wilshire Blvd., Suite 715, Beverly Hills, CA 90212 (*©* **310/271-6665**); and 205 N. Michigan Ave., Suite 3770, Chicago, IL 60601 (*©* **312/327-0290**).

On the island, go to the **Office Municipal du Tourisme** adjacent to La Capitanerie (the Port Authority Headquarters) on the pier, quai du Général-de-Gaulle (*©* **590/27-87-27;** no website).

The unofficial source for information on the web is www.st.-barths. com. The web-only *Insider's Guide to St. Barths* (www.sbhonline. com) offers details on arts, dining, shopping, and nightlife listings, as well as constructive readers' forums and trip reports.

ISLAND LAYOUT & NEIGHBORHOODS

St. Barts lies 24km (15 miles) southeast of St. Martin and 225km (140 miles) north of Guadeloupe. The island's capital and only seaport is enchanting **Gustavia,** named for a Swedish king. This dollhouse-scale port rings a splendid harbor where little fishing boats bob alongside sleek yachts. Its narrow streets—lined with 18th-century Swedish or French stone buildings housing gourmet eateries,

St. Barthélemy

HOTELS

Carl Gustaf **21**
Eden Rock **6**
Hostellerie des Trois Forces **14**
Hôtel Guanahani and Spa **11**
Hôtel St. Barth Isle de France **2**
La Normandie **15**
Le P'tit Morne **1**
Le Sereno **12**
Le Toiny **13**
Le Village St-Jean **19**
Les Ilets de la Plage **3**
Les Mouettes **8**
Les Ondines **12**
Salines Garden Cottages **16**
Tropical Hôtel **19**

RESTAURANTS

Au Port **23**
Bar'tó **11**
Eddy's **25**
The Hideaway **4**
L'Esprit Saline **17**
La Mandala **22**
La Plage **5**
La Route des Boucaniers **25**
Le Gaïac **13**
Le Sapotillier **23**

Le Tamarin **18**
Maya's **27**
Wall House **24**

NIGHTLIFE

Bar de' l'Oubli **26**
Bar'Tó **11**
Do Brazil **20**
Le Bête à Z'Ailes **26**
Le Select **26**
Le Ti St. Barth **9**
Nikki Beach (Casa Nikki) **7**
Taïno Lounge **10**
The Yacht Club **24**

SHOPS

Diamond Genesis **25**
Gold Fingers **26**
La Ligne St. Barth **15**
L'Atelier de Fabienne Miot **26**
Laurent Eiffel **25**
Le Comptoir du Cigare **25**
Les Artisans **25**
Made in St.-Barth **4**
St. Barts Style **25**
Stéphane & Bernard **26**
SUD, SUD **4**

galleries, chic boutiques, and an excellent **Municipal Museum**—are easily explored on foot. Traveling northwest from Gustavia, you reach the typical villages of **Corossol** and **Colombier,** where women weave lantana straw handicrafts from hats to handbags in cotton-candy-colored *cazes* (traditional wooden houses) garlanded with flowerpots and fishing nets.

Right by the airport, **St-Jean** is the closest thing to a resort town: a tropic St-Tropez, brimming with smart boutiques and beachfront bistros. A few minutes' drive east is serene **Lorient,** site of the first French settlement with a popular locals' beach; beautifully adorned graveyards; 19th-century Catholic church, convent, and bell tower; and reconstructed 17th-century Norman manor. Further east, **Grand Cul-de-Sac** (Point Milou) is the island's second major resort center, its wide swath of sand surveyed by top-notch eateries.

GETTING THERE

One reason why St. Barts has retained its quaint character and isn't overrun by the masses is the simple fact of getting there. The flight from St. Maarten is just 10 minutes long, but for many people, landing on a tiny airstrip between two volcanic hills and braking mere feet from sunbathers on the beach is 10 minutes of terror. Those who go by boat or high-speed ferry have the unpredictable, sometimes stomach-churning seas to contend with. So you pick your poison.

BY PLANE   The makeshift landing strip at St-Jean airport on St. Barts is just 2,170 feet long. It accommodates only STOL (short takeoff and landing) aircrafts no bigger than 19-seaters. And even on these small planes, landing on St. Barts has often been compared (and not favorably) to touching down on an aircraft carrier. The pilot must divebomb between two mountains (one with a giant white Swedish cross), then pull up abruptly: no extra charge for the thrill ride. (In fact, any pilot who plans to land in St. Barts is required to qualify for a special permit first.) No landings or departures are permitted after dark.

There are no nonstop flights to St. Barts from North America. From the United States, the principal gateways are St. Maarten, St. Thomas, and Guadeloupe. **Tradewind Aviation** (© **800/376-7922;** www.tradewindaviation.com) offers two daily first-class charter flights to St. Barts from San Juan; the flight is an hour long and roundtrip cost (including taxes and surcharges) start at $395. At any of these islands, you can connect to St. Barts via interisland carriers.

/ Tips   **Airline Advice**

Always reconfirm your return flight from St. Barts with your interisland airline. If you don't, your reservation will be canceled. *Note:* On rare occasions, a flight will be rescheduled if the booking doesn't meet its fuel quota. Also, don't check your luggage all the way through to St. Barts, or you may not see it for a few days. Instead, check your bags to your gateway connecting destination (usually St. Maarten), then take your luggage to your interisland carrier and recheck it to St. Barts. Just in case pack a change of clothes, any required medicine, and a bathing suit in your carry-on.

Most people from the U.S. or Canada first fly to St. Maarten; for details on getting to St. Maarten, go to "Getting There: By Plane," in chapter 2. From St. Maarten, your best bet is **Windward Islands Airways International** (known by everybody as **Winair;** ② **866/466-0410** in the U.S. and Canada, or 590/27-61-01; www.fly-winair. com), which usually offers 10 to 20 daily flights to St. Barts. One-way passage costs around 64€ ($80)—but that figure excludes taxes and surcharges, which can more than double the cost. Flight duration is a mere 10 minutes.

St. Barth Commuter (② **590/27-54-54;** www.stbarthcommuter. com) flies four flights Monday through Saturday (two Sun) from L'Espérance Airport in Grand Case, St. Martin (one-way fares 60€/$90 adults, 45€/$68 children 2–11). It flies once daily from St. Maarten's Princess Juliana Airport (one-way fares 65€/$98 adults, 50€/$75 children 2–11).

Air Caraïbes (② **877/772-1005** in the U.S. and Canada, or 590/82-47-00 and 590/27-71-90; www.aircaraibes.com) flights depart four or five times a day from Pointe-à-Pitre's Pôle Caraïbes Aéroport in Guadeloupe. Roundtrip passage to St. Barts starts at 227€ ($340); trip time is 45 minutes.

BY BOAT   The **Voyager** vessels (② **590/87-10-68;** www.voyager-st-barths.com) make frequent (usually daily, sometimes twice a day) runs between St. Barts and either side of St. Maarten/St. Martin. The schedule varies according to the season (and the seas), but the *MV Voyager II* usually departs Marigot Harbor for St. Barts every morning and evening. *MV Voyager I* travels from Oyster Pond to Gustavia. Advance reservations are a good idea; fares run around 50€ to

58€ ($75–$87) adults, 30€ ($45) children 2–12 one way (plus taxes). The trip can take around 45 minutes and can be rough; it's recommended that those with queasy tummies take seasickness medication before the trip.

The technologically advanced, speedier, more luxurious, and stable 68-foot hydrofoil *Rapid Explorer* (© 590/27-60-33; www.st-barths.com/rapid-explorer) offers three daily 45-minute crossings between St. Maarten's Bobby's Marina in Philipsburg and Gustavia. Reservations are essential; the fare is 59€ ($89) adults, 47€ ($70) children one way (plus taxes).

GETTING AROUND

BY TAXI   Taxis meet all flights and are not very expensive, mostly because destinations aren't far from one another. Dial © 590/27-75-81 or 590/27-66-31 for taxi service. A typical rate, from the airport to Cul-de-Sac, is 20€ ($30). Fares between 8pm and 6am, and on Sundays and holidays are 50% higher. Taxi service must be arranged between midnight and 6am—call ahead. There are taxi stands at the St-Jean airport and in Gustavia.

The government imposes official fares on **tours by taxi.** Many travelers simply approach a likely looking taxi driver and ask him to show them around. The official rates for one to three passengers are 40€ ($60) for 45 minutes, 44€ ($66) for 60 minutes, and 60€ ($90) for 90 minutes. For four or more passengers, add 8€ ($12) to each of the above-mentioned prices.

BY RENTAL CAR   A rental car is highly recommended to get around the island and beach-hop like a local. You can reserve one yourself or have your hotel rent one for you, with your specifications, of course. A number of rental agencies are located at the airport, although most rental agencies are happy to deliver cars straight to your hotel or villa.

Star Location Car Rentals (© 690-42-28-42; www.star-loc.com) offers rates with a 1€=$1 equivalency—a great deal for Americans. It's located right at St-Jean Airport, with a wide range of rental cars, from automatic-drive Suzuki SUVs and four-wheel-drives to stickshift vans. Rates run from 38€ to 130€ a day, depending on the season. Also at the airport is **Gumbs Car Rental** (© 590/27-75-32), a longtime island car-rental company with a fleet of 65 cars; the reasonable rates start at around 20€ ($30) a day. Those with an itch to drive a Mini Cooper convertible around the island can rent one for around 120€ ($180) a day from **Pure Rental,** on Rue du Roi Oscar II, in Gustavia (© 590/27-64-76).

> **Tips Read All About It**
>
> The English-language *Saint-Barth Weekly* is an excellent resource for events and local gossip; you can also download the latest edition in a PDF file from the tourist office website. The bilingual *Ti Gourmet Saint-Barth* is a free, invaluable, pocket-size guidebook providing contact information, minireviews, and general prices of restaurants; pick one up almost anywhere.

Budget (✆ **800/472-3325** in the U.S., or 590/29-62-40; www.budget.com) rents various 4WD Suzukis and automatic Daihatsus for 60€ ($90) a day, with unlimited mileage. Be sure to reserve at least 3 business days before your arrival.

Hertz (✆ **800/654-3131** in the U.S. and Canada; www.hertz.com) operates on St. Barts through a local dealership, **Henry's Car Rental,** with branches at the airport and in St-Jean (✆ **590/27-71-14**). It offers open-sided Suzuki Samurais for 65€ ($97) a day, and more substantial Suzuki Sidekicks for 70€ to 90€ ($105–$135) per day.

At **Avis** (✆ **800/331-1212** in the U.S. and Canada, or 590/27-71-43; www.avis.com or www.avis-stbarth.com), you'll need a reservation a full month in advance during high season. In the winter, cars range from 68€ to 98€ ($102–$147) a day. In the off season, rentals are 44€ to 90€ ($66–$135) a day.

Note: For Budget, Hertz, and Avis, if you reserve your car in the U.S. you will be charged in dollars, not euros.

Driving is on the right and maximum speed is 50kph. Never drive with less than half a tank of gas on St. Barts. There are only two gas stations on the island, and both are closed on Sunday: one near the airport (open only 7:30am–noon and 2–7pm—with an all-night automatic pump that usually accepts MasterCard and Visa), the other in Lorient (open 7:30am–noon and 2–5pm). All valid foreign driver's licenses are honored. *Warning:* Honk your horn furiously while going around the island's blind corners to avoid having your fenders sideswiped. The corkscrewing roller coaster roads could make a Grand Prix racer blanch: Always inspect brakes and gears before accepting a vehicle.

BY MOTORBIKE & SCOOTER Denis Dufau operates two affiliates (✆ **590/27-70-59** and 590/27-54-83). A helmet is provided (helmets are required), and renters must either leave an imprint of a valid credit card or pay a deposit. Rental fees vary from 24€ to 35€ ($36–$52) per day, depending on the size of the bike. For all but the smallest models, presentation of a valid driver's license is required and you must be 21 or older.

FAST FACTS: St. Barthélemy

Banks The two main banks, both of which have **ATMs,** are: **Banque Française Commerciale,** rue du Général-de-Gaulle, Gustavia (© 590/27-62-62, or © 590/27-65-88 in St-Jean); and the **Banque Nationale de Paris,** rue du Bord de Mer (© 590/27-63-70). Open hours for both are Monday to Friday from 8am to noon and 2 to 3:30pm.

Currency As of press time 1€ equaled US$1.50. Before you leave home, check the current exchange rate on the web at **www.xe.com**.

Documents U.S. and Canadian citizens need a passport to enter St. Barts. If you're flying in, you'll need to present your return or ongoing ticket. Citizens of the European Union need only an official photo ID, but passports are always recommended.

Electricity The electricity is 220-volt AC (50 cycles); U.S.-made appliances will require adapter plugs and transformers.

Emergencies Dial © **17** for **police** or **medical** emergencies, © **18** for **fire** emergencies.

Hospital St. Barts is not the greatest place to find yourself in a medical emergency. Except for vacationing doctors escaping their own practices in other parts of the world, it has only seven resident doctors and about a dozen on-call specialists. The island's only hospital, with the only emergency facilities, is the **Hôpital de Bruyn,** rue Jean-Bart (© 590/27-60-35), about .4km (¼ mile) north of Gustavia. Serious medical cases are often flown to St. Maarten, Martinique, Miami, or wherever the person or his/her family specifies.

Language The official language is French, but English is widely spoken.

Pharmacies The **Pharmacie de Saint-Barth** is on quai de la République, Gustavia (© 590/27-61-82). Its only competitor is the **Pharmacie de l'Aéroport,** adjacent to the airport (© 590/27-66-61). Both are open Monday through Saturday from 8am to 7:30pm; on Sunday, one or the other remains open for at least part of the day.

Safety Crime is rare on St. Barts; it's one of the safest islands in the Caribbean. But it's always wise to protect your valuables. Don't leave them unguarded on the beach or in parked cars, even if locked in the trunk.

Taxes You're assessed a $5 departure tax if you're heading for another French island. Otherwise, you'll pay $10. Taxes are included in your airline ticket. There is no sales tax and no tax on restaurant meals.

Telephone St. Barts is linked to the Guadeloupe telephone system. To call St. Barts from the United States, dial **011** (the international access code), then **590** (the country code for Guadeloupe), then **590** again, and finally the six-digit local number. To make a call to anywhere in St. Barts from within St. Barts, dial only the six-digit local number, and ignore the prefix 590. Cellphones use the **690** prefix, then the six-digit number. To reach an AT&T operator from anywhere on the island, dial ℂ **0800-99-00-11.** To reach **MCI,** dial ℂ **0800-99-00-19,** and to reach **Sprint,** dial ℂ **0800-99-00-87.**

Time When standard time is in effect in the United States and Canada, St. Barts is 1 hour ahead of the U.S. East Coast and 4 hours behind Greenwich Mean Time. When daylight saving time is in effect in the United States, clocks in New York and St. Barts show the same time—5 hours behind Greenwich Mean Time.

Tipping Hotels usually add a service charge of 10% to 15%; always ask if this is included in the price you're quoted. Restaurants typically add a service charge, too. Taxi drivers expect a tip of 10% of the fare.

Water The water on St. Barts is generally safe to drink.

Weather The climate of St. Barts is ideal: dry with an average temperature of 72°F to 86°F (22°C–30°C).

2 Accommodations

Excluding the priciest hotels, most places here are homey, comfortable, and casual. In March, it's often difficult to find lodgings unless you've made reservations far in advance. Small surprise that accommodations in high season often exceed the cost of minor plastic surgery, nearly doubling during Christmas week; a service charge of 10% to 15% is usually added to your bill. Several properties close between August and October; off-season rates plummet and often include a rental car for stays of a week or more.

St. Barts has a sizable number of villas and apartments for rent by the week or month. Most are dotted around the island's hills—very few are on the beach. Instead of an oceanfront bedroom, you get a panoramic view (and usually a pool). Because beach-hopping is de rigueur, regardless of where you bunk, many regulars prefer the villa experience. One of the best agencies to contact for villa or condo rentals is **St. Barth Properties,** 693 E. Central St., Suite 201, Franklin, MA 02038 (© **800/421-3396** or 508/528-7727 in the U.S. and Canada; www.stbarth.com). Peg Walsh, a longtime St. Barts aficionado, and her capable son, Tom Smyth, will make arrangements for car rentals and air travel to St. Barts, then upon your arrival book babysitters, chefs, personal trainers, and restaurant reservations. Rentals can range from a one-room "studio" villa away from the beach for $980 per week off season, up to $40,000 per week for an antiques-filled minipalace at Christmas. Most rentals average between $2,500 and $4,000 a week between mid-December and mid-April, with discounts of 30% to 50% the rest of the year. Amenities vary according to villa, from built-in gyms to wine cellars to pools. Ms. Walsh can also arrange accommodations in all categories of St. Barts's hotels. Another excellent option with similar rates and services is **Wimco** (P.O. Box 1481, Newport, RI 02840; © **800/449-1553** or 401/847-6290; www.wimco.com), whose on-island partner, **Sibarth** (© **590/27-62-38;** www.sibarth.com), was founded 30 years ago by Brook and Roger Lacour. Rates and services are similar; Mrs. Lacour represents nearly 250 villas in every conceivable style (hilltop Spanish hacienda, postmodern beachfront stunner, or cozy *caze*) and size, from one to seven bedrooms.

Note: At press time the François Plantation was closed for renovations but was scheduled to reopen in late 2008 or early 2009. Go to www.francoisplantation.com for more information.

Up-and-coming: In the works is a 40-room luxury hotel on Grand Cul-de-Sac, the **Niilaaia Hotel Resort & Spa** (www.niilaaia. com). It is being built on the oceanfront site where the St. Barth Beach Hotel stood before it was razed.

VERY EXPENSIVE

Carl Gustaf ★★   *Note:* At press time the hotel was scheduled to reopen in late 2008 after an extensive half-year refurbishment. When it reopens, Gustavia's most glamorous hotel promises to be even more glam, with a newly designed restaurant, a state-of-the-art spa, and a new four-bedroom suite, the Royale Suite. The hotel oversees the town's harbor from a steep hillside. Each room is in one of a dozen pink or green, red-roofed villas. Access to each building is via a central staircase, which tests the stamina of even the most active guests. The wood-frame units are angled for maximum views of the boats bobbing far below in the bay and panoramic sunsets, best enjoyed from the plunge pool on the private patio bisecting each suite. Bedrooms are exceedingly well furnished and promise to be even more so at their grand unveiling. Guests walk across Italian marble floors under a pitched ceiling to reach their luxurious bed. Beaches are within a 10-minute walk.

Chef Emmanuel Motte has revitalized the classic French kitchen—and now it has a new redesign to match. The "Goose," as it's affectionately known, has always been *the* spot for sunset cocktails.

Rue des Normands, 97099 Gustavia, St. Barthélemy, F.W.I. © **800/322-2223** in the U.S., or 590/29-79-00. Fax 590/27-82-37. www.hotelcarlgustaf.com. 15 units. Winter 1,140€ ($1,710) 1-bedroom suite, 1,685€ ($2,527) 2-bedroom suite; off season from 640€–740€ ($960–$1,110) 1-bedroom suite, from 850€–1,050€ ($1,275–$1,575) 2-bedroom suite. Rates include continental breakfast and airport transfers. AE, MC, V. **Amenities:** Restaurant; piano bar; outdoor pool; health club; sauna; deep-sea fishing; sailing; scuba diving; water-skiing; windsurfing; room service; massage; laundry service; dry cleaning; nonsmoking rooms; helicopter rides. *In room:* A/C, TV/DVD, CD players, fax, dataport, Internet access, kitchenette, minibar, fridge, hair dryer, iron, safe.

Eden Rock 𝕽𝕽𝕽   Greta Garbo checked in as Suzy Schmidt for a 3-day holiday but ended up staying 3 weeks. That was long ago, but this legendary hotel still exerts a magnetic pull on the rich and fabulous. Eden Rock occupies the most glamorous site on St. Barts, a quartzite promontory cleaving St-Jean Bay into two perfect white-sand crescents. When the island's former mayor, Remy de Haenen, paid $200 for the land years ago from an old woman, she ridiculed him for paying too much. Today, the story is part of island lore.

In 1995, the new British and Zimbabwean owners David and Jane Spencer Matthews embarked on a continuing reinvention that transformed Eden Rock into one of the Caribbean's most glamorous addresses, where even celebrities people-watch. A $25-million renovation/expansion, completed in December 2006, absorbed the adjacent Filao Beach property without sacrificing intimacy or style. Individually decorated accommodations either climb the rock or are perched steps from the water on either side. The original "Rock" rooms are filled with antiques, family heirlooms, silver fixtures, steamer trunks, four-poster beds, and watercolors of local scenes by Jane (an accomplished artist herself) and her children. Larger suites might contrast lemon chairs with lavender throw pillows, or mauve walls with mahogany armoire and marble accents. The newer units include eight suites with decks opening onto the beach as well as five one- to three-bedroom beach houses with outdoor Jacuzzis and plunge pools (two have full swimming pools). The 450-sq.-m (1,500-sq.-ft.) **Howard Hughes Loft Suite,** atop the Main House on "the rock," features hardwood floors, three verandas offering 360-degree panoramas, and two bathrooms uniquely clad in welded copper. The newest luxury villa is **Villa Nina,** with two bedrooms and its very own art gallery, a private pool, and a beachside location. In the pipeline is the **Rockstar** villa, a stunner with four master suites, a screening room, a recording studio, a private pool, and a dedicated butler.

Getting plenty of buzz is the **Eden Rock Art Gallery,** opened by Jane Matthews to showcase local and international artists. She's delivered on the latter, big-time, with recent shows by such heralded artists as Richard Prince and Will Cotton.

The casual beachfront **Sand Bar** is a fabulous lunch spot with reliably delicious food. An equally incomparable dinner (and people-watching) is served at the swanky **On-The-Rocks Restaurant.**

Baie de St-Jean, 97133 St. Barthélemy, F.W.I. (© 877/563-7105 in the U.S., or 590/ 29-79-999. Fax 590/27-88-37. www.edenrockhotel.com. 33 units. Winter 665€– 985€ ($997–$1,477) double, 1,265€–3,065€ ($1,897–$4,597) suite/house; off season 475€–625€ ($712–$937) double, 760€–2,425€ ($1,140–$3,637) suite/ house. Rates include buffet breakfast, airport transfers, taxes, and service charges. AE, MC, V. **Amenities:** 2 restaurants; bar; snorkeling; windsurfing; room service; babysitting; laundry service; dry cleaning. *In room:* A/C, TV, dataport, minibar, hair dryer, safe.

Hôtel Guanahani and Spa (⭑⭑⭑ (Kids

St. Barts's largest hotel would be a jewel of a small boutique hotel anywhere else. Don't let its casual good nature fool you: Guanahani defines excellence. Service is as good here as you'll get anywhere, with the staff knowing what you need before you even know it yourself.

This award-winning hotel enjoys a spectacular situation on its own peninsula bracketed by two scenic beaches, one facing the Atlantic ocean, the other, the Grand Cul-de-Sac Bay, overlooking Marigot Bay. The resort looks compact, but it spills down a lush hillside to the spacious beach. And its spa, the Clarins Spa, is a world-class facility, with an herbal tea room and a good-size swimming pool. Of the resort's 68 rooms, 35 are suites—and 14 of those have private pools. Guanahani has six unique villas that offer the ultimate in space and privacy. Of these, the Pelican Suite is perfect for families; a pitched-roof cottage trimmed in gingergread details, with two bedrooms, two bathrooms, its own private backyard (with roving chickens), sweeping views of Grand Cul-de-Sac, and an outdoor hot tub. The ocean-view Marigot Suite has two bedrooms and private access to the spa and spa pool; the Wellness Suite also has private access to the spa. (Both the Marigot and Wellness villas have built-in spa packages.) Each villa comes with private butler service, which means every day is full of little surprises. After mentioning that we were planning an island beach-hopping trip, for example, we were delighted to find a basket full of beach goodies at our door: umbrella, towels, sunscreen—even printed directions to the St. Barts beaches.

The room interiors are a delight as well, with a bright lime-plum-and-turquoise color scheme that mirrors the surrounding gardens where butterflies and hummingbirds flit and flutter. Guanahani is not for those who have mobility problems or just don't relish huffing up and down steep slopes. There's a big variation in price, view, size, and decor, though all units have a private patio, the latest gadgetry from iPod docking stations to LCD flatscreen TVs, Bulgari and Clarins toiletries, and a brightly tiled, shower-only bathroom.

Though intimately scaled, Guanahani presents an amazing array of activities. The two restaurants, airy, alfresco **Indigo** and the formal (in the St. Barts sense of the word) **Bar'tó** (see "Dining," later in this chapter), offer creative continental cuisine. Staffers are remarkably cordial and beyond competent; little luxuries include chilled Bulgari towels in the airport shuttle. And kids are welcomed throughout the resort, with two children's programs (Kindergarten and Junior's) and a big toy box on the beach.

Grand Cul-de-Sac, 97133 St. Barthélemy, F.W.I. ℭ **800/223-6800** in the U.S., or 590/27-66-60. Fax 590/27-70-70. www.leguanahani.com. 68 units. Winter 580€–935€ ($870–$1,402) double, from 1,055€ ($1,582) suite; off season 350€–580€ ($525–$870) double, from 705€ ($1,057) suite. Extra person 100€ ($150). Rates include full American breakfast and round-trip airport transfers. AE, MC, V. **Amenities:** 2 restaurants; 3 bars; 2 outdoor pools; 2 tennis courts; fitness center; spa; Jacuzzi; boat rental; catamaran; canoes and paddleboats; fishing; sailing; scuba; windsurfing; children's programs (ages 2–12); car rental; salon; 24-hr. room service; babysitting; laundry service; dry cleaning; horseback riding; boutique. *In room:* A/C, ceiling fan, LCD flatscreen TV, DVD, Wi-Fi, minibar, hair dryer, safe, butler services (villas only).

Hôtel St. Barth Isle de France ✮✮✮ Effortless elegance distinguishes this family-run hotel, which continues to rack up awards ("Best Hotel in St. Barts": *Conde Nast Traveler U.K.*; "Top Five Hotels in the Caribbean": *Conde Nast Traveler U.S.*) for its luxurious, supremely comfortable lodging and excellent service. It opens right onto glorious Flamands beach. The architecture blends the richly saturated colors of Corsica with Caribbean and colonial New England influences. Guest rooms are unusually spacious for St. Barts. Each top-notch unit contains a private patio or terrace overlooking the pool, beach, or lavishly landscaped grounds. Individual decor marries antique mahogany and rattan furniture, contemporary *bergères* (wing chairs), local straw work, Limoges porcelain, dainty French fabrics, 19th-century engravings collected from neighboring islands, and the odd dramatic flourish (cherry red lampshade or magenta throw pillow). Beds are luxurious, fitted with fine linen. Commodious marble-clad bathrooms are well-equipped with dual basins, large tubs (some with whirlpool jets), and showers. For a sense of privacy, you might opt for the Tropical Villa, set in the hotel's tropical garden with its own private plunge pool; the Hillside Bungalow, which overlooks the gardens and has a terrace; and the Fisherman's Cottage, which has two en-suite bedrooms, a kitchenette, and its own interior courtyard.

The on-site Molton Brown Spa and quintessential beachfront *boîte*, **La Case de l'Isle** (sophisticated island-tinged French fare), complete the memorable experience.

97098 Baie des Flamands, St. Barthélemy, F.W.I. ℂ **800/810-4691** in the U.S., or 590/27-61-81. Fax 590/27-86-83. www.isle-de-france.com. 35 units. Winter 845€–1,280€ ($1,267–$1,920) double, from 1,545€ ($2,317) suite, from 1,065€ ($1,597) villa/bungalow/cottage; off season 525€–795€ ($787–$1,192) double, from 1,055€ ($1,582) suite, from 670€ ($1,005) villa/bungalow/cottage. Rates include continental breakfast and roundtrip airport transfer. AE, MC, V. Closed Sept 1–Oct 15. **Amenities:** Restaurant; bar; 2 freshwater pools; tennis court; gym; spa; car rental; 24-hr. room service; babysitting; laundry service. *In room:* A/C, TV, minibar, fridge, beverage maker, hair dryer, safe.

Le Sereno ✮ Lighting designer Arnold Chan (Miami's Delano, L.A.'s Mondrian) and French decorator Christian Liaigre (New York's Mercer) collaborated on the sleek, minimalist, "ethno-Zen" design aesthetic of this latest entrant in the super-deluxe category, which debuted in December 2005. Standard rooms are cramped (in great part due to trendily oversize beds) but include private minigardens; larger units offer private access to the resort's 180m (600-ft.) beachfront. Scandinavian and Asian influences predominate: white-on-white color scheme with wood accents, the severe geometry (elevated black granite square wash basins, triangular chrome lamps) softened by gauzy white curtains and plush armchairs. Add custom-made D. Porthault linens, Parisian toiletries, personal iPods and docking stations, flatscreen LCD TVs, in-room Wi-Fi access, individual parking spaces, not to mention beach beds and designer martini bar, and *voilà:* instant boutique hotel buzz. The **Restaurant des Pecheurs** is the on-site restaurant, serving fish fresh delivered to the hotel daily by local fishing boats. Highly touted is the restaurant's bouillabaisse, filled with fresh fish from the Mediterranean flown in every Thursday.

Grand Cul-de-Sac (B.P. 19), 97133 St. Barthélemy, F.W.I. ℂ **590/52-83-00.** Fax 590/27-75-47. www.lesereno.com. 37 units. Winter 680€–1,190€ ($1,120–$1,785) suite, 1,480€–2,180€ ($2,220–$3,270) villa; off season 480€–780€ ($720–$1,170) suite, 1,130€–1,780€ ($1,695—$2,670) villa. Rates include breakfast and airport transfers. AE, MC, V. Closed Sept—Oct. **Amenities:** Restaurant; bar; outdoor pool; fitness center; spa treatments; 24-hr. room service; laundry service; dry cleaning; boutique. *In room:* A/C, ceiling fan, flatscreen LCD TV, DVD, dataport, minibar, Wi-Fi, iPod and iPod docking station, hair dryer, safe, robes.

Les Ondines ⓕ *(Finds)* This postmodern suite-hotel, cleverly sequestered by a private garden lagoon opening onto Grand Cul-de-Sac beach, is named for a mythical sea nymph. The one- and two-bedroom suites, most with glorious ocean views, range from 60 to 139 sq. m (643–1,500 sq. ft.)—enormous by St. Barts standards. The decor stylishly fuses classic and contemporary elements. Beamed vaulted ceilings and natural wicker or teak furnishings (including four-poster beds) contrast with trompe l'oeil jungle artworks, ethereal paintings depicting the eponymous sea creatures, and brilliantly hued fabrics. All feature such necessities as fully equipped kitchens, high-speed Internet access, and fax (two-bedroom units have washer/dryer and dishwasher). Creative touches extend to modish kitchens and track-lit bathrooms (stunning bas-relief moldings and mosaics).

Grand Cul-de-Sac, 97133 St. Barthélemy, F.W.I. ℂ **590/27-69-64.** Fax 590/52-24-41. les.ondines@wanadoo.fr. 6 units. Winter 350€–690€ ($525–$1,035) double; off season from 215€–450€ ($322–$675) double. Winter rates include continental breakfast, airport transfers, tax, and service charge. AE, MC, V. Closed Sept–Oct. **Amenities:** Outdoor pool; kayaks; 20% discount on activities at the nearby watersports center; room service. *In room:* A/C, ceiling fan, TV/DVD, kitchen, hair dryer, safe.

Le Toiny ⓕⓕⓕ One of the Caribbean's most glamorous and chillingly expensive resorts has been refreshed and revitalized, thanks to new ownership (a Texas consortium that includes Tour de France champ Lance Armstrong), new management (Guy and Dagmar Lombard), and a sweeping renovation of its 15 villas, scattered among a half-dozen buildings clinging to a gently sloping hillside overlooking the windswept southeast coast. This Relais & Châteaux enclave now has direct beach access—a pleasant five-minute path through a coconut grove. Abundant flowering shrubs protect privacy-seekers from prying eyes, though Brad Pitt, on vacation with his then-girlfriend Gwyneth Paltrow, was supposedly so relaxed that he dropped inhibitions and more for the paparazzi. Each sumptuous suite features its own private pool, teak and mahogany furnishings, espresso machines, and beds swaddled in Frette linens. Floors and coffered ceilings utilize tropical woods, from teak to gaïac (a rare species that grows on-site), while giant bathrooms impress with impeccable hand-painted moldings, walk-in closet, and separate outdoor garden shower. Service ranges from merely attentive to downright intuitive, with staff proffering thoughtful extras from snorkeling gear to jet-lag lotions. In the new Serenity Cottage, you can get a spa treatment featuring spa products from Le Ligne of St. Barts. The outstanding restaurant, **Le Gaïac,** reviewed in "Dining," below, will be thoroughly renovated in 2009.

Anse de Toiny, 97133 St. Barthélemy, F.W.I. © **800/278-6469** in the U.S., or 590/27-88-88. Fax 590/27-89-30. www.hotelletoiny.com. 15 units. Winter 1,195€–1,600€ ($1,792–$2,400) 1-bedroom suite, 2,650€ ($3,975) 3-bedroom suite for up to 6; off season 495€–675€ ($742–$1,012) 1-bedroom suite, 1,150€ ($1,725) 3-bedroom suite for up to 6. Rates include French continental breakfast and airport transfers. AE, DC, MC, V. Closed Sept 1–Oct 25. **Amenities:** Restaurant; bar; outdoor pool; fitness equipment; bike rental; car rental; room service; massage; babysitting; laundry service; dry cleaning; rooms for those w/limited mobility, Wi-Fi; DVD library. *In room:* A/C, flatscreen plasma TV/DVD, CD player, fax, broadband Wi-Fi, kitchenette, minibar, beverage maker, hair dryer, iron, safe, stair-stepper and stationary bike available upon request.

EXPENSIVE

Les Ilets de la Plage ⚑ *Kids*   With a location that's hard to beat, set down on the sands of St-Jean beach, this charming entry to the hotel scene is already making waves. It has 11 villas, with one-, two-, and three-bedroom units available (four are right on the beach), all with room to spare and fully equipped kitchens. The villas are charmingly outfitted and feel very private—and you're just 10 minutes away from great St-Jean restaurants.

Plage de St-Jean, 97133 St. Barthélemy, F.W.I. © **590/27-88-57.** Fax 590/27-88-58. www.lesilets.com. 11 units. Winter 435€–685€ ($653–$1,028); off season from 220€–365€ ($330–$548). AE, MC, V. **Amenities:** Outdoor pool; concierge services; car rental; babysitting; library. *In room:* A/C, ceiling fan, TV/DVD/VCR (available on request), CD player, Wi-Fi, kitchen, hair dryer, safe.

MODERATE

Hostellerie des Trois Forces ♣ *(Finds)*   Breton astrologer Hubert Delamotte (a Gemini) and wife, Ginette, created this hilltop sanctuary dedicated to enriching the flow between life's primary three forces: mind, body, and spirit. Yet it's too special to be labeled just another New Age retreat; patrons of all persuasions—seers to CEOs, Meryl Streep to Ram Dass—seek refuge and refreshment here. Even the site was divined by the ancient eco-art of geomancy: organizing environments to optimize harmony between user and space. The inn occupies panoramic grounds in Vitet about a 10-minute drive from Cul-de-Sac and Lorient beaches. The gingerbread bungalows are staggered to maximize privacy and sweeping ocean vistas. Each is named for a sign of the zodiac and decorated with the appropriate color scheme: scarlet for Leo (natural performers), meditative navy for Pisces, pink for nurturing Cancer. Astrology even influenced Hubert's handmade beds (Libras, the Zodiac's romantics, sleep in a stately four-poster with lacy linen and gauzy mosquito netting). Holistic services include massage therapy, yoga, past-life regression therapy, osteopathy, and psychic readings. Hubert believes, "The stomach is a spiritual gate," and his on-site restaurant's superlative French fare earned him membership in France's prestigious gastronomic order Confrérie de la Marmite d'Or. The excellent, affordable wine list will delight any oenophile.

Morne Viet, 97133 St. Barthélemy, F.W.I. © **590/27-61-25.** Fax 590/27-81-38. www.3forces.net. 7 cottages. Winter $220–$270 double; off season $120–$170 double. AE, MC, V. **Amenities:** Restaurant; outdoor pool; laundry service. *In room:* A/C, kitchenette (in 2 units), fridge, safe, private terrace.

Le P'tit Morne ♣ *(Value)*   This is hardly the most luxurious lodging on an island legendary for its glamorous five-star hotels. But its relatively low rates, remote but remarkably pretty hillside setting 10 minutes' drive from Petite Anse and Flamands beaches, and the warm welcome extended by island-born owners, M. and Mme. Felix and their daughter Marie-Joëlle, make it a worthy vacation site. Colonial-influenced buildings hold commodious units with completely unpretentious furniture, comfortable king-size beds, functional kitchens, and compact shower-only bathrooms. Each has a terrace or balcony designed to catch the tradewinds while offering breathtaking views of the crashing surf and tiny offshore cays (Superior and Deluxe rooms have two terraces). The best room, New Moon, offers tasteful hardwood furnishings, dramatic red-and-black color scheme, a panoramic sun deck cleverly carved from the cliff, a private pergola, and its own outdoor dining room.

Colombier (B.P. 14), 97095 St. Barthélemy, F.W.I. ℂ **590/52-95-50.** Fax 590/27-84-63. www.timorne.com. 14 units. Winter 185€–230€ ($278–$345) double; off season 95€–150€ ($143–$225) double. AE, MC, V. Closed Sept. **Amenities:** Outdoor pool; limited room service; babysitting. *In room:* A/C, ceiling fan, kitchen, fridge, beverage maker, hair dryer (in some), iron.

Les Mouettes *(Value)* While these well-kept bungalows are pretty basic, their price and admirable beachfront situation rank them among the island's better bargains. Families particularly appreciate the convenience: Each unit features an additional twin bed or pull-out sofa, and outdoor patio with kitchenette and grill, which you can stock at the minimart and sublime *boulangerie* (bakery) across the street, revered for its almond croissants and éclairs. The location, sandwiched between sand and a major intersection, is also its biggest drawback; weekend noise and traffic snarls are common, but only the cheapest bungalow, no. 7, abuts the street itself (and lacks full ocean views). The mostly duplex bungalows sport red corrugated iron roofs, white gingerbread trim, and bright aqua railings; interiors are similarly simple yet appealing with handsome armoires, handcrafted straw lamps, and shell-patterned fabrics. The cordial, English-speaking owners (the Greaux family) genuinely enjoy sharing advice and anecdotes with guests.

Lorient, 97133 St. Barthélemy, F.W.I. ℂ **590/27-77-91.** Fax 590/27-68-19. www.st-barths.com/hotel-les-mouettes. 7 units. Winter 140€–215€ ($210–$322) double; off season 95€–140€ ($142–$210) double. No credit cards. *In room:* A/C, ceiling fan, kitchenette.

Le Village St-Jean *(R)* This family-owned cottage colony hideaway, a 5-minute hike uphill from St-Jean Beach, typifies what the French call a *hôtel bourgeois,* offering charm, warmth, comfort, and value. Stone-and-redwood buildings cling precariously to the hill, holding five handsomely furnished rooms (with fridge only) and 20 cottages (both one- and two-bedroom) with well-equipped kitchens, tiled shower-only bathrooms, sun decks or gardens, tiered living rooms, and balconies with retractable awnings and hammocks strategically placed to enjoy the breeze and spectacular ocean views. Each is attractively appointed with polished hardwood furnishings, abstract or primitive artworks, fresh flowers daily, and striped or solid fabrics in bold colors. (The deluxe superior cottages were recently redecorated with fabrics from Pierre Frey and London's chic Designers Guild.) The complex has a lovely new restaurant offering

Mediterranean specialties and local seafood, **Restaurant Le César,** with a sprawling terrace on a platform above the sloping terrain. The new Well-being Cottage holds a gym and a "Beauty Cabin" (for massages and other body treatments) next to the pool.

Baie de Saint-Jean (B.P. 623), 97133 St. Barthélemy, F.W.I. (℃) **590/27-61-39.** Fax 590/27-77-96. www.villagestjeanhotel.com. 25 units. Winter 220€ ($330) double, 260€–620€ ($390–$930) cottage; off season 130€ ($195) double, 170€–400€ ($255–$600) cottage. Extra person 70€ ($105), children 4 and under 35€ ($52). Hotel rooms include continental breakfast. MC, V. **Amenities:** Restaurant; bar; Internet cafe; outdoor pool; pétanque court; "Well-being Cottage"; gym; Jacuzzi; car rental; limited room service; babysitting; laundry service; dry cleaning. *In room:* A/C, ceiling fan, flatscreen TV, kitchen, fridge, hair dryer.

Salines Garden Cottages ⭐ *Finds*   This is excellent value on pricey St. Barts. Guests stay in very stylish gingerbread *cazes* (traditional Creole houses), three with kitchenettes, nestled amid flowering trees and bushes just steps from one of the island's loveliest beaches. Each has a private tiled terrace shaded by bougainvillea. Interiors have brilliant batik fabrics, island crafts in various media, and four-poster or cast-iron beds. Asian and African antiques, collected by the peripatetic owners, enliven public spaces and grounds. Romantics and independent types can cherish utter seclusion while finding sustenance at two fine restaurants within walking distance.

Anse de Saline, 97133 St. Barthélemy, F.W.I. (℃) **590-51-04-44.** Fax 590/27-64-65. www.salinesgarden.com. 5 units. Winter 140€–190€ ($210–$285) double; offseason 90€–120€ ($135–$180) double; 30€–50€ ($45–$75) additional person. Continental breakfast, airport transfers, taxes, and service charges included. AE, MC, V. **Amenities:** Outdoor pool; babysitting; laundry service. *In room:* A/C, ceiling fan, kitchen (in some), hair dryer, safe.

Tropical Hôtel *Value*   The facade of this small, unpretentious hotel looks like a picture-postcard Caribbean colonial inn. Originally built in 1981 and restored in 1997, it's perched on a hillside about 40m (130 ft.) above St-Jean Beach. Each immaculate room contains a shower-only bathroom, a king-size bed with good mattress and lace coverlet, tile floors, beamed ceiling, charming straw or brick accents, and a fridge. Nine units have sea views and balconies; no. 11's patio opens onto a lush garden.

The hotel has an antiques-filled hospitality center where guests read, listen to music, or order drinks and snacks at a paneled bar. The pool is small, but watersports are available on the beach.

St-Jean (B.P. 147), 97133 St. Barthélemy, F.W.I. (℃) **800/223-9815** in the U.S., or 590/27-64-87. Fax 590/27-81-74. www.tropical-hotel.com. 21 units. Winter 210€–266€ ($315–$399) double; off season 136€–192€ ($204–$288) double. Rates

include continental breakfast and airport shuttle (upon request). AE, MC, V. Closed
June to mid-July. **Amenities:** Outdoor pool; car rental; babysitting; laundry service.
In room: A/C, ceiling fan, TV, dataport, fridge, hair dryer.

INEXPENSIVE

La Normandie ✦ This modest, unassuming, family-owned
Antillean inn has undergone a transformation: No longer a plain
Jane, the Normadie has become a smart boutique inn with completely updated rooms. The owners, however, are committed to
keeping the rates down, and lucky for you—this is very good value
in pricey St. Barts. A new Brazilian-wood deck connects the two
buildings that hold the guest rooms. The Normandie is located near
the intersection of two major roads, about 200m (660 ft.) from Lorient Beach.

97133 Lorient, St. Barthélemy, F.W.I. ℭ **590/27-61-66.** Fax 590/27-98-83. www.
normandiehotelstbarts.com. 8 units. Year-round rates 90€–165€ ($135–$247) double. Rates include continental breakfast and afternoon wine. MC, V. **Amenities:** Outdoor pool. *In room:* A/C, flatscreen plasma TV, Wi-Fi, fridge, beverage maker.

3 Dining

Fueled by hot young French chefs and hotel dining rooms that keep
ratcheting up the excellence quotient, the St. Barts dining scene is
superb. It's also really, really expensive—and the weak dollar only
makes dining out in St. Barts that much more pricey for Americans.
But the island is not just about five-star hotel dining. You can eat
very well at the many casual beachfront, hilltop, and harbor-side
restaurants. Keep in mind that prized tables are often booked along
with hotel reservations in high season. You might snag a seat at lunch
or at the bar.

New at press time was the ultra-casual **O'Corail Restaurant,** a
beach bar that opened in April 2008 on the sands between Le Sereno
and the former La Gloriette in front of the Ouanalao Dive shop. It
has lovely views out over the bay at Grand Cul de Sac and good,
fresh-tasting food, from burgers to lobster salad to paninis. The
restaurant serves breakfast and lunch daily and is open from 9am to
5pm.

IN GUSTAVIA

Au Port FRENCH/CREOLE   Unpretentious ambience, straight-
forward brasserie fare, generous portions, and an utter lack of snobbery have made this restaurant an enduring island favorite—in fact,
it's the oldest restaurant on the island. Set one floor above street

Eating Well with the Plunging Dollar

Eating out in St. Barts is pricey to begin with, but it's practically become the sole domain of multimillionaires as the dollar continues its slide against the euro. You can, however, find ways to eat at many fine restaurants for less. Many of the island's most popular spots offer an affordable and filling lunchtime *plat du jour* (daily special) for 10€ to 12€ ($15–$18). Restaurants offering plats du jour include **La Marine,** the **Wall House,** and **Le Repaire** in Gustavia, and **The Hideaway** in St-Jean.

level, in the center of town, it features neo-colonial decor with antique accessories. Appetizers feature such treats as creamy, vanilla-infused Caribbean pumpkin soup and a homemade duck foie gras. Fine seafood specialties include sautéed scallops in a Champagne sauce and a casserole of lobster and vegetables. Meat and poultry are also treated with tender loving care, especially the breast of honey-roasted duck and the typical island dish—goat stew with bananas au gratin.

Rue Sadi-Carnot. ℂ **590/27-62-36.** Reservations recommended, especially for veranda tables. Main courses 16€–33€ ($24–$49); fixed-price menu 33€ ($49). AE, MC, V. Mon–Sat 6:30–10pm. Closed June 15–July 31.

Eddy's ❀ *Value* CREOLE   Charismatic Eddy Stackelborough has long satisfied in-the-know locals and regulars with simple but honest island fare (green papaya salad, shrimp curry barbecued ribs, chicken in coconut sauce, passion fruit mousse). The setting resembles a Caribbean translation of *The Secret Garden* with a virtual jungle punctuated by ethno-tropic trappings (masks, boldly hued art naïf, vetyver grass mats, and woven ceiling). It's a miracle how Eddy keeps prices affordable by most standards (perhaps the roving location keeps rents down).

Rue du Centenaire (near rue Général du Gaulle), Gustavia. ℂ **590/27-54-17.** No reservations taken. Main courses 15€–22€ ($22–$33). No credit cards. Mon–Sat noon–10:30pm; closed Sun.

La Mandala ❀ *Finds* THAI/FRENCH/SUSHI   The location alone—a house on Gustavia's steepest street with a dining deck overlooking a swimming pool—guarantees memorable cocktails and tapas as the setting sun fireballs across the harbor. New owners haven't tampered with the whimsical decor (Buddhas, hand-shaped ashtrays, enormous earthenware frogs), but now serve a menu that includes a sushi bar and Thai/French fusion cuisine.

Rue de la Sous-Prefecture. ℂ **590/27-96-96.** Reservations recommended. Main courses 22€–34€ ($33–$60). AE, MC, V. Thurs–Tues 7–11pm; sushi and cocktails 5–7pm; closed Wed.

La Route des Boucaniers ⚐ *(Finds* FRENCH/CREOLE   Having written a five-volume primer, owner/chef Francis Delage is considered the definitive authority on Creole cuisine. The decor evokes a rum shack—there's even a boat wreck—but this belies his sophisticated fare, which has lured the likes of Cameron Diaz and Steven Seagal. The restaurant has a prime perch overlooking Gustavia harbor. The menu offers such tempting dishes as spiny lobster and pumpkin bisque; coq au vin de Bourgogne; sea scallops and shrimp with crispy risotto and passionfruit sauce; and a traditional West Indian chicken Colombo curry with Creole sauce. The *assiete Creole* (spicy Caribbean platter) contains codfish fritters, conch gratin, marinated Bonito puff pastry of crab, and a *feroce d'avocat* (local avocado recipe and green salad).

Rue de Bord de Mer, Gustavia. ℂ **590/27-73-00.** Reservations required in winter. Main courses 20€–28€ ($30–$42). AE, MC, V. Daily 10am–10pm.

Le Sapotillier   ⚐⚐   FRENCH/SEAFOOD   Brittany-born Stéphane Guidal is the hot chef at Le Sapotillier, and his credentials are impeccable—among other apprenticeships, Guidal worked most recently with Alain Ducasse in Paris. What has not changed at Le Sapotillier is the memorable fine-dining experience. Dine outside on the candlelit patio under a magnificent sapodilla tree or inside the clapboard-covered Creole cottage where stone walls are hung with vivid art naïf and charming hand-painted chairs contrast with splendid china and linens. Among Guidal's influences is the traditional cuisine of his grandmother, but his creativity with classics shines through. You might start with the homemade duck terrine of foie gras served with tomato confit chutney or seared frogs' legs. Fish figures prominently as a main course, with delicious renderings of Dover sole, Atlantic turbot, and sea bass. For gussied-up comfort food, try the shepherd's pie of confit duck magret with black truffles and foie gras sauce.

Rue Sadi-Carnot. ℂ **590/27-60-28.** www.le-sapotillier.com. Reservations required. Main courses 31€–39€ ($46–$58). MC, V. Nov–Apr daily 6:30–10pm. Closed Sept–Oct.

Wall House ✿✿ FRENCH/CREOLE   Charming owners Franck
Mathevet and Denis Chevallier perfected the recipe for success: daz-
zling harbor views, warm service, lively ambience, and bistro fare
with flair at fair prices. Franck specializes in rotisserie items—witness
spit-roasted five-spice honey-pineapple duck. He also juggles ingredients and influences: signature dishes include mahimahi steak in
lime-ginger mousseline sauce; sautéed foie gras on gingerbread with
rhubarb compote; and the divinely creative lobster and mozzarella
on crispy polenta bruschetta with pesto. The prix-fixe menus are
remarkable values. The cozy salon-wine bar, which hosts rotating art
exhibits, is a great spot to sip an aperitif or after-dinner cordial.

La Pointe. ✆ 590/27-71-83. www.wallhouserestaurant.com. Reservations recommended. Main courses 14€–29€ ($21–$43); prix-fixe menu 25€ ($37). AE, MC, V.
Lunch Mon–Sat noon–2:30pm; dinner daily 7–9:30pm. Closed June–Oct.

IN THE GRANDE SALINE BEACH AREA
L'Esprit Salines ✿ ASIAN/CREOLE   Three Maya's alumni—
Christophe Cretin, Guillaume Hennequin, and chef Jean-Charles (J.
C.) Guy—collaborated on this supremely sexy beachside bistro. The
open-air, pastel-painted cottage nestles between a virtual jungle garden and a gunmetal bluff. Crashing waves, slinky Euro-pop, and a
model (in both senses) waitstaff enhance the seductive ambience.
The menu changes daily but might include Grand-mere's fresh corn
soup or crab and chives fritters with sour cream. Main courses might
include pan-fried yellowfin tuna with shiitake mushrooms or a
lavender and rosemary grilled rack of lamb. Beware the lethal lemongrass rum that caps dinner.

Plage de Saline. ✆ 590/52-46-10. Reservations recommended. Main courses 29€–
34€ ($43–$51). AE, MC, V. Open Wed–Mon noon–10pm. Closed June–late Oct.

Le Tamarin ✿ FRENCH/CREOLE   The perfect place for a lazy
afternoon on the beach, this open-air bistro sits amid rocky hills and
forests on the road to Plage de Saline, in a thatched gingerbread cottage with teak-and-bamboo interior. Lunch is the more animated
meal, with many customers dining in T-shirts and bathing suits. If
you have to wait, savor an aperitif in one of the hammocks stretched
under a tamarind tree—or even take a dip in the swimming pool.
The menu focuses on light, summery fare that complements the
steamy sun. Inventive examples include mahimahi tartare, conch
ravioli, and chicken with a gingerbread crust.

Plage de Saline. ✆ 590/27-72-12. Reservations required for dinner. Main courses
25€–34€ ($37–$51). AE, MC, V. Nov 16–Apr 30 daily 10am–1am. Closed May
1–Nov 15.

Finds **Picnic Fare on St. Barts**

St. Barts is so expensive that many visitors buy at least one meal (perhaps a "gourmet lunch to go" package) from an epicurean takeout deli, or *traiteur*. The most centrally located, **La Rôtisserie,** rue du Roi Oscar II (© **590/27-63-13**), is proud of its endorsement by Fauchon, the world-famous food store in Paris. On display are bottles of wine, crocks of mustard, pâté, herbs, caviar, chocolate, and exotic oils and vinegars, as well as takeout *plats du jour* from pâtés to *pissaladière* (onion tart) usually sold by the gram, costing around 8€ to 18€ ($12–$27) for a portion suitable for one. The place is open Monday through Saturday from 7am to 7pm, Sunday from 7am to noon; go early for the freshest items. There are two other worthy *traiteurs* in St-Jean. **Maya's To Go** (© **590/29-83-70**) is operated by the famed island restaurateurs (see below). Its windswept patio (with Wi-Fi access) is a great place to watch the planes and enjoy such takeout specialties as papaya and shrimp salad, Thai beef salad, and sauteed noodles with lemongrass. It's open from Tuesday to Sunday 7am to 7pm. American-born I. B. Charneau named **Kiki-é Mo** (© **590/27-90-65**) after her sons Keefer and Marlon. It channels the Italian *salumerias* of her Short Hills, New Jersey, childhood with pizzas, pastas, and panini—and the best espresso on island. And if you want to stock up on basic supplies and groceries, St. Barts has a number of grocery stores with excellent selections of imported French delicacies. There's a very good **Match supermarket** (© **590/27-68-16**) right across from the airport, and it's open on Sundays.

IN THE GRAND CUL-DE-SAC BEACH AREA

Bar'tó ✸✸ FRENCH/MEDITERRANEAN   Yes, it's pricey, and yes, it's located inside one of the island's most exclusive hotels, Guanahani. But Bartoloméo manages to be unthreatening, informally sophisticated, and gracefully upscale. It's a lovely setting, on a wooden deck that's partially covered by a white-slat-wood ceiling and the rest under cream-colored umbrellas beneath the blue-black night sky. Tables are spaced liberally apart, and slatted salmon-rose walls are romantically lit. The food is impeccable: You might start with a foie gras terrine with figs, black currants, and port coulis, or the St. Barts lobster and preserved duck spring rolls. Pan-fried sea bass is dressed with rosemary, tomato, and black olives. For meat, you can order lamb, veal, or a Black Angus beef filet.

In the Hôtel Guanahani, Grand Cul-de-Sac. (℃) **590/52-90-14**. Reservations recommended, especially for nonguests. Main courses 32€–46€ ($48–$69). AE, DC, MC, V. Daily 7:30–10pm. Closed Sept.

IN THE PUBLIC BEACH AREA

Maya's 🏶 INTERNATIONAL   After several seasons, this beach-front *boîte* just northwest of Gustavia remains the island's premier stargazing (in both senses) spot, thanks to its artful simplicity and preferential treatment for regulars. The much-rebuilt Antillean house attracts crowds of luminaries from the worlds of media, fashion, and entertainment. It's the kind of *pieds dans l'eau* (feet in the water), picnic-table-on-the-beach place you might find on Martinique, where its French Creole chef, Maya Beuzelin-Gurley, grew up. Maya stresses "clean, simple" food with few adornments other than island herbs and lime juice. You might follow cold avocado soup with lobster with grilled fish in a Creole sauce or a veal chop with portobello mushrooms. Almost no cream is used in any dish, further endearing the place to its clientele. Views face west and south, ensuring glorious sunset watching.

Public Beach. (℃) **590/27-75-73**. Reservations required in winter. Main courses 31€–43€ ($46–$64). AE, MC, V. Mon–Sat 7–10pm. Closed Sept–Oct.

IN THE ST-JEAN BEACH AREA

The Hideaway 🏶 *Value* INTERNATIONAL   How can you not love a place that advertises "corked wine, warm beer, lousy food, view of the car park" with a staff "hand-picked from the sleaziest dives, mental institutions, and top-security prisons?" Savvy locals and celebrity regulars know that the sound system, food, and prices rock at this beloved haunt nicknamed Chez Andy after Brit owner Andrew Hall. Worthy specialties include a hot goat-cheese salad with bacon, bell peppers, and onions; crispy battered Creole cod balls, shrimp Creole; pastas; and thin-crust pizzas from the wood-burning oven. Andy will finish off your evening (and you) with a bottomless carafe of free vanilla or orange rum.

Vaval Center, St-Jean. (℃) **590/27-63-62**. Reservations recommended. Main courses 16€–24€ ($20–$30). AE, MC, V. Tues–Sun noon–2pm and 7–10:30pm.

La Plage 🏶 SEAFOOD/FRENCH   This feet-in-the-sand beach bar has been an instant island classic since it opened, with rich tropical colors and comfortable lounges. Tables spill out onto the St-Jean sand under the starry sky. Expect a lively, welcoming scene, with

DJ-spun music—but also expect a relaxed vibe and solid food. Dine on grilled fish and lobster and island-inspired flavors.

Tom Beach Hotel, Plage de St-Jean. 𝄐 **590/27-53-13.** Reservations recommended. Main courses 18€–40€ ($37–$60). AE, MC, V. Daily noon–3:30pm and 7pm–midnight.

IN THE TOINY COAST AREA

Le Gaïac 𝑅𝑅 FRENCH   This swooningly romantic restaurant is for folks who want to dine among the rich and famous at Le Toiny—St. Barts's most expensive hotel—but aren't willing to mortgage their futures for a room. Guests dine in an open-air pavilion adjacent to the resort's infinity pool, with a view that sweeps out over the wide blue sea. Lunchtime menu items—perhaps ravioli with red pepper and goat cheese—are simple yet exquisitely prepared, and the sumptuous all-you-can-eat Sunday champagne brunch (43€/$64) is a must. Top examples include lacquered lime filet of grouper with local bananas; rack and saddle of lamb breaded with shredded coconut and spices; veal chop spiked with black truffle and baked in sea salt; and ricotta and Portobello tortellini served in a marjoram broth. The first-rate cuisine, setting, and service make for a truly memorable meal.

In Hôtel Le Toiny, Anse de Toiny. 𝄐 **590/27-88-88.** Reservations recommended in winter. Main courses lunch 20€–29€ ($37–$43), dinner 30€–40€ ($45–$60). AE, DC, MC, V. Mon–Sat 8–10am, noon–2:30pm, and 7–10pm; Sun 11am–2:30pm. Closed Sept 1–Oct 23.

4 Beaches

St. Barts has some 21 white-sand beaches. Few are crowded, even in winter; all are public and free. Topless sunbathing is common (nudity is officially permitted on two). The best known is **St-Jean Beach** 𝑅𝑅, which is actually two beaches divided by the Eden Rock promontory. It offers watersports, restaurants, and a few hotels, as well as some shaded areas: There's fine snorkeling west of the rock. Lovely, comparatively uncrowded **Flamands Beach** 𝑅𝑅, to the west, is a wide, long beach with a few small hotels and some areas shaded by lantana palms. In winter, the surf here can be rough, though rarely hazardous.

   Lorient Beach, on the north shore, is quiet and calm, with shaded areas. An offshore reef tames breakers save on the wilder western end, where French surfer dudes hang out and hang ten.

   For a beach with hotels, restaurants, and watersports, **Grand Cul-de-Sac Beach** 𝑅, on the northeast shore, fits the bill. It's narrow, breezy (the preferred site for wind- and kite-surfing), and protected by a reef.

North of Gustavia, the rather unromantic-sounding **Public Beach** is a combination of sand and pebbles more popular with boaters than swimmers—it's the location of the St. Barts Sailing School. There is no more beautiful place on the island, however, to watch the boats at sunset, perhaps over the imaginative Asian/Creole/Latin tapas—cod carpaccio to coconut ceviche—at trendy **Do Brazil**, a favored lunch spot as well (see "Nightlife," below). Located near a small fishing village, **Corossol Beach** offers a typical glimpse of French life, St. Barts style. This is a calm, protected beach, with a charming little **seashell museum.**

South of Gustavia, **Shell Beach** or **Grand Galet** is awash with seashells—or it is when the conditions are right. Rocky outcroppings protect this beach from strong waves. It's also the scene of many a weekend party.

Gouverneur Beach ⊛⊛, on the southern coast, can be reached by driving south from Gustavia to Lurin. Turn at the popular **Santa Fe** restaurant (ⓒ **590/27-61-04;** stop for drinks on the way back to savor sensational sunset views) and head down a narrow road. The uncrowded strand is gorgeous (as are the mostly nude beachcombers), ringed by steep cliffs overlooking St. Kitts, Saba, and Statia (St. Eustacius), but there's no shade. You'll find excellent snorkeling off the point. **Grande Saline Beach** ⊛⊛, to the east of Gouverneur Beach, is reached by driving up the road from the commercial center in St-Jean; a short walk past disused salt ponds over the sand dunes and you're here. Lack of shade doesn't deter the buff sunbathers (the late JFK, Jr., was famously photographed here), or the many families who find the shallow ocean bottom ideal for swimming.

Colombier Beach ⊛ is difficult to get to but well worth the effort. It can only be reached by boat or by taking a rugged goat path from Petite Anse past Flamands Beach, a 30-minute walk. The lookouts here are breathtaking; several adjacent coves are usually patrolled only by peacocks and mules. Shade, seclusion, and snorkeling are found here, and you can pack a lunch and spend the day. Locals call it Rockefeller's Beach because for many years David Rockefeller owned the surrounding property (Harrison Ford allegedly bought his blue pyramidical house).

5 Sports & Other Outdoor Pursuits

FISHING   Anglers are fond of the waters around St. Barts. From March to July, they catch mahimahi; in September, wahoo. Atlantic bonito, barracuda, and marlin also turn up frequently. **Yannis Marine,** Gustavia (© **590/29-89-12;** www.yannismarine.com), charters a 9m (31-ft.) Contender outfitted for deep-sea sport fishing. A half-day trip for five costs 750€ ($1,125), which includes a captain, fuel, snacks, drinks, and fishing equipment. Yannis also offers boat rentals, snorkeling trips, and island excursions; sunset cruises (7–11 guests) cost 650€ to 900€ ($975–$1,350).

KITESURFING   Kitesurfing is fast becoming one of the most popular sports here. Former champion Enguerrand Espinassou gives expert lessons at **7e Ciel of St. Barth Kiteschool,** at the Ouanalao Dive center (see below) on Grand Cul-de-Sac (© **690/69-26-90**), open daily from 8am to 5pm. Kitesurfing costs 300€ ($450) for a 3-hour lesson, 450€ ($675) for a 5-hour lesson, and 800€ ($1,200) for 10 hours. Reservations are recommended, especially in high season.

SAILING   Charter the beautiful *Lone Fox,* a wooden sailing yacht built in 1957, for a day of sailing, swimming, snorkeling, and exploring the St. Barts coastline. You'll have a captain and crew on board to do all the heavy lifting. The maximum number of passengers is 12, and the cost is 900€ ($1,350) to 1,400€ ($2,100), depending on the season (© **690/33-27-91;** www.lonefoxcharters.com).

SCUBA DIVING   **Marine Service,** quai du Yacht-Club, in Gustavia (© **590/27-70-34;** www.marine-service.fr), is the island's most complete watersports facility. It operates from a one-story building at the edge of a marina on the opposite, quieter side of Gustavia's harbor. Catering to both beginners and advanced divers, the outfit is familiar with at least 20 unusual sites scattered throughout the protected offshore Réserve Marine de St-Barth. The most interesting include Pain de Sucre off Gustavia harbor and the remote **Grouper,** west of St. Barts, close to the uninhabited cay known as Île Forchue. The only relatively safe wreck dive, the rusting hulk of *Kayali,* a trawler that sank in deep waters in 1994, is recommended for experienced divers. A resort course, including two open-water dives, costs 110€ ($165), as does a "scuba review," for rusty certified divers, while a one-tank dive for certified divers begins at 60€ ($90). Multidive packages are available. **Ouanalao Dive St-Barth** (© **590/27-61-37;**

www.ouanalao-dive.com), located in the Grand Cul-de-Sac, is another recommended outfit with single and double-tank dives, night dives, and an open-water PADI diving school course (590€/$885; they also offer kitesurfing). An equally reliable Gustavia outfit for both diving and snorkeling is **Plongée Caraïbes,** Quai de la République next to the post office (℄ **590/27-55-94;** www. plongee-caraibes.com); rates are competitive.

SNORKELING   Hundreds of shallow areas right off beaches such as Anse des Cayes teem with colorful aquatic life. **Marine Service** (see above) runs daily snorkeling expeditions. Group excursions cost from 65€ ($97) per person. Private snorkeling trips cost 600€ ($900) for a half-day trip, 1,000€ ($1,500) for a full day. They can also rent snorkeling gear and suggest top locations.

SURFING   Beach clubs rent out equipment for surfing St. Barts' main surfing beaches, including Anse des Cayes, Toiny, Miliou, and Lorient. Contact the **Reefer Surf Club** (℄ **590/27-67-63**).

6 Shopping

Duty-free St. Barts offers liquor and French perfumes at some of the lowest prices in the Caribbean—often cheaper than in France itself. You'll find good buys, albeit a limited selection, in haute couture, crystal, porcelain, watches, and other luxuries. Gustavia's Quai de la République (nicknamed "rue du Couturier") matches Paris's rue du Faubourg St. Honoré or avenue Montaigne for designer boutiques, including Bulgari, Cartier, Dior, and Hermès. If you're in the market for **island crafts,** look for intricately woven straw goods (baskets, bags, bonnets) and striking art naïf including models of Creole *cazes* and fishing boats.

Aside from Gustavia, St-Jean is the island's center of shopping action, with five small shopping centers along the main road leading toward Lorient: **La Savanne, Les Galeries du Commerce, La Villa Creole, La Sodexa,** and **L'Espace Neptune.**

Diamond Genesis   This well-respected jeweler maintains an inventory of designs strongly influenced by European tastes. Although the prices can go as high as 10,000€ ($15,000), an appealing and more affordable 18-karat-gold depiction of St. Barts sells for around 200€ ($300). You can also peruse the selection of watches by Jaeger-LeCoultre, available only through this store, as well as Breitling, Chanel, and Tag Heuer. 12 rue du Général-de-Gaulle/Les Suites du Roi Oscar II. ℄ **590/27-66-94.** www.diamondgenesis.com.

Gold Fingers ⓡ   This is the largest purveyor of luxury goods on St. Barts. The entire second floor is devoted to perfumes and crystal, the street level to jewelry and watches. Prices are usually 15% to 20% less than equivalent retail goods sold stateside. Ask about sales when you visit. Rue de la France. ⓒ 590/27-64-66.

La Ligne St. Barth ⓡ   This store features Hervé Brin's scents and skincare products extracted from Caribbean flora according to generations-old recipes. Exquisitely packaged offerings include papaya peeling cream, melon tonic lotion, pineapple masks, vetyver grass shower gel, algae shampoo, various eaux de toilette, soaps, sponges, scented candles, and lovely boxes fashioned of papier mâché or banana leaf. Route de Saline, Lorient. ⓒ 590/27-82-63. www.lignestbarth.com.

L'Atelier de Fabienne Miot   This shop features Fabienne's stunning creations, such as black pearls or turquoise set in jagged gold nuggets, as well as jewelry by such noted designers as Kabana and Bellon. Rue de la République, Gustavia. ⓒ 590/27-63-31.

Laurent Eiffel   Found here is clever *"comme-il-faux"* fashion—everything at this upscale boutique is either "inspired by" or crafted "in imitation of" designer models that cost 10 times as much. Look for belts, shoes, and bags—knockoffs of Versace, Prada, Hermès, Gucci, and Chanel. Rue du Général-de-Gaulle. ⓒ 590/27-54-02.

Le Comptoir du Cigare   This place caters to the December-to-April crowd of villa and yacht owners. It's sheathed in exotic hardwood, and enhanced with a glass-sided, walk-in humidor storing thousands of cigars from Cuba and the Dominican Republic. Smoke the Cubans on the island—it's illegal to bring them back to the United States. There's also a worthy collection of silver ornaments, lighters, pens suitable for adorning the desk of a CEO, artisan-quality Panama hats from Ecuador, and remarkable cigar boxes and humidors. 6 rue du Général-de-Gaulle. ⓒ 590/27-50-62. www.comptoirducigare.com.

Les Artisans   This top gallery specializes in fanciful crafts and custom jewelry. They can also arrange visits to ateliers of leading local artists in various media (names to watch include Robert Danet, Jackson Questel, and Hannah Moser). Rue du Roi Oscar II. ⓒ 590/27-50-40.

Made in St-Barth   This is the best place for handicrafts. The women of Corossol sell their intricate straw work, including those ever fashionable wide-brim beach hats. Other crafts include local paintings, pottery (gorgeous glazed tiles), infused rums, essential oils, and decorative ornaments. Villa Créole, St-Jean. ⓒ 590/27-56-57.

St. Barts Style   This store offers racks of beachwear and shoes by such makers as Banana Moon and Claire Mercier in citrus colors like lemon, lime, grapefruit, and orange; chic accessories like toe rings; and psychedelic-looking T-shirts from about a dozen different manufacturers. Rue Lafayette, near rue du Port. ✆ 590/27-76-17.

Stéphane & Bernard   This is the playground of Stéphane Lanson and Bernard Blancaneau, who often best the prices and inventory of individual couturier boutiques thanks to their flawless fashion sense and high-powered connections. Expect the latest handpicked Gaultier, Lacroix, Leger, Galliano, and Missoni creations. Rue de la République, Gustavia. ✆ 590/27-65-69. www.stephaneandbernard.com.

SUD, SUD   This store carries stylish women's-only clothing, both day and evening wear, for the high-fashion model or the heiress trying to look like one. Galerie du Commerce (adjacent to the airport), St-Jean. ✆ 590/27-98-75.

7 St. Barts After Dark

Most visitors consider a sunset aperitif followed by a French Creole dinner under the stars enough of a nocturnal adventure. Beyond that, the lounge and live music scenes have exploded, enlivening the once quiet evenings.

In Gustavia, one of the most popular gathering places is **Le Select** ✷, rue de la France (✆ 590/27-86-87), a 50-year-old institution named after its more famous granddaddy in the Montparnasse section of Paris. It's utterly simple: vaguely nautical decor inside the glorified shanty, though most patrons congregate at tables in the open-air garden (called "Cheeseburgers in Paradise" in homage to honorary St. Barthian Jimmy Buffett), where a game of dominoes might be under way as you walk in. You never know who might show up here—perhaps Mick Jagger. The place is open Monday to Thursday 10am to 10pm, and Friday to Saturday 10am to 11pm. There's live entertainment weekly, but the schedule is erratic; expect anyone, including Mr. Parrothead himself. Locals adore this classic dive where many a rumor is started on its speedy path around the island.

Bar de l'Oubli, 5 rue de la République (✆ 590/27-70-06), occupies Gustavia's most prominent corner (opposite Le Select), at the intersection that most locals simply term "Centre-Ville." The setting is hip, the color scheme marine blue and white, and the background music might be the Rolling Stones. It's open daily from 7am, when breakfast—*croque monsieurs*—is served to patrons puffing Gauloises while recovering from various stages of their hangovers, to midnight or later, depending on business.

Former French tennis star and singer/performer Yannick Noah is one of the owners of **Do Brazil** (© 590/29-06-66; www.dobrazil. com), right on the Plage de Shell Beach. This bar and café is a great place to hang out after a swim on Shell Beach. It serves a "Zen" menu (French-Thai) as well as French-Brazilian cuisine.

Casa Nikki (Nikki Beach) *⊛*, Baie de St-Jean (© 590/27-64-64; www.nikkibeach.com), may well be the notoriously exclusive chain's most decadent outpost. The anything-goes ambience (think runway show–meets–frat party) starts with staffers arguably even more gorgeous than the celeb crowd. They float around in white tees and diaphanous pants by day (changing to less potentially revealing black at night since they often end up in the water). Expect the Hilton girls, Sean Combs, Ivanka Trump, and Mariah Carey competing over who can buy the most champagne to shower fellow guests and recruiting other glam folk to table dance.

Ex-Swedish model Alex Dumas defected from Nikki Beach to supervise proceedings at the Guanahani's sizzling **Bar'Tô Lounge,** Grand Cul-de-Sac (© 590/27-66-60), a virtual U.N. of sights, sounds, and tastes (the latter courtesy of supper menus and desserts from the Bar'tó restaurant next door). **Taïno Lounge** in the Christopher, Pointe Milou (© 590/27-63-63), headlines chanteuse Nilce and pianist Philippe Nardone. Oh, how the sultry Brazilian Nilce smokily wraps her throat around classics from Aznavour to Astrud Gilberto.

Le Bête à Z'Ailes (also known as the Baz Bar) on the harbor in Gustavia (© 590/92-74-09) is a happening live music club, where an eclectic assortment of bands play soul, jazz, blues, urban folk, and indie tunes, accompanied by excellent sushi and creative cocktails.

Draped in red, **Le Ti St. Barth** (Pointe Milou; © 590/27-97-71; www.ksplaces.com) calls itself a Caribbean tavern, and the setting, in a pitched-roof Creole-style cottage, manages to be both unthreateningly charming and terrifically sexy at once. DJ Francky spins the tunes, and the theme parties are legendary.

Le Ti St. Barth's Carole Gruson transformed the **Yacht Club,** 6 Rue Jeanne d'Arc (© 590/27-86-39; www.ksplaces.com), into the dawn patrol's favored haunt, with breathtaking harbor views through billowing white drapes, and competitive dressing.

Index

See also Accommodations and Restaurants indexes below.

RESTAURANTS

NOTES

NOTES

FROMMER'S® COMPLETE TRAVEL GUIDES

Alaska
Amalfi Coast
American Southwest
Amsterdam
Argentina
Arizona
Atlanta
Australia
Austria
Bahamas
Barcelona
Beijing
Belgium, Holland & Luxembourg
Belize
Bermuda
Boston
Brazil
British Columbia & the Canadian
  Rockies
Brussels & Bruges
Budapest & the Best of Hungary
Buenos Aires
Calgary
California
Canada
Cancún, Cozumel & the Yucatán
Cape Cod, Nantucket & Martha's
  Vineyard
Caribbean
Caribbean Ports of Call
Carolinas & Georgia
Chicago
Chile & Easter Island
China
Colorado
Costa Rica
Croatia
Cuba
Denmark
Denver, Boulder & Colorado Springs
Eastern Europe
Ecuador & the Galapagos Islands
Edinburgh & Glasgow
England
Europe
Europe by Rail

Florence, Tuscany & Umbria
Florida
France
Germany
Greece
Greek Islands
Guatemala
Hawaii
Hong Kong
Honolulu, Waikiki & Oahu
India
Ireland
Israel
Italy
Jamaica
Japan
Kauai
Las Vegas
London
Los Angeles
Los Cabos & Baja
Madrid
Maine Coast
Maryland & Delaware
Maui
Mexico
Montana & Wyoming
Montréal & Québec City
Morocco
Moscow & St. Petersburg
Munich & the Bavarian Alps
Nashville & Memphis
New England
Newfoundland & Labrador
New Mexico
New Orleans
New York City
New York State
New Zealand
Northern Italy
Norway
Nova Scotia, New Brunswick &
  Prince Edward Island
Oregon
Paris
Peru

Philadelphia & the Amish Country
Portugal
Prague & the Best of the Czech
  Republic
Provence & the Riviera
Puerto Rico
Rome
San Antonio & Austin
San Diego
San Francisco
Santa Fe, Taos & Albuquerque
Scandinavia
Scotland
Seattle
Seville, Granada & the Best of
  Andalusia
Shanghai
Sicily
Singapore & Malaysia
South Africa
South America
South Florida
South Korea
South Pacific
Southeast Asia
Spain
Sweden
Switzerland
Tahiti & French Polynesia
Texas
Thailand
Tokyo
Toronto
Turkey
USA
Utah
Vancouver & Victoria
Vermont, New Hampshire & Maine
Vienna & the Danube Valley
Vietnam
Virgin Islands
Virginia
Walt Disney World® & Orlando
Washington, D.C.
Washington State

FROMMER'S® DAY BY DAY GUIDES

Amsterdam
Barcelona
Beijing
Boston
Cancun & the Yucatan
Chicago
Florence & Tuscany

Hong Kong
Honolulu & Oahu
London
Maui
Montréal
Napa & Sonoma
New York City

Paris
Provence & the Riviera
Rome
San Francisco
Venice
Washington D.C.

PAULINE FROMMER'S GUIDES: SEE MORE. SPEND LESS.

Alaska
Hawaii
Italy

Las Vegas
London
New York City

Paris
Walt Disney World®
Washington D.C.

FROMMER'S® PORTABLE GUIDES

Acapulco, Ixtapa & Zihuatanejo
Amsterdam
Aruba, Bonaire & Curacao
Australia's Great Barrier Reef
Bahamas
Big Island of Hawaii
Boston
California Wine Country
Cancún
Cayman Islands
Charleston
Chicago
Dominican Republic

Florence
Las Vegas
Las Vegas for Non-Gamblers
London
Maui
Nantucket & Martha's Vineyard
New Orleans
New York City
Paris
Portland
Puerto Rico
Puerto Vallarta, Manzanillo & Guadalajara

Rio de Janeiro
San Diego
San Francisco
Savannah
St. Martin, Sint Maarten, Anguila & St. Bart's
Turks & Caicos
Vancouver
Venice
Virgin Islands
Washington, D.C.
Whistler

FROMMER'S® CRUISE GUIDES

Alaska Cruises & Ports of Call

Cruises & Ports of Call

European Cruises & Ports of Call

FROMMER'S® NATIONAL PARK GUIDES

Algonquin Provincial Park
Banff & Jasper
Grand Canyon

National Parks of the American West
Rocky Mountain
Yellowstone & Grand Teton

Yosemite and Sequoia & Kings Canyon
Zion & Bryce Canyon

FROMMER'S® WITH KIDS GUIDES

Chicago
Hawaii
Las Vegas
London

National Parks
New York City
San Francisco

Toronto
Walt Disney World® & Orlando
Washington, D.C.

FROMMER'S® PHRASEFINDER DICTIONARY GUIDES

Chinese
French

German
Italian

Japanese
Spanish

SUZY GERSHMAN'S BORN TO SHOP GUIDES

France
Hong Kong, Shanghai & Beijing
Italy

London
New York
Paris

San Francisco
Where to Buy the Best of Everything.

FROMMER'S® BEST-LOVED DRIVING TOURS

Britain
California
France
Germany

Ireland
Italy
New England
Northern Italy

Scotland
Spain
Tuscany & Umbria

THE UNOFFICIAL GUIDES®

Adventure Travel in Alaska
Beyond Disney
California with Kids
Central Italy
Chicago
Cruises
Disneyland®
England
Hawaii

Ireland
Las Vegas
London
Maui
Mexico's Best Beach Resorts
Mini Mickey
New Orleans
New York City
Paris

San Francisco
South Florida including Miami & the Keys
Walt Disney World®
Walt Disney World® for Grown-ups
Walt Disney World® with Kids
Washington, D.C.

SPECIAL-INTEREST TITLES

Athens Past & Present
Best Places to Raise Your Family
Cities Ranked & Rated
500 Places to Take Your Kids Before They Grow Up
Frommer's Best Day Trips from London
Frommer's Best RV & Tent Campgrounds in the U.S.A.

Frommer's Exploring America by RV
Frommer's NYC Free & Dirt Cheap
Frommer's Road Atlas Europe
Frommer's Road Atlas Ireland
Retirement Places Rated